One Man's County

A perambulation of Northumberland

Bibliography

Northumberland. Its History, Features and People
    James Christie

The Oxford Names Companion

The Romance of Northumberland   A.G. Bradley

The Buildings of England: Northumberland.   Nikolaus Pevsner.

The King's England: Northumberland.   Arthur Mee

Northumberland Villages   Godfrey Watson

Castles and Peles of the English Border   Robert Hugill

Short Guide to the Roman Wall
Waters of Tyne   T.H. Rowland

Famous Northern Battles
Hexham and Corbridge: History & Guide   Frank Graham

Northern Heritage: Newcastle upon Tyne

Bygone Westerhope   J.T. Allison and A.D. Walton

Bradshaw's Railway Guide, 1922

Castles and Tower Houses of Northumberland   Mike Salter

The Castle on Devil's Water &
Tracking a Legend   Frances Dickinson

Pennine Way Companion   A. Wainwright

Northumbrian Coastline   Ian Smith

Someone asked me: which was the best place? I've always thought an impression of anywhere is dependent on circumstances: the weather, the accommodation, the evening meal you had (and the wine that went with it) – as well as the place itself, of course. On that basis, the 'best place' was Warkworth: church, river, castle, hermitage, all in spring sunshine. The 'street rising to the castle', remember? And yet, for me, even this comes second place to the sight of Warkworth castle standing proudly above the trees as seen from the banks of the Coquet. Absolutely wonderful. But Northumberland was, and is still, the land of the far horizons. Yes: I am proud of Northumberland; long may it be not only England's farthest north, but England's best, kept that way by future generations. And long may they fly the flag.

There remains, of course, a question. In my days of 'retirement' (I use the word loosely; I will never retire from writing until the inevitable day I have to), why am I living in Cumbria? The answer is simple: the Lakeland fells, once my escape from the stresses and strains of a detective inspector's role, I decided to make my home. For me there is nothing to replace the 'friendly giants', as I believe Wainwright once described the fells, or the clouds that cling on to them, or the becks that flow from them and the glorious lakes among them. I can see them from my study window as I write these words. But Northumberland isn't so far away; and I can only live in one place, after all.

Now, in Tynemouth, it was time for the fish and chips, easily located along Front Street. Excellent they were. They put them in a wee cardboard box these days. I sat on a bench near the Priory entrance and scoffed them slowly, enjoying every bite. I sat there alone, savouring the memories of my journey. And when it was time to go I took my memories with me.

One Man's County

A perambulation of Northumberland

Paul Heslop

Froswick

British Library Cataloguing-in-publication data
A catalogue record for this book is available from the British Library.

Copyright © 2010 by Paul Heslop

Published by Froswick Press, P.O. Box 125, Keswick, Cumbria, CA12 4PE

All rights reserved. No part of this work may be reproduced or stored in an information retrieval system or transmitted in any form or by any means electronic, mechanical, photocopying, recording or otherwise without prior permission of the author. This book is sold subject to the condition that it shall not by way of trade or otherwise be lent, resold, hired out or otherwise circulated without the author/publisher's consent in any form of binding or cover other than that in which it is published.

ISBN 978-0-9538066-2-1

Front cover design: Ray Liberty and Darian Bridge

All photographic images by the author.

Printed and bound in Great Britain by
CPI Antony Rowe, Chippenham and Eastbourne

Dedicated to the memory of Robert Waugh

By the same author

The Job – 30 Years a Cop

The Walking Detective – an account of a Walk from Cornwall to Caithness

Old Crimes of Northumberland and Tyne & Wear

Bedfordshire Casebook – a reinvestigation into murders and other crimes

Hertfordshire Casebook – a reinvestigation into murders and other crimes

Cumbria Murders

Murderous Women – Sarah Dazley to Ruth Ellis

Cover illustrations (clockwise, from top right): Woodhorn Colliery; Hareshaw Linn; St Laurence's Church, Warkworth; Cathedral Church of St Nicholas, Newcastle upon Tyne.

Author's note

This book is about an adventure: a journey made over seven visits around Northumberland. Walking has long been in my blood; walking is what I do. So too, is writing; writing is what I do too. It was natural to blend the two together.

When writing this book I decided to produce an account of my journey, together with local history appertaining to places visited, miscellaneous anecdotes and my opinions, good or bad, but always frank, about unrelated topics that fall randomly into place. It's not easy to blend these things together; one has to strike a balance to ensure that (a) the narrative is entertaining, and (b) it doesn't detract too far in one direction at the expense of another. In places I have digressed from the theme, but never, I hope, at the expense of entertaining the reader.

Much (though by no means all) the factual content of the 'local history' narrative was gleaned through research, and where relevant I have accredited sources in the bibliography. Finally, if the reason one writes is to 'entertain', which it is, I hope *One Man's County* succeeds in this regard.

Paul Heslop
September, 2010.

Northumberland is a land of contrasts: from the urban metropolis of Tyneside in the south to the lonely, rounded Cheviots in the north; from the wild moors in the south-west to the sea in the east. Everywhere the land is soaked in history, from Ancient Britons to the Romans, English-Scots wars, the arrival of Christianity and the Norsemen.

And even though it's quite a big county (nearly 2,000 square miles, not including the Metropolitan Districts of Newcastle upon Tyne and North Tyneside, neither strictly in Northumberland), I decided to explore it, or parts of it, almost exclusively on foot.

Tyne and Wear was one of the new Metropolitan Counties created in 1974. But as far as I am concerned, and certainly for the purposes of this book, the ground north of the Tyne is all part of Northumberland.

Standing at a position half a mile out to sea at the end of a long finger of concrete may seem a strange place to begin a journey around one's native county. But the decision to do so was down to good reason: in exile since the 1970s, I wanted to revisit the past as well as explore the present. What better place to begin than at the end of Tynemouth pier, with the view deep into the very throat of the Tyne, close by the magnificent ruins of the priory and castle?

The pier was about sixty years old when we first became acquainted. Now it is over 100, and I'm not getting any younger either. But I was happy to return: I was in Northumberland, 'England's farthest north', as my schoolteacher told us with more than a hint of pride. Could I be proud of Northumberland now? I would know soon enough.

CONTENTS

Part One	All this and Heaven too	1
Part Two	Tyne Valleys	41
Part Three	Far Horizons	75
Part Four	A Frontier of Empire	103
Part Five	North Tynedale and Kielder	133
Part Six	Cheviot Landscapes and the Tweed	164
Part Seven	A Glorious Coast	198
Part Eight	Coquet to Tyne	236

Part I

All this, and Heaven too

It was one of those days when you can see for miles. A clear, blue autumn sky, with the special feeling one gets on a crisp morning. Alone, I stood at the lighthouse at the end of the pier and took stock. It had been many a moon since I first came here as a boy with my parents. It would have been on one of those trips the local workingmen's club organised, ten busloads to the seaside, kids singing 'She'll be wearing Woolworth's bloomers when she comes...'. Weren't we rude.

So, what was different? Not a lot. Same Old Man River, the Tyne, heaving silently between the pier on which I stood and its longer twin, reaching out from South Shields, the ruins of the priory and castle on the headland they have graced for centuries. Beyond, the haphazard buildings of North Shields shimmered in the sunshine, two ashlar towers of the high and low lights prominent. And north, along the coast, to good old Whitley Bay and beyond, to the far distance where, shiver me timbers, there was something new after all: wind turbines, powering up some kid's Scalectrix in Scunthorpe or somewhere in the name of saving the planet.

It was the river that fascinated most. So wide, so deep. There's been some fine sights from this pier: ocean-going liners and sleek warships; humble fishing boats, huge oil tankers, Scandinavian ferries. And the 'tall ships'. Many were built on the Tyne and made their maiden journeys between these piers. Those were the days. Today nothing graced river or sea. Not so much as a stick of driftwood.

I'd loved to have got into the lighthouse: 'completed in 1909', as the sign says. Sadly, a locked iron gate thwarted such ambition. Instead, I lingered, looking out to sea, then back at the priory and across to South Shields. Then I noticed some men casting lines from the pier, and never mind the sign: 'No fishing'. There are too many signs, don't you think? Do this. Don't do that. Go back to Old Kent Road. Too many worthies in high places telling folk what to do. Or what not to do. In the name of health and safety usually. Go on, guys, fish away. If you can catch anything in these waters these days you'll be lucky.

A lone fellow appeared by the lighthouse. He looked like a bank manager. He neither spoke nor in any way acknowledged my presence. No matter. I wasn't here to speak to strange men. No, I was here to begin an adventure. And sure enough, when I turned my gaze seaward again for a last, lingering look, lo and behold I saw a ship, a tiny speck on the azure main. And, what's more, it was heading my way. Its presence seemed to send a message: the action starts *now!*

I've always been someone to savour a moment. A moment like this. I felt fit. I felt good. As I walked, I remembered the old crane that once straddled the pier and ran along it on rails. The crane is gone but the rails remain, now flaked with rust. The pier is set at two levels; the higher level was where I walked now, the lower, inner level was now occupied by more fisherfolk, all ignoring the 'Don't do it' signs. Ahead were towering sandstone cliffs, strengthened against further erosion by concrete. It's as well. It wouldn't do for the castle and priory to fall into the sea, would it? The priory, my finishing line, was the burial place of three kings. I was keeping something special till last.

My immediate goal was the grand monument to Cuthbert, Lord Collingwood, second-in-command to Nelson at Trafalgar. You can't miss the monument, which is a beacon to approaching shipping. First, though, I arrived at the Spanish Battery, a former 16th century fortress that housed about twenty guns in anticipation of invasion of the Spanish Armada. Now it's a car park, which motorists visit in daylight to take in the view, or in darkness for any other reason. Just behind, on higher ground, I discovered twenty or more benches, all unoccupied, but which, on a summer's day will be occupied by many posteriors, bums on seats, as they say.

And what a view, of the river mouth and out to sea. This was another place to linger, and linger I did, selecting a bench at random. The approaching vessel was getting bigger and would soon be passing between the piers, the only object afloat on a wide and expansive ocean. I spent some time reading the memorial plates on the benches, their messages testimonies to deceased friends and family. 'Gone fishing. His ship is anchored safe and sound'. 'A wonderful mother'. 'All this and heaven too'. And one to a serviceman, killed in the Gulf in 1992, 'Only the wanderer knows England's graces'. Such moving epitaphs. My parents brought me here, and when he was dying I brought my dad here. In the last two months of his life he could not speak, but as he stood here that day I fancy he was savouring special memories.

Setting off to see Collingwood, I encountered my mute friend again. He seemed to have something on his mind. He didn't appear to be enjoying being here, not as I was. Maybe he had defrauded the bank and wanted to give himself up but just couldn't find the courage. That was it. He thought I was Old Bill and he wanted to clear his slate but didn't have the bottle. Would a sympathetic word have brought out an outpouring of guilt? Would he be happy to get it off his chest? Come on, mate, you needed the money but you made a mistake. We all make mistakes, don't we? Well, then. Anyway, it was time to call on Cuthbert.

Lord Collingwood was a true Geordie, a hero of his time. Born in Newcastle in 1750, he was sent to sea as a midshipman at the age of eleven. He rose to Vice-Admiral, serving at the siege of Boston in the American War of Independence, and as lieutenant with Nelson in 1778. He commanded a ship in battle in 1794, blockaded Cadiz in 1797-98, and Brest in 1799-1805 before being promoted to Vice-Admiral. On 21 October, 1805, Second in Command at Trafalgar, he led the fleet into action and sustained the sea-fight for up to an hour until other ships were in gunshot range, which caused Nelson to exclaim, 'See how that noble fellow Collingwood takes his ship into action.' He took command on Nelson's death, and later saw service off Spain and the Dardanelles and Sicily. His peerage was granted on merit, not lineage, which says much for the man.

Collingwood lived at Morpeth, not that he was home much. And although he survived Trafalgar, he never saw England again, dying at sea on the *Ville de Paris*, on 7 March, 1810. Died on a French ship, or at least one with a French name – how ironic! He was buried next to Nelson, in St Paul's Cathedral. It's lucky his statue was built at all, as those who would fund it, prominent 'men of means', expected it to be erected in Newcastle. When they discovered Collingwood was to stand at the mouth of the Tyne some of them withdrew their funding. He's there thanks to public subscription. Over twenty feet tall, you can't miss him, standing high and proud on his pedestal, together with four of the guns from the *Royal Sovereign*, his ship at Trafalgar.

Collingwood has been a welcome sight for those entering the Tyne for years, the symbol of home. I climbed the twenty stone steps to the dais and spent some time with him, staring out to sea, as he has since he was erected here in 1847. After a while I did something the great man could never do, and looked upriver towards North Shields, then across to South Shields on the Durham side. D'you know, if they had cast Collingwood's face a little more to the right he would have had a perpetual view of Penshaw Monument.

On the subject of public subscription, I wonder what that meant exactly in Victorian times. Was it voluntary contributions of workers who grafted during the industrial revolution for a pittance, or was it taken out of their wages by all-powerful employers who needed the money for the 'cause', in this case Collingwood's statue? Somehow I can't see a working chap with a wife and kids to support happily handing over a few bob so that Collingwood could gaze out to sea in perpetuity. They wouldn't even have heard of him, most of them, and probably wouldn't have cared tuppence if they had. They probably couldn't have spared tuppence, either.

Looking across the wide and navigable river mouth here, it's hard to imagine the Tyne was the scene of so many shipping disasters. But if navigation looks straightforward today, it wasn't always so. Dangerous rocks, the Black Middens, were responsible for many tragedies. Five ships in three days were wrecked in blizzards in November, 1864. One, the *Stanley*, struck the rocks with the loss of thirty lives. People saw it all from the cliffs, and afterwards a hundred men volunteered to help the Coastguard save lives, and thus was formed the Volunteer Life Brigade. Today Black Middens was occupied by a score of seabirds, perched only inches above the lapping waters of the river.

There were a few people about, locals enjoying a stroll. People said 'good morning', as one does when all seems right with the world. Suddenly the large vessel I had seen approaching the river earlier appeared. She was the *Queen of Scandinavia*, and she wasn't half pushing a huge wave out from her bows. Her passengers were tiny figures, some of whom were waving. There's always someone who waves when a boat or ship passes by, isn't there?

North Shields grew around Clive Street's high-sided houses, 'crowded and unhealthy and subject to plagues', narrow alleys with steep flights of steps leading up from the river. From 1694 the streets were 'forbidden to pigs', so we can assume from then on things improved. In the 18th and 19th centuries the town traded with the colonies; there were 76 steam trawlers based at North

Shields landing 20,000 tons of herring annually, and factories for curing and processing fish. By then the town was overcrowded, and new houses were built on the higher ground above the river. These were occupied by the better-off, businessmen and the like, whilst the workers occupied the slums below.

With cuts in fishing quotas, courtesy of the European Union, I wonder if we still have a fishing industry. I'm all for managing stocks, but English fishing boats restricted in English waters, whilst foreign vessels are allowed to? I wonder how the Spanish would react if fishermen from North Shields fished off Cadiz. *Buenos dias, mis amigos. Bienvenidos a España!* I don't think so. Let's have our territorial waters back and the right to manage our own fishing grounds, that what I say. That's what lots of English people say.

Today, the Quay is a fine place to sit and watch the world – and the river – go by. So exotic you could be in the Med somewhere. Almost. It wasn't always so. Time was sewage ebbed and flowed with the river, as far as Newcastle and beyond. It was hardly the place for a picnic. It was a place of employment, of industry. Now it's unrecognisable from not so many years ago. The change is for the better, environmentally. There were fisherfolk here today, a few guys with their lines cast into the river as they waited for the hoped-for bite.

I fished here myself once, in the 1970s. Caught something someone described as a 'poddler', a smallish fish that moments before had been swimming happily among human waste, and an evil-looking eel-like creature with snapping teeth. The first I took home, gutted and ate (I wasn't fishing for fun), the second I didn't know what to do with until someone ran up and thrust a knife through it's writhing body and that was that. What fun!

Union Street Stairs are not to be recommended to anyone with heart problems. They climb steeply and directly to Tyne Street and the Wooden Doll pub. The steep-sided embankment, erstwhile location of the slums, is now clear, and as for the view – superb doesn't do it justice: upriver, and across to the other Shields – and Penshaw Monument, of course.

Today, the colour was blue: blue river, blue sea. And here was the Old High Light. The Old High Light and Old Low Light were built in 1727 to guide ships into the river. Approaching on a dark night, ships' navigators would line up the lights, one above the other, and set their course to avoid sandbanks and the risk of grounding. The Tyne was shallow at the mouth in the old days, and had to be dredged constantly. The old lights were rendered redundant when the sandbanks shifted over the years, hence the New High Light and New Low Light of 1808, those ashlar towers, so visible today and still used by approaching shipping in the same way as the old lights before.

Walking along Tyne Street, high above the river, I spotted the familiar figure of Stan Laurel. His statue stands in Dockwray Square, with Stan in characteristic pose, holding his hat in one hand and scratching his head with the other. Arthur Stanley Jefferson, as he was, was born at Ulverston, Lancashire – now part of Cumbria – in 1890, and lived at No 8 Dockwray Square from 1897 until 1901, after which the family moved to Bishop Auckland. Both his parents were active in the theatre, so it's not surprising Stan followed suit. He ended up in the States, where he met Oliver Hardy. The pair appeared in a silent movie and the rest is history. In the far corner of the Square a plate on the wall of a house indicates the spot where Stan lived, although the original house has gone. Dockwray Square has been tastefully rebuilt, and it was a pleasure to walk around it.

At the end of Tyne Street, a large black anchor rests meaningfully on a stone dais: 'For all those lost at sea – Lord grant them safe harbour'. Those lost at sea include fishermen, and the anchor is a tangible reminder of the perils they face. There were poppies, just as there are at war memorials. Quite right, too. I moved on to Northumberland Square before heading for Albion Road, where I hoped to have sight of the old Jubilee school, for of this place I have a tale to tell.

It was 1966 and I was a young copper not long unleashed on the streets of central Newcastle. We walked the beat in those days, a visible presence on the streets so much missed today. Patrolling alone was a bit fraught, as in those pre-personal radio days we had no means of calling assistance. I weighed under ten stones, hardly your typical rozzer. Then I met Arthur McKenzie, international discus thrower, member of North Shields Polytechnic and policeman.

Arthur was a former pupil of Jubilee School, on Albion Road, North Shields. Years later, as a policeman, he went there weight training. What did that mean exactly? I asked. Lifting weights for strength, he replied. I could do with some of that, I thought. So it was I found myself being transported in Arthur's Austin A55 along the Coast Road to North Shields. The old school building was disused, but it was OK, said Arthur, we had permission to use it. Not that he had a key. No, his means of entry, which must have been difficult for him until he met me, was to pick me up, and slide me sideways through a narrow, insecure window, whereupon, safely deposited, I let him in by opening the door from the inside.

Inside the cold, empty building, Arthur had his weights. Under his guidance I did the same exercises, with less weight (slightly), and over the course of time, through Arthur's coaching, I was able to lift far more than I ever imagined. My self confidence and overall fitness improved, moreso when I helped out in Arthur's discus training. In case you're wondering how it's possible to help someone who throws the discus, it's simple really: Arthur threw it, I ran and fetched it. Laugh if you will, but he threw the damn thing a long way, I can tell you.

Today, the old school building has gone, and a small park now occupies the spot where it stood. It seems to me that for a man who served his town so well at athletics, and later became a successful writer, it's Arthur McKenzie, not Stan Laurel, who should have his achievements commemorated by a statue, and they could put it right here, on the site of the old Jubilee school.

It was time to catch the Metro.

The good folk of Tyneside will hardly regard the Metro as novel. After all, it's operated since 1980. To someone who left Tyneside just a couple of years before that, it was something new. My plan today was to visit Segedunum Roman Museum. Arrival at Wallsend Metro station was evidence of how Britain's great new industry, tourism, has taken effect; the signs being in Latin as well as English. 'No Smoking' is 'Noli Fumare'; 'Platform 2' is 'Suggestus II'. Fair enough, as long as naïve schoolkids don't get to think the Romans built the station. By all accounts they aren't taught much history these days. Do they know who Collingwood was? Or Nelson? Or even the Romans?

And so to the fort: *Segedunum*. The Romans chose this site for their fort at the Wall's end, the river being unfordable at this point, and on a bend, which enabled the garrison to see vessels approaching from either direction. The fort is the easternmost end of Hadrian's Wall. The Wall was supposed to end at Pons Aelius – Newcastle – but the Romans decided to extend it to prevent raiders entering through ravines leading off from the river around what is now Byker. Excavated at Segedunum are gateways and walls, soldiers' barracks, headquarters building, commandant's house, granary and hospital. Six hundred soldiers, including cavalry, were billeted here. The fort covered four acres and had three principal gateways – one on each side except that facing the river. The true 'Wall's end' ran from the south-east corner of the fort to the river. The section now seen was discovered in 1903 when they were enlarging Swan Hunter's shipyard for the construction of *Mauretania*.

Segedunum was occupied for 300 years, after which the Romans departed and the land was turned over to farming. In 1781 Wallsend Colliery was sunk at the site. This was followed in the 1880s by the construction of terraced housing and the expanding shipyard of Swan Hunter's, later Swan Hunter and Wigham Richardson. Considering this industrial activity it's amazing the site was ever recovered for posterity. I wonder what the 'Iron Tsar', Nicholas I of Russia, made of it. In 1825, invited to inspect the colliery, Nicky put on a miner's helmet and was all set to go down the pit, but baulked at the black hole at his feet, which he declared to be 'the mouth of hell'. None but a madman would enter it, he said, so we can assume he didn't join the lads at the coal face. If that's how an Iron Tsar did at the site of a pithead, God knows what an ordinary one would have done.

Segedunum today has four main attractions: the excavated site, the museum, reconstructed Bath House and viewing tower. In the museum, I watched the 'interactive' screen that takes you on a tour of the fort, and met the guide, a bloke in full Roman regalia who spoke with a Geordie accent. He looked the part, but sadly didn't sound it. Unless, that is, the Romans spoke Geordie. 'Hoy, Septicus, it's your torn t'patrol the waal.' 'Aye, but not if tha's hassel in Newcassel.' Somehow I doubt it. Segedunum is worth anyone's time, not only to see the remains, but to read the information notices displayed strategically by the sites of former buildings. The cavalry barracks, one says, were originally timber, then stone, with a large pit in each room for the collection of horses' urine (to avoid sleeping in it). The granary buildings, says another, had projecting buttresses against the walls because of the weight of the grain.

The Bath House was outside the fort. This may be because Roman forts were originally constructed of wood, and a bathhouse, with its underfloor heating system, the *hypocaust*, was the last thing they would want so close to wooden buildings. The location of the original bathhouse is unknown, so they've constructed a working replica of the one at Chesters. The Romans certainly made an occasion of bathing. First, a cold room with a cold bath, to wash off dirt. Then came the warm room to relax in and warm up, and to have a massage. The hottest room was like a modern-day Turkish bath. Here, the daily grime was sweated out, scraped away from their masters and mistresses by slaves. Then came the dry room, with sauna-like high temperatures. There were toilets, *lavatrina*, but not with privacy. Toilet seats were sited over a running stream or pit. There was no toilet paper. Instead they used sponges, dipped into a water channel in front of the toilet. Another job for the slaves – cleaning the loos. Somebody had to.

From Level 9 in the viewing tower is a panoramic view of the excavated fort and beyond, right into Newcastle. I had the viewing room to myself, save for a woman guide who would have long-since tired of looking down on the remains, if she ever found them interesting in the first place. Eyeing me up as a major distraction (not attraction), she eventually spoke. 'Are y' walkin' Hadrian's Way?' she asked, as if the obvious answer would be yes. After all, everyone wearing boots and carrying a rucksack was walking the route of the Wall – weren't they? 'No,' I replied, resisting the temptation to say 'I'm walking *my* way,' but withheld further dialogue, which only served to stimulate her curiosity. She couldn't resist. 'Well, where are y' walkin' then?' 'Around Northumberland,' I said. 'Well, that should be easy enough,' she replied. I didn't argue.

Right by Segedunum world famous Swan Hunter's shipyard once employed thousands of men. They built passenger ships, merchant ships, warships, ships of every shape and size and type, as well as floating docks and supertankers. The *Mauretania* may lay claim to the Tyne's most famous passenger ship. At nearly 32,000 tons, she was launched in 1906 and held the Blue Riband for the fastest crossing of the Atlantic longer than any other vessel: 22 years for the eastward crossing, 20 years westward. The giant supertankers of the 1960s included *Esso Northumbria*, at 253,000 tons. In the 1980s came modern-day naval vessels *Ark Royal*, and the following year *Illustrious*.

Now shipbuilding on the Tyne is all but over. The proud names of Swan Hunter's and others are now confined to history, a part of Britain's decline as an industrial nation. Almost everything is made abroad now, including ships. But what really sticks in the craw is that when they wound up Swan Hunter's they dismantled the cranes and sent them to India so they could make ships there instead; the cranes that had graced the Tyne for years, the very tools of a workforce which for generations had turned out such quality goods. We buy ships built by foreigners using our own cranes. How sad it all is.

Back at the Metro station, I perused a list of fare-dodgers – names, addresses, amount fined – as I awaited the train for Newcastle Central Station. As the train rattled along, I looked with interest over the east end of Newcastle at places I had last visited long ago. Over there, unseen, among the city streets, was Fossway, where my first girlfriend lived. Over there, unseen, beyond the city streets, was the famous old river, the Tyne. And over there, in the distance, was Penshaw Monument.

So, what was I doing exactly? This 'walking around Northumberland', as I told the woman at Segedunum.

Well, I was born in Northumberland. But I've walked for years in many areas of Britain: from climbing the Lakeland fells and Scotland's Munros, to roaming the landscapes of the Home Counties and Chilterns and elsewhere, and otherwise putting one foot in front of the other wherever my fancy takes me. But always in Britain. For me, Britain is best. Britain has such a diverse landscape, still largely unspoilt – although, let it be said, we are making a jolly good fist at changing things.

I grew up in Westerhope when it was a small village, and when it was in Northumberland, pre-1974 local government changes. I left school at fifteen, and served my time as an electrician. At 21 I joined the Newcastle upon Tyne City Police, and twelve years later moved to Hertfordshire, where I lived until I retired from the force in 1995. By that time, I had succumbed to the lure of the Lake District. But I've always loved Northumberland. And so, a man in his sixties, I decided to explore it by walking around it over a series of seven visits. True, I took the Metro, and there were a few other places where I relied on wheels, but the Metro was something I wanted to use, and elsewhere the occasional bus was taken where it suited me. Some of the places I had been to before; others were for the first time. The journey, the subsequent research and writing about it all, was a labour of love.

My journey would be, broadly, clockwise, beginning at the end of Tynemouth Pier, and ending at the magnificent Priory and Castle ruins on the headland nearby. As far as Newcastle city centre was concerned, I had decided to visit selected places, walk familiar streets and relive past memories. I was armed with my own knowledge, long since fixed in my mind through living and working there, and through Nikolaus Pevsner's *Northumberland*, along with other books, leaflets and any other means available to me.

Newcastle has evolved over the years, but I was going to revisit, in just the course of a few hours, some familiar places. One of them dates back to my early childhood: the Central Station. Memories of the sight and sound and smell of steam-driven locomotives, driver and fireman, faces blackened but smiling from the engine footplate, the shriek of the guard's whistle when the last carriage door is slammed shut. Then the *whoosh* of steam as the train moves off, bound for London or Aberdeen. I was arriving at Newcastle Central now. Coming home, you could say.

The old steam trains have gone. The Victorian railway stations have been modernised (sort of). But one thing hasn't changed: the message over the intercom. 'We r*gr*t the d*p*rt*ure of the *.15 to L*nd*n K*ng's Cr*ss h*s b**n d*l*y*d due to l*av*s on the l*ine s*uth of B*rw*ck. Th*s train w*ll n*w l**ve Pl*tf*rm ** at *.45. N*rm*l s**vice w*ll b* r*s*med *s s**n *s p*ss*ble.' It doesn't matter where you are; the message is either indecipherable or, just as likely, booms out just as an Inter-City express is rumbling into the station and the vital information about your delayed departure is drowned out.

So it was today, as I emerged from the Metro into Newcastle Central. So it was in the fifties, when I travelled by train for the first time on the *Aberdonian*. Mam was a Scot, born and bred in Banffshire, and we were off to stay at my uncles' farms near Aberchirder. Jimmy and Willie, together with Mam and their brother, Bob, 'emigrated' with their parents to England's North East. Jimmy and Willie worked in the steelworks at Consett, which they hated, so they went home and bought small farms. Who could blame them?

Apart from the Booking Hall the Central Station hasn't changed much. It was designed by John Dobson and opened on 29 August, 1850, by Queen Victoria and Prince Albert, a new station for a new railway, the York, Newcastle and Berwick Railway Company. The line north to Berwick had been made possible the previous year by the building of the High Level Bridge, and Dobson's station was regarded as one of the finest in

13

England. His original design was even finer, and won an award at the Paris Exhibition in 1858. An Englishman winning an award for architectural design in France must be a rare achievement. Dobson's original design wasn't realised due, probably, to lack of funds; the portico we see today was not added until 1863 and was designed by Thomas Prosser.

Dobson was born in North Shields in 1787. He studied art in London but refused to stay there, preferring to move to Newcastle where he set up in his own business, designing houses and buildings of beautiful sandstone. If Dobson was Newcastle's great architect, Richard Grainger was its great builder. He was born in the city and died in the city. He came into contact with men of influence, notably the town clerk, John Clayton. Dobson, Grainger, Clayton and another architect, Thomas Oliver, are the men who gave the heart Newcastle has today, the so-called 'Grainger Town', based on Grey Street, Grainger Street and Clayton Street. Strangely, I have no recollection of an Oliver Street.

Building Grey Street was far from straightforward: how to create an elegant street of fine buildings when there's a stream flowing down the middle of it. The Lort Burn split the city in two, and was bridged by High Bridge and Low Bridge, names that survive. The burn still flows – underground. Grainger Town was designed as a commercial and shopping centre, although subsequently was usurped as far as the latter was concerned by the development of Northumberland Street. No matter, these streets and buildings remain today, much as Dobson, Grainger *et al* left them. Except for the ones they knocked down in the name of progress, that is.

Emerging from the Central Station, I found myself on familiar territory: Neville Street, part of the former Newcastle City Police Central Division. Just outside the station was a police box, and opposite was the Victoria and Comet pub, now called O'Neill's. We had enjoyable times in the Vic and Comet, or the Sick and Vomit, as we sometimes called it, walking in at closing time, feet colliding with bottles and broken glass, calling, 'Come on, let's have yer,' as the clientele supped the last of their beer before kindly leaving the premises. The Vic and Comet famously appeared in the movie, *Get Carter*, when Michael Caine, as a Cockney gangster, came up to Newcastle to sort the locals. A bloke from London sorting Geordies? How credible is that?

Grey's Monument seemed an appropriate place to aim for. Some of my earliest memories are of the monument. My parents took me past it on our way 'along Saville row to Cook's'. As I made my way up Grainger Street I was delighted to see the monstrous office block they built over the bottom of Westgate Road has gone, enabling one to see the fine buildings along Collingwood Street beyond. I passed the top of the Bigg Market, where I made my first arrest for crime (a bloke who stole a moped, nicked by Regional Crime Squad officers diligently checking the pubs and handed to me, moped and all, thank you very much).

I confess to never knowing why Charles Grey merited being stuck on top of a Doric column 135-feet high. Amazing, when you think that for over half a century I'd walked past the monument, did point duty at its base and on occasion, as a youngster, climbed the 164 steps leading to the railed platform.

Northumbrian born, Grey became a Whig MP at 22. He believed there was a strong need to improve the British parliamentary system (has anything changed?), with more equal representation of the people in parliament: 'A man ought not to be governed by laws in the framing of which he has not a voice, either in person or by his representative.' One assumes he would therefore have had no truck with the European Union. Anyway, times were a-changing, due mainly to the Industrial Revolution. Hitherto, rich landowners held sway in parliament in a system going back to the 1600s, whilst the wealth creators of the new industrial towns were not represented. The Tory government was never going to change things, since the votes of rich landowners favoured their own re-election.

In 1793 Grey introduced a Parliamentary Reform bill, but his proposals for change were rejected by the Commons. When his father died, he inherited his title and moved to the House of Lords. In 1830, when he became Prime Minister, his new reform bill was defeated again in the Commons, and in 1831 another reform bill was passed only for the Lords to reject it. Yet another bill was passed by the Commons, and this time, sensing another rejection by the Lords, Grey asked William IV to create another fifty Whig peers to ensure its passage. The king refused, but after rioting in different parts of the country – a reminder of what had happened in France's revolution – Grey's Reform Act of 1832 came into being. Whilst the electoral system remained far from perfect – no universal suffrage and still with some property qualifications to vote – it was a step in the right direction. Grey was Prime Minister when, in 1833, slavery was abolished throughout the British Empire. He was a good guy.

Grey's statue was the work of Edward Hodges Baily, who also carved Nelson's statue in Trafalgar Square. It's sad that the two men occupy such lofty positions that their sculptured features are too far away for anyone to have a close look. It's OK with Nelson; we all know what he looks like. But Grey's features, despite occupying a central position in Newcastle, remain much of a mystery. Incidentally, his head is a replace-ment; the first one fell off in a thunderstorm. All I can say I'm pleased it didn't happen when I was directing trolley buses on Grey Street point.

I'm sure Grey would be proud if he knew his statue was standing at the top of the street named after him, especially if he also knew what John Betjeman said of his visit there in 1948: 'I shall never forget seeing the curve of Grey Street to perfection on a misty Sunday morning. Not even old Regent Street, London, can compare.' For the glory that is Grey Street, we have John Dobson to thank for most of the east side; two architects from Grainger's office, John Wardle and George Walker, were responsible for the west. I walked down Grey Street now, where much of the top end has been pedestrianised. This part of the city has a cosmopolitan feel as a result.

Newcastle has many impressive churches. Top of the list in the humble view of the author is that dedicated to St Nicholas, a parish church until 1882 when it attained cathedral status and Newcastle became a city. St Nicholas, it seems, was popular as saints go: patron saint of children, seamen, scholars, brides and the hungry. He may be popular, but his cathedral isn't, reputedly being the second least visited in England, after Bradford. I wonder how they know.

The cathedral dates back mainly to the 14th and 15th centuries. It's the 15th century tower that catches the eye, nearly 200 feet high, with its famous lantern spire. Lord Collingwood was baptised and married in the cathedral. There's a monument to him inside, inscribed: 'He held command of the Mediterranean for nearly five years, during which time he never quitted his vessel for a single day…On the decline of his health, he became anxious to visit his native land, but having learnt that his services could ill be spared in those critical times, replied that his life was his country's and persevered in the discharge of his arduous duties until worn out by fatigue. He died at sea on 7 March, 1810, aged 60'.

I wandered around the cathedral (as you do). Old flags, faded and slowly turning to dust, hang horizontally from poles, whilst on the floor are huge slabs, worn smooth by the passing of feet over the years. I checked the Holy Bible, lying open on the lectern, at Isaiah, 60: 18: 'Violence shall no more be heard in thy land, wasting nor destruction within they borders…'. If only.

St Nicholas' Cathedral holds special memories for me. In 1961 I was a bright young sparky, serving his apprenticeship under the guidance of my mate Tommy. Our company had a contract to clean and repair the electric lighting in the nave of the cathedral, large bulbs backed by circular white shades, pointing downward to reflect the light. It was my job to clean the shades with a damp cloth, and replace any faulty bulbs. Simple enough, except they were located up at roof level, 50 feet or so I would guess, above the pews and stone floor. To access them, Tommy and I, with the help of the verger, an Uncle Fester look-alike called Walter, placed a wooden ladder on the floor which they held as best they could whilst I shimmied up, carrying spare bulb and a damp cloth. The ladder had three wooden sections, which were raised, when perpendicular, by means of a rope and pulley system. It weighed the proverbial ton and might have pre-dated the cathedral.

Standing at the top of the ladder, sometimes having to thrust a foot out and jam it against the wall for balance, I'd hang on to the ladder with one hand and with the other remove the faulty bulb, then clean the shade. Any slippage of the ladder on the floor, or my foot slipping from the rung, would have been fatal, as I would have fallen onto the pews or the floor. I will never forget Tommy's and Walter's faces, peering up at me, feet jammed against the ladder, which they gripped tightly to hold it steady. I wonder what today's health and safety bods would make of it.

I paid for my visit to the cathedral by generously dropping some £1 coins into a large metal box, secured by two padlocks. They landed with a resounding, metallic 'clang'. Either the box had recently been emptied, or I had just discovered why they know how so few people visit the cathedral.

Outside the cathedral sits a grim-faced Queen Victoria, carved out in bronze. She reclines beneath a wrought-iron canopy that's supposed to echo the architecture of the cathedral lantern, producing a 'balance of naturalism and fantasy'. The statue was unveiled in 1903, shortly after Queen Vic's death. There are statues of our longest reigning monarch – 'Queen of the United Kingdom of Great Britain and Ireland, and Empress of India' – all over this island, and I don't think I've ever seen her smiling. Or even looking indifferent.

The castle keep stands on the site of a former fortification, the Roman fort, *Pons Aelius*, named after the bridge it was built to protect. The present-day keep is pre-dated by the first castle built here in 1080 – the *new castle* – by Robert Curthose, eldest son of William I, the Conqueror. Curthose means 'short legs', or, just as likely, 'short arse' to the locals.

The invading William conquered England in 1066, but he didn't have much control in the far north where resistance by the natives was fierce and protracted. The new castle – that is to say, the old castle – was effectively a wooden stockade, built on a mound. The Normans chose the site for the same reason as the Romans, its superb defensive position above the river. Only the west side was vulnerable, so they cut a deep ditch, maximising the defensive position of the castle.

In 1168, Henry II built another new castle. It cost £1,144. Henry's castle consisted of the present-day stone keep (without the turrets, which are Victorian), and a stone curtain wall. In 1248 Henry III added a barbican on the north side, now known as the Black Gate after Patrick Black, who leased it as a residence in the 17th century. When Newcastle built its town wall in the 13th century, the castle was effectively rendered redundant.

I have read conflicting accounts of which was the true *new castle*. Most favour the first, although maybe the second seems more likely. Today, we cannot appreciate the superb defensive setting of the castle because much of the land around it has been filled in, and the presence of the anachronistic Victorian-built railway, elevated here, between the keep and the Black Gate.

An exploration of the keep is a must for anyone interested in Newcastle's history. In the Garrison Room are iron rings attached to the walls, to which felons awaiting trial were chained. And there's the Blue Stone, which was fixed to the old stone bridge over the Tyne, marking the boundary between Newcastle and Durham. Criminals on the run could claim immunity from the law if they passed the Blue Stone, thus passing from one jurisdiction to another. The whole castle experience ends with a climb up on to the roof, with superb views of the city and Gateshead.

In 1400, when Newcastle became a county in its own right, the castle remained in Northumberland, along with other buildings that sprung up within its walls. The whole area then became a refuge for undesirables, who fled there to be out of the jurisdiction of the town's authorities. Thereafter the castle site became a rubbish dump. In 1809, Newcastle Corporation bought the keep and furnished it with a new roof and built battlements to tart it up, so that when the newly constructed Moot Hall, which held the county assizes, was opened, the approach to it was via a presentable building instead of the crumbling ruin the keep had become. Even so, the keep served as the Northumberland county gaol until 1828. Sadly, when the Victorians built their railway they destroyed the gateway in the outer wall. But the keep stands defiant, having resisted the changes that have taken place all around it.

And so to the Quayside.

The Romans were first to exploit the natural resource of the Tyne, where they built their bridge, *Pons Aelius*, the first part of their Roman Wall project. It's hard to imagine now, but it seems the river could be forded then, at low tide, when it was wider and just followed its natural course seaward. But as Newcastle expanded piers were built to enable ships to dock, then the docks were gradually filled in with rubbish and so the Quayside came to be.

The area became one of high population and commercial activity, 'inhabited by men that have their living by Shipping, such as Merchants, Hostmen [coal fitters], Brewers, a great Place of Resort for the business of the Coal Trade. You see almost nothing but a whole street of Signposts and Taverns, Alehouses, Coffee-houses. At the Quay is a safe Station for Ships, where they lye free and secure from the dangers of wind and water, where they unload their Wares and Commodities, their Wood, and by a Crane their wines, Flax and heavier Commodities'. (Henry Bourne: 'History of Newcastle').

By the time I relieved PC Denys Younger on 16-beat, the Quayside and its environs were quiet places, almost deserted on night shift. Taverns and coffee houses? Forget it. There was nought but offices and warehouses and traffic passing over the Swing Bridge on its way to somewhere else. 16-beat in the sixties was no place for a keen young bobby, whose only company was rats or the occasional tramp.

Today, the Quayside has changed; coffee and ale aplenty, and the river cleaned up so you can breathe fresh again where before it was the smell of sewage and industrial pongs. I never thought I'd see the day I could stand midstream, courtesy of the Gateshead Millennium Bridge, and look with pleasure and pride to the bridges in one direction, downriver towards Walker the other, and at the regeneration that has taken place here. But I digress, for I have a tale to tell, the story of a man who proves that if you want to succeed you jolly well can.

John Scott was born in 1751 in Love Lane, just off the Quayside. His father, William, had been a coal fitter who had accumulated property worth £20,000. John went to the Royal Grammar School at Newcastle, where he played truant and was whipped for it, and generally didn't have a particularly creditable childhood. After obtaining a degree at Cambridge, he met and fell in love with Elizabeth Surtees, the daughter of Aubone Surtees, an eminent banker. Bessie's father considered Scott's station in life too lowly for his daughter so he packed her off to her uncle's for a while, hoping she would forget her lowly suitor. But the pair corresponded and met when they could, and when Bessie's father arranged for his daughter to marry someone else, young John and Bessie decided to do something about it.

On 18 November, 1772, John Scott placed a ladder against Bessie's parents' house at 41, Sandhill. Bessie climbed from an upstairs window into John's waiting arms and the pair eloped to Scotland, where they were married. If either parent was worried about John's prospects, they needn't have been. Scott went on to become a successful barrister, then an MP, after which he was knighted. In 1793 he was appointed Attorney General, and in 1799 he received a peerage as Lord Eldon, and two years later was appointed Lord Chancellor, a position he held almost continually for twenty-six years. The moral of the story is: if you want something, go for it.

Bessie Surtees's house is still there, a handsome, timber-framed building. These houses, and others nearby, are five storeys high and once had shops at street level. If I was bored on 16-beat I shouldn't have been, but a 20-odd year old bloke in the 1960s wasn't someone who appreciated such wonderful architecture and a sense of history when he saw it. He does now.

Newcastle is famous for its bridges. Take the High Level Bridge. It was designed by Robert Stephenson and opened by Queen Victoria in 1849. I hope she managed a smile. There were nineteen proposals for the new bridge. Suffice to say they wanted a high level route to cross the river for trains and road traffic and Stephenson's design fitted the bill. Trains would run on the upper deck, road traffic on the lower. The latter included horses, which hitherto had to haul heavy carts up the banks on each side of the river.

The Swing Bridge of 1876 is believed to stand on the site of the Roman bridge. It is pre-dated by a medieval bridge that was washed away in the Great Tyne Flood of 16 November, 1771, and another of 1781 which was removed less than a century later to make way for a bridge that would enable sea-going vessels to pass – a swing bridge. The medieval bridge must have been quite a sight. From Gray's Chorographia (1649): 'The bridge over the Tine [sic] consisteth of arches high, having many houses and shops and three towers upon it, the first on the south side, the second in the middle and the third on the Newcastle side. Lately they built upon an arch a magazine and an old chappell'.

The Great Flood swept away every bridge along the river save the one at Corbridge. Fortunately, there was plenty warning; the river had swelled through the night and it wasn't until the following afternoon that the bridge was swept away, by which time any sensible person would have been well clear.

I have heard that the Tyne Bridge was designed as a forerunner to the Sydney Harbour Bridge, Australia. It was opened first, after all. But this is not true. The Tyne Bridge was conceived and work began two years *after* Sydney Harbour's.

Sydney Harbour Bridge was designed and built by Dorman Long of Middlesbrough. Work commenced in July, 1923, and the bridge was opened in 1932. The Tyne Bridge was designed by Mott, Hay and Anderson and was also built by Dorman Long. Work commenced in August, 1925, and the bridge was opened by King George V and Queen Mary in 1928. Thus, even though started later, the Tyne Bridge was opened first. It was bound to take less time to erect, considering the difference in their sizes: the span of the Tyne Bridge being 177 yards, Sydney Harbour's 550 yards.

Approval for construction of the Tyne Bridge was granted by the Corporations of Newcastle and Gateshead, their intention being to provide a bridge high enough above the river to give clearance to the tallest of ships, to provide jobs, much needed after the General Strike and to have the Swing Bridge removed upon the completion of the new bridge. Happily, only the first two of these ideas were realised, and today the Tyne Bridge is *the* symbol of Newcastle, the place more than any other that means home.

But if the Tyne Bridge hogs the limelight, the river's latest crossing belongs, strictly, to Gateshead. The Millennium Bridge was born out of a competition, launched by Gateshead Council in 1996, to find a design for a bridge that would allow ships to pass, didn't overshadow the view of the existing bridges and didn't obstruct the Quayside. A tilting bridge was the answer, and today pedestrians and cyclists can cross the river at low level. It was opened by the Queen in 2002. (I bet she was smiling). When I first saw it I didn't much like that spindly, curved arch. But I like the concept of being close to the now clean waters of Tyne when I cross the river, which is done without the noise and clatter of traffic. Still not sold on the shape of the thing, but if it has to tilt, as it does, one has to accept the curve is necessary.

All in all, the Quayside is an agreeable place now: cleaner, sweeter, vibrant. Those were my thoughts as I left it to walk up Dean Street, where, at the junction with Mosley Street I glanced to my right to see Swan House, 'a product of the 1960s', as Pevsner describes it, almost with a sneer. As it stands on the site of the celebrated Royal Arcade, which was demolished to make room for it, one can see where he's coming from. The Royal Arcade was designed by Dobson and completed in 1832. It was supposed to be 'an elegant shopping experience'. Sadly, it was not a success, being badly sited, the western entrance some distance from the town centre, the eastern opening up on to a less desirable part of the city.

Connecting the two entrances was the arcade itself, 250 feet long with six fluted Corinthian columns and an arched ceiling 'decorated in the Grecian style'. How grand it sounds. Sadly they knocked it down in 1963, numbering the stones, presumably in the hope of re-erecting it elsewhere, or even selling it to the Yanks. But the stones were either abandoned or purloined by locals who found them, apparently abandoned, and took them home for their rockeries.

But is Swan House so bad? It was originally an office block; now it's private apartments. The building, which stands high above the modern road system below, I've always thought to be quite aesthetic, with its symmetrical appearance of many windows and not too high. But it's not Swan House I want to talk about, but rather the man it's named after.

Most people, even English people, seem to think the electric light bulb was the invention of an American, Thomas Edison. I recall reading as much in my *Boy's Book of Inventions*. But hang on a mo': what about Joseph Swan – 'pharmacist, chemist, physicist and inventor'?

Since man first discovered how to light a fire – I forget who it was right now – mankind has adopted different ways of providing light. Firelight first. Then candles, oil, paraffin and gas. When electricity came along John Wellington Starr, an American, had some success in producing an electric light bulb, but it was ineffective. There were two other pioneers, Thomas Edison and Joseph Swan. Swan worked at a pharmaceutical company in Newcastle, Mawson, Swan and Morgan, at 13 Mosley Street.

In 1860 Swan developed an electric lamp, but the bulb had a poor vacuum and produced an inefficient light. In 1877 he produced a bulb with a good vacuum, and with the insertion of a carbonised filament he produced a light bulb that worked. The vacuum was the key to his success; because there was little residual oxygen in the bulb, the filament glowed. He patented his bulb in 1878, a year before Edison patented his. On 3 February, 1879, Swan demonstrated his incandescent lamp to the Royal Society of Chemistry at the Literary and Philosophical Society in Newcastle. Edison was unable to demonstrate his until the following October. Swan then installed electricity into his home in Kells Lane, Gateshead, the first house in the world to be lit by electric lighting.

Swan, it seems, was less concerned with making money than Edison and agreed that Edison could sell his light bulbs in America. The Edison and Swan United Electric Light Company was established, selling light bulbs fitted with a cellulose filament invented by Swan. The company was later known as EdiSwan, a name that became familiar to me when I began my apprenticeship as an electrician.

Swan's talents didn't end with light bulbs. He also improved photographic developing techniques, devising a means of drying wet photographic plates, initiating the age of convenience in photography. He also patented a new process for squeezing nitrocellulose through holes to form fibres for use in the textile industry. In 1904 he was knighted. Quite right, too. And it's equally right that we take a pride in our history and teach our children the facts. And maybe they should name somewhere else in Newcastle after him again too, since they've changed the name of Swan House to '55 Degrees North'.

I headed up Pilgrim Street, to the naked lady on top of the Northern Goldsmith's clock. She kept me company on nightshift, just over the road from 9-beat, and before that held my undivided attention when I came to town shopping with Mam. Then I continued to Northumberland Street.

It's hard to imagine that Northumberland Street once carried the A1 between London and Edinburgh. Cars, buses, lorries; in the 60s this was the scene of a continuous traffic jam, so busy there were two police controlled pedestrian crossings. I stood on them myself from time to time, all smart in white coat and white gloves. Today I was able to sit on a bench in the middle of what was the Great North Road and watch the world go by: a world of office workers, shoppers, students, newsvendor's, a small market stall and even a beggar, approaching people, hand outstretched, unhindered by the unlikely arrival of the law. There was no noise, no congestion, no exhaust fumes; instead, peace and a quiet hubbub of conversation. I have always believed city and town centres are for people, not traffic. Northumberland Street is better now.

I continued to St Thomas's Church. When I was 'on the beat' this was one of favourite parts of the city: the church backed by the Civic Centre. I remember fine summer mornings, checking property – pushing doors, looking out for broken windows, all part of a policeman's job then – and ending up here, around 4.30 in the morning, wandering around the church, saying 'Morning' to the occasional tramp sleeping on a bench in the church grounds. Eyes would open before they drifted back into sweet repose. I always let them be; they were harming no-one. Birdsong was the only sound. I'd end up facing the memorial to the Northumberland Fusiliers: marching soldiers, their families alongside, bronze figures on a block of white granite. The figures look grand in sunshine, showing them in light and shadow. The bold inscription: 'Non sibi sed patriae. The Response 1914'. The Latin part of the inscription means 'Not for self, but for country'. A suitable motto, don't you think, to be inscribed over every doorway in Parliament so that our Dishonourable Members can read it, and read it again and again, though whether any will grasp its meaning is doubtful.

I walked now to Eldon Square. The Square, formerly 'three ranges of houses treated with Greek simplicity', was one of Grainger's earliest enterprises. There are only two ranges now, the western one having been demolished to make way for the Eldon shopping centre. Thankfully they left the square of grass and footway, and the war memorial, showing St George slaying the dragon: 'A tribute of affection to the men of Newcastle and district who gave their lives in the cause of freedom'. The good citizens of Newcastle were asked to donate one shilling each towards to its cost. The target of £13,260 was quickly passed, and the surplus donated to charity.

Thankfully, they never knocked St Andrew's Church down. It's the oldest church in the city and some of the masonry was there before they built the town wall. Stepping into the churchyard is an amazing experience: in just a moment you leave the busy pavement for a world of tranquillity. Today's modern buildings tower above, but the church stands defiant, resistant to change.

The inscriptions on some of the headstones are interesting. On one: 'The family burial place of Francis Trewhitt, *Shipbuilder*, who departed this life in December, 1777, aged 62 years'. On another: 'To the memory of James Glynn, *Ironfounder*, who died

April 4th, 1826' Shipbuilder and ironfounder. We don't have many of those these days. Listing the occupations of those buried was commonplace: carpenter, plumber, butcher... One headstone, on the north side of the church, marks the resting place of the Rev Richard Elliott, 'a zealous, active and useful preacher of the Gospel in the Methodist connexion...died deeply and justly lamented, July 7 1813'. Not a bad epitaph. The Rev is in dubious company; they used to bury murderers on the north side of St Andrew's after execution on the Town Moor and elsewhere.

Emerging through the north gate of the churchyard, I could not help but reflect on the number of times I passed this way on the bus to Westerhope, as a boy and during my teenage years and afterwards when, in my twenties, I wandered hereabouts on the beat as a boy in blue. Yet I never took particular interest in the church or the churchyard, never would have dreamed of noting inscriptions on headstones. Today I find it all fascinating. Maybe I would have been interested then if someone had given me a push, as it were, if I had thought there might be a reason to look. Or maybe such things are barred by default to someone so young, whose interest might have been directed elsewhere. Girls, for instance.

Also in the northern part of the churchyard stands part of the town wall, a significant part of Newcastle's history yet never mentioned in any history lesson at school that I recall. Murage, the authority to build the wall, was granted in 1265. Its purpose, not surprisingly, was to defend against the Scots, and it is interesting now to note the course it took, having regard to the city today.

Building work began along the line of present-day Blackett Street, and carried on simultaneously in both directions, before reaching the river at points east and west of the town. First, heading west, the wall reached the New Gate, before enclosing St Andrew's Church behind the Andrew Tower. Gallowgate was not a gate at all, but a route to the gallows on the Town Moor. The gallows stood on the right hand side of what is now Barrack Road, beyond Leazes Park.

The wall turned south-west at the New Gate – present-day West Walls, where it still stands – and continued with other towers to the West Gate, running along the line of Pink Lane, through the site of the Central Station to the Close. Eastwards along Blackett Street, it ran to the Pilgrim Gate at the top of present-day Pilgrim Street, along the course of Newbridge Street, before turning south at the Carliol Tower. It continued past the Plummer Tower and enclosed the village of Pandon before reaching the river at the Sand Gate. It then ran along the Quayside to Sandhill where the Tyne was bridged, defences here including a further gate on the Newcastle side.

The wall was two miles long, between seven and ten feet thick and twenty to thirty feet high. There were six principle gates and other lesser gates and posterns, and seventeen towers, which were semi-circular and projected from the wall, enabling defenders to fire sideways on anyone attempting to scale the wall. There was a parapet and wall-walk, a lane that ran continuously along the inner part of the wall and a ditch on the outside. John Leland, 'the father of English local history', said the strength and magnificence of the walling of Newcastle 'far passith all the waulls and cities of England and most of the cities of Europe'.

The wall was breached in 1644, when a Scottish army of 20,000 under the command of Lord Leven, fighting on the side of the Parliamentarians against Charles I's Royalists, turned up at the gates. John Marley, with 800 Royalist troops refused entry. Leven bombarded the wall, but the people inside resisted, ignoring propaganda leaflets offering 'honourable surrender'. The Scots threatened to destroy the spire of St Nicholas's Church, but declined when told that Scots prisoners had been placed there. The message was clear: 'that at the same Moment he destroyed the beautiful Structure he should bathe his hands in the Blood of his Countrymen'. The town held out for three months before the Scots broke through and captured the town, which they plundered, although not to the extent they might have done. Whether this was due out of respect to the town's courageous defenders, or because the defenders had nowt worth plundering, isn't clear.

John Marley withdrew to the castle, but surrendered after four days. When he came out he might have been torn to pieces by the townspeople who blamed him for their suffering. He was thrown into the dungeon, but on being taken for execution to the Tower of London he escaped. Charles I ended up in the castle too, before being taken to the Tower; there would be no escape for him. The Stuart cause became closely linked with Newcastle, and thanks to the heroic stand of the great seige the town was invested with the motto that stands today: *Fortiter Defendit Triumphans* – Triumphing by a brave defence.

Beyond the section of the town wall next to St Andrew's churchyard, is the giant emporium and haunt of masochists known as St James's Park, home of Newcastle United FC, the Theatre of Dreams. Strictly, the term applies to Old Trafford, home of Manchester United, but it to me it belongs to the Magpies. I used to think of St James's Park as the Theatre of Nightmares, but this is incorrect. There have been grand occasions there in my lifetime, but the fact is the last time Newcastle United won anything they were in black and white and I don't mean the strip. For over half a century the club has not won a major domestic trophy, the last meaningful silverware to adorn the trophy cabinet (if they still have one) being the Inter-Cities Fairs Cup, in 1969. This, despite having the greatest support in the land. Thus St James's Park is the true Theatre of Dreams. Old Trafford is the Theatre of Success.

I was there for every match when they won the Fairs Cup, on duty, a boy in blue, privileged to be on the perimeter of the pitch next to the action. I remember the first European goals, four of them against Feyenoord. What an atmosphere, with the crowd invading the pitch in hysteria every time they scored. Being obliged to uphold the law, I had to run on to the pitch too. I was in the middle, right next to Wyn Davies, Pop Robson and Co.

Actually, I didn't patrol the side of the pitch for every home game. For the semi final tie against Glasgow Rangers I stood alone on the flat roof at the Gallowgate end.

I will never forget Wednesday, 21 May, 1969. I was on duty in the city centre when busloads of Rangers fans arrived. If we expected a carnival atmosphere we were soon shocked into reality, for many of them had been drinking and were well served by the time they arrived in Newcastle. They seemed to be everywhere: on every street, on every corner. By match time it was obvious there would be trouble. The problem was exacerbated when hundreds of them climbed the outer wall of the ground in the (drunken) belief they had got into the stadium. When they realised they hadn't they weren't best pleased.

Still, things settled down and the game started. Unfortunately, when Newcastle scored to make it 2-0 the Rangers fans, crammed into the Gallowgate end, started throwing bottles onto the pitch. I'd seen plenty of 'trouble' in my time at the ground, but it had always been by youths and kids. These were drunken men, their battle cries indecipherable to civilised folk like Geordies. Both teams left the field, but there was the real possibility that the Rangers fans would get onto the pitch *en masse*, so the police formed a thin blue line and sanity reigned – just. I saw it all from my flat rooftop.

I was alongside the pitch again when United played the Hungarian side Ujpest Dozsa in the final. The crowd: 60,000. I invaded the pitch again when Bobby Moncur scored – twice! Jimmy Scott got the other. Newcastle won the return leg in Hungary too. Since that memorable night United have appeared in three FA Cup Finals, losing them all without scoring, and one League Cup Final, which they lost. Then there was the magic of Keegan, as player and manager, and in 1996 they all but won the Premiership. They deserved to, but didn't. In fact they haven't won the title since 1927.

The following should put things into perspective (if you don't want to know, look away now): 1927 was the year of the first transatlantic telephone call between New York and London, when Charles Lindberg made the first non-stop transatlantic flight from New York to Paris, when the first television demon-stration before a live audience was broadcast, when Ford stopped making Model Ts, when the BBC was founded, when the first talkie movie, 'The Jazz Singer', starring Al Jolson, was released. Scary, eh?

And now, a true walk in history, along the narrow lane behind West Walls, the town wall towering on the right, as it has for over seven hundred years. I came to the Mordern Tower, complete with upper storey 'added around 1700 by the Company of Plumbers, Glaziers, Pewterers and Painters'. Close by was the postern gate used by the Blackfriars monks who were granted access here to pass through the wall. Next comes the Heber Tower, built in the late 13th century, and restored in 1770 by a company of 'Armourers, Curriers and Feltmakers' who used the tower as a meeting hall. Here the wall turns sharply south-west to the Durham Tower, still there with its barrel vault. A short distance further is Westgate Road – site of the West Gate – long gone, like all the gates, alas.

Nearby, albeit of more recent construction, is the Tyne Theatre, built as a theatre and opera house in 1867, but used after 1919 as a 'talkies' cinema known as the *Stoll*. The ornate 'Italianate front' still catches the eye of the discerning onlooker, and I can vouch for the magnificent interior of three tiers of balconies and boxes and the high proscenium arch. But these features, commendable that they are, were not the reason for my nocturnal visits here. No, I, and a mate or two, came to feast our eyes, not on the merits of architecture and design, but the screen, or rather what was on it in vivid Technicolor. This was the age of the X-rated movie, Brigitte Bardot and the naked anatomies of any female who happened to be appearing in a (usually) French movie.

You had to be sixteen to get in. We weren't, but tried to look it. The word 'nonchalant' was invented specially for us as we handed our money to the stern-faced woman in the kiosk, before entering that wonderful auditorium of tiered balconies where we sat in darkness to await the forthcoming sexual revelations. It was a long wait: Pearl and Dean, trailers for forthcoming features (all X-rated), *Coal News*, a regular documentary-cum-propa-ganda feature with miners hacking coal to music. Then, at last, the movie, along with sub-titles, usually with an irrelevant story but always, at some point, showing naked flesh, if only for a fleeting moment. But for young, testosterone-driven lads it was a moment worth waiting for.

And wait for it we did, all over again, as we sat through the rest of the movie, Pearl and Dean, the trailers and *Coal News*, with the knowledge that when the main event figured there would be silence, total and absolute, throughout the auditorium, followed by collective male sighs as naked flesh was fleetingly exposed for the last time that evening, after which 95% of the audience left. There was little point in staying, since no-one was interested in the plot, that's if there was one in the first place. Those who remained were courting couples, whose interest was in each other, not the movie. All of this was nothing compared to the pornographic images available today at the cinema, on the internet and in magazines, to everyone, no matter how old. We were innocents in a relatively innocent world, although it didn't feel that way at the time.

Today, I wandered through Blackfriars, derelict ruins in the sixties, now tastefully revitalised, and Stowell Street, Newcastle's Chinatown. I used to stand here for hours in the darkness, waiting for people to break into cars. Policing on the beat, it was called. A worthwhile activity in the days when thieves were punished. Which reminds me: all the way from Tynemouth and right through Newcastle city centre and no sign of plod. Why don't they come out and meet the public? We won't bite. Honest.

And so to Newgate Street. We used to catch the bus here for Westerhope, just at the corner of Low Friar Street. It was the Number 3, or Armstrong's bus to Stamfordham, Ingoe or Matfen. Or Bell's Bus, which ran hourly between Newgate Street to Throckley and back. The same bus, that is. Back and forth. Back and forth. You could set the time by it. It was a special bus, lower than your average double decker to allow it to pass under low bridges, not that there were any on the Throckley run. It had a low roof and long seats on the upper deck, accessed by a passenger footwell on the offside, set low so that you didn't have to stoop when walking along it. Unfortunately the low footwell encroached into the space downstairs, so that if you happened to be seated downstairs at the window on the offside, you had to remember to lower your head when you stood up. I remember the number of Bell's Bus: LHN 933. I wonder how many miles it had on the clock by the time it went to the knacker's yard. And I wonder too how many times forgetful passengers (like me) smacked our heads as we stood up to get off. Happy days!

If arrival in Newcastle from the south is dramatic – the river, the bridges, the city skyline – arrival from the north along the Great North Road, or the north-west from Cowgate, either way taking you across the Town Moor, is unusual. It's just that having entered the city limits to the usual build-up of houses, the stranger unexpectedly finds himself back in open country, complete with grazing cows. Hardly anyone visits the Moor (except when the 'hoppings' – 'the biggest travelling fair in the world' – comes to town) yet almost everyone cherishes it. There are plenty of developers who'd love to get their hands on it, but it's protected by Act of Parliament so no-one is allowed to build on it.

Not that an Act of Parliament is a guarantee against development. Britain's laws are subject to the rule of the EU. Frankly, I'm waiting for the day that someone applies to build a whopping great mansion or theme park in the middle of the Moor, claiming their 'human right' to do so. Time will tell about our right to protect it and lots of other places.

I was on the bus for Westerhope. The village dates back to 1890, when a group of men formed the Northern Allotment Society. Their aim was to 'further the growth of fruit and flowers, and the cultivation of smallholdings with objects educat-ional and practical'. At the time the population of the west end of Newcastle was crowded into grim terraced houses; men worked at the pits, on the river, in the factories. Yet there, just up the road – if there was a road – lay open countryside. So the Society bought part of Red Cow Farm on the Montagu estate and named it Westerhope.

I have read that the name derives from the fact that they came 'west with hope' to create a new community, but I'm not convinced. They came west (from Newcastle) right enough; but 'hope' is a common northern place-name, meaning an enclosed plot of land. That sounds more like it to me. Then again, maybe arrival with hope from the grim streets of Newcastle was the reason for the name. It would certainly have been true.

For the first twelve years of my life I lived at Lily Terrace, part of 'Bainbridges Buildings', three terraced streets owned and named after three women who occupied a house on the corner, Lily, Edna and Mary Bainbridge. The street lighting was gas, but I swear that even in the gloom of those dark evenings nothing ever happened. I'm talking about crime. There wasn't any, apart from scrumping and knocking on people's doors and running away. I admit it, and I'm sorry. But no-one was mugged or molested. There were no break-ins. We had a village bobby, which would be one reason why there was no crime – but only one reason; there were others, such as being brought up in caring family environments and taught under discipline conditions at school.

PC Armstrong lived in a stone house at the Black Swine (it's still there) and stared at us when he rode by on his bike. He stopped me once, as I rode my bike along a country lane and asked me if I'd been stealing apples from the grounds of the Newbiggen Hall Hotel (spelt Newbiggen, not Newbiggin, as the later housing estate was named). I told him I hadn't, which was the truth (I'd been stealing them from the orchard behind the *Runnymede*). Anyway, this might be a good time to mention my family.

My father, and his father, were pitmen at North Walbottle Colliery, or High Pit as it was known. Granddad came from Tindale Fell, Cumberland, to Northumberland, where there was work – at the pit. Dad left school at 14 and worked down the pit for 49 years of his life. He didn't earn much, never mind he was on his knees hacking, cutting, drilling coal. He drank at the local workingmen's club, taking Mam at weekends. He had big, strong hands yet was a most gentle man, with never a raised voice or a hint of temper.

And I'll tell you something else: even though he was a working class chap who spent his life at the sharp end I never heard him swear. Oh, he'd say the 'soft' swear words, but never the filth modern-day 'comedians' rely on to get a laugh. When I was a teenager and knew everything, I listened to Pick of the Pops on the radio every Saturday night. Lonnie Donegan. Roy Orbison. Elvis. Dad was unmoved. 'Bing Crosby is all their daddies,' he would say. He meant Bing is King. He should have written to the BBC and said so. It might have caught on.

I never knew my maternal grandparents. Mam moved to Newcastle when she was twelve years old. I don't know how she met Dad, but their marriage lasted for over half a century until Dad died in 1988, Mam the following year. Their marriage was a happy one, a solid one. A typical one, I might say, since no-one seemed to part in those days when kids always had their 'mam and dad'. My folks never went far, save for holidays, and then only to relatives or on caravan holidays in the Lake District.

I didn't realise it at the time, but I had the most wonderful parents. As a kid it's something you take for granted. It's not until you're older and you've lived a life you realise what you had, and how much you would love to bring them back if you could, if only to thank them for everything – your life, your security, bringing you up properly. I'll do it here. Thanks, folks.

I couldn't possibly omit Aunty Julie, an old lady who loved me as she would her own son. She lived a few doors along Lily Terrace, providing me with a sort of second home. She cooked me Sunday lunch for years, as well as evening meals on Fridays, including after I had started to work for a living. I sometimes slept at her house in a huge metal-framed bed and was generally spoilt rotten. Sunday lunch was preceded by listening to the wireless: Educating Archie, the Billy Cotton Band Show – *Wakey – Wakey!* The former was a massive con – a ventriloquist on the radio – the latter was pretty dire, Alan Breeze singing the same dreary songs every week. Then it was off to Sunday School at the Methodist Chapel. I could write another book on my childhood memories. Couldn't we all.

Lily Terrace is a quiet cul-de-sac. I got off the bus and went there now. Not much has changed. Some of the houses have dormer windows. Some of the backyard walls are lower than they were. The brick walls between the backyards are still there, still with rounded header bricks on top. We had outside lavs. An oil lamp would burn in winter to prevent the pipes freezing. We didn't have loo rolls. Instead, the *News of the World* was cut into squares and Bob's your uncle. Don't let anyone ever tell you it's not a good newspaper.

The pig bin's gone. That's the bin that stood by the gas lamp, halfway along the lane. Potato peelings and vegetable scraps were deposited into it, for pigs, presumably. Recycling is nothing new. The pig bin was somewhere housewives who lived on the terrace met. It was a focus, a place to linger, have a fag (or tab, as they'd say) and a natter. The ceramic gutter running the length of the lane is still there, the same one, but where housewives knelt on a mat on the ground and scrubbed it clean, now the gutter was grubby, with weeds growing in places. I'm not criticising today's residents; it's just that things were different.

Beaumont Terrace was named after a coal seam at North Walbottle Colliery. I lived there from the age of twelve until I was twenty. 'The Terrace', as everyone called it, comprised 119 houses with back yards facing each other, the back doors being the front doors, if you get my drift. The houses originally had 'earth closets', where a lucky guy with a shovel collected your excrement through a small door accessed from the public footpath (before my time I hasten to add). They're bricked up now. Another small door, higher up, was the 'coal hole'. Long gardens ran off from the fronts. Some gardens were cultivated, some were wilderness, some had pigeon crees made up of old doors, planking, you name it. Dad grew flowers and veg and kept his tools in a small hut at the top of the garden. What's the odds they'd get nicked today?

I had considered walking to my old school, Westerhope County Primary. Or the site of it, anyway; but since they've knocked the old building down there didn't seem much point. I guess we all remember our schooldays: the school itself, the teachers, our schoolmates. Of the former I remember two buildings: the infant and primary schools. They were simple buildings, but perfectly adequate for teaching purposes. Teachers are more important than buildings.

In class, we sat in rows, facing the front. I have never believed in what appears to be the modern method of sitting kids in groups, facing one other. Kids looking at one another have licence to be mischievous; pulling faces, chattering. Kids want to have fun. Fine. But a classroom is a place for learning, not fun. No, they should be facing the teacher and the teacher should be facing them. We were taught the three Rs, of course (and our 'times tables'), and quite a bit of history and geography too.

I have complained in these pages of our teachers' failure to take us to some historic sites on our doorstep, but this was later, at Secondary school. I won't go into that part of my life; I prefer to focus on Westerhope. My teachers at junior school, their names and faces, remain quite vivid in my mind. Headmaster: Mr Peggs – Peggsy; others include Misses Stevenson and Nairn, lovely ladies who were dedicated to their job and rapping our knuckles with a ruler when we weren't paying attention. There was Mr Griffiths, known as Goofy due to his lower, protruding jaw. Kids will always allocate nicknames to their teachers. Bet you can think of a few yourself. Mr Griffiths – I'll spare him the nick-name again – was a big Welshman who drove a 'Baby Austin'. It looked like a toy car when he was inside it.

Then there was the arithmetic teacher, Mr Riley. He had a serious injury, a war wound, which took the form of a deep indentation to his forehead, the sort of thing that ordinarily might have earned him an unkind nickname by heartless kids. But he never had a nickname, he had something else: respect. We knew without being told he'd suffered the injury on our behalf. Our class were all 'war babies', and although we were too young to remember anything about the war, the mid-1950s was nevertheless a time when the war, or its consequences, still permeated through Britain.

What I remember most about Mr Riley was that when he was teaching, he couldn't forget about the war. He's teaching arithmetic, but just one contrived question from someone about the war meant an instant diversion from the meaning of pye-r-squared to a pincer movement somewhere in France as Jerry was forced to retreat. Whatever sums had been scrawled on the blackboard would give way to hastily drawn lines, indicating the position of the Germans in relation to British tanks, usually including American positions if only to make his point that the Yanks were useless. Such distractions, of course, were much preferred to arithmetic. Whatever I learned about the war I learned from Mr Riley. He was at Dunkirk. He was there on D-Day. For all I know he may have single-handedly liberated Belgium. What is certain is that the man had a ghastly and permanent injury, sustained on behalf of everyone in that class. Sustained for you, today.

Our schoolmates we recall, partly from memory, partly because we have school photographs. I can't remember any of my school chums getting 'into trouble'. The appearance of the village bobby on his bike was enough to focus minds. What has this to do with perambulating around Northumberland? Nothing particularly, except that I lived and went to school in Northumberland so you might say it's part of Northumberland's history – *social* history if you like.

Where was I? Oh aye, Beaumont Terrace. I walked the length of the Terrace now, to the one-time cinema, now bingo hall, the *Orion*. Built in 1912, the *Orion* was 'the pictures' for years. Nobody said 'movies'. The pictures was where we went on Saturday mornings to watch Hopalong Cassidy and Tom Mix. And Superman, of course, in those days portrayed as a sort of cardboard cutout 'flying' across the New York skyline, so corny we kids laughed at it even then. He was in comics too, along with Captain Marvel, 'The World's Mightiest Mortal'. Where Superman was really a bloke called Clark Kent who changed clothes in a telephone booth or somewhere, Captain Marvel just said 'Shazam!', upon which he changed into an heroic-like figure resplendent in a cloak. I suppose he could fly too, but I can't remember now.

As for Superman, I remember my mother presenting me with an old blanket, which I wore as a Superman cloak. I daubed it with a huge 'S', climbed into the coalhouse and jumped out of the coalhole in a vain attempt to emulate my hero. As this was about five feet high it's a miracle I didn't break a leg or something. I did manage to get myself covered in coal dust, which is more than Superman, carboard or otherwise, ever achieved.

Sometimes the *Orion* matinee showed Nyoka, the Jungle Girl, a weekly serial where, at the end of each episode, our heroine was left in peril and you had to come back next week to see what happened. Somehow it didn't quite work like that. There was Nyoka, scantily clad, incidentally, lying on the floor, desperately trying to stop an advancing wall (in an obvious film set) from pushing her into a crocodile-infested pit (filled with obvious crocodiles). Just as she was on the brink of a ghastly demise it would end – until next week, you'd have thought, except next week it was the same episode again. We went again anyway. She was scantily-clad, after all. Who cared about crocodiles?

But it was Cowboys and Indians that brought kids to the matinee. Heroes on horses, plugging the baddies and shooting up the sheriff. After the show the doors would open and dozens of kids in short trousers would emerge, riding imaginary horses and firing imaginary guns at imaginary baddies. Roy Rogers was the all-American hero. He featured in countless films with his horse, Trigger, his one-two-three-four-legged friend. He's stuffed now. Trigger, that is.

One evening, at the *Orion*, when I was about fourteen, a movie about nudists was on. A few of us lads went, eager to see moving naked flesh, as opposed to the black and white images we perused in the crumpled editions of *Health and Efficiency*, and smiling models posing in their corsets in our mothers' catalogues. I was surprised at the film not being an X-Certificate, but I suppose it was because it didn't include scenes of a sexual nature, as they say today. We skulked in our seats, mortified at the prospect of being seen by our dads. Mercifully, none of our dads was there. Then I realised if they had been they would have been just as mortified at the prospect of being seen by their goggle-eyed sons. The movie was good. In fact I've loved women ever since.

The *Orion* looked small to me now, but isn't that the way of things? You go back to places and they look smaller. I wondered what it was like inside these days. Sadly, its doors were locked. It was time to move on. I caught the bus to Newburn.

Part II

Tyne Valleys

Newburn's place in our industrial history should not be underestimated. In the early 19th century, John Spencer built a mill for the manufacture of files, and later, his son, also John, managed a factory manufacturing materials for the railway, armaments and mining industries worldwide. After the Great War demand for steel diminished and some of the factories closed, but there was still a 'Spencers' in the 1950s at the bottom of Walbottle Road, at least that's what we called the building that stood there. Maybe it was because people had always called it that.

Newburn to me is synonymous with the Salvation Army. It's just that when I was a kid 'Aunty Julie', who was of a religious disposition, visited the Sally Ann most Sunday evenings, at Newcastle City Temple, Wallsend, Boldon Colliery or Newburn. She never wore the uniform, but simply attended and sang the hymns. I remember singing with the congregation at 'the Army'.

At Newburn a vivid picture remains in my memory, of a diminutive chap – in full Salvation Army uniform of course – leading from the front:

> Shall we gather at the river,
> The bew-ti-ful the bew-ti-ful the river,
> Shall we gather at the river
> That flows by the throne of God?

The congregation comprised good, working-class folk, who had little but lived in houses either rented from private landlords or owned by the colliery. They didn't own cars, didn't have television in most cases and didn't complain. Nor did they aspire to climb the social ladder, and I suspect they had no debt either. But they did have happiness. I see it still in their faces. They were good people, salt of the earth, people who would have done anything to help anyone, to be there for friends.

The church of St Michael and All Angels stands on a small hill and probably dates back to the 13th century. It was locked to me, but there was still the churchyard to explore. Here were the graves of two men with much in common: they were young, they were coal miners, they were killed working down the pit and they are buried at Newburn. One is Thomas Fatkin, 26, killed at Throckley Colliery on 24 April, 1917. The other is Robert Browell, 'who met with an accident whilst following his employment at Walbottle Colliery, 1 May, 1893, aged 30'.

Other miners, killed at work, are also buried here, men in their prime who worked down a black hole to win coal so that others could light their home fires, fuel their factories, sail their ships. There's also the family burial site of the Hedleys, where William Hedley, the 'locomotive engineer', is interred, and the grave of Robert Hawthorn, engineer, marked by a handsome obelisk. As I recall, I heard not a word about them at school (unlike Thomas Edison).

Hedley is an unsung Geordie, the inventor of *Puffing Billy*, a steam locomotive. He is associated with the wagonway that ran from Wylam to the staiths at Lemington. It was a far from simple task to transport coal in the mid 18th century. At first, horses pulled wagons along wooden rails, then steam engines were used to draw wagons along rails by a method whereby the engine was fixed and the wagons were towed by a cable. Hardly practical over great distances. A steam locomotive had been designed and invented for use at a colliery near Leeds, but used the pinion engaging system, where teeth engaged with slots in the track. This was too expensive and complex. Step forward William Hedley.

Hedley was the resident engineer at Wylam. The colliery owner, Christopher Blackett, was frustrated to mine coal only to find it difficult to get it to Lemington. So he tasked Hedley to design a steam locomotive that pulled wagons efficiently and cheaply. In 1814, Hedley, assisted by Jonathan Forster, an enginewright, and Timothy Hackworth, a blacksmith, produced a locomotive with two vertical cylinders outside the boiler. The pistons rods extended upwards to pivoted beams, which were connected by rods to a crankshaft under the frames, from which the gears drove the wheels.

Hedley introduced a system of smooth rails, which many regarded as unsatisfactory, saying the wheels would spin and the locomotive would not be propelled forward, as indeed was the case. He solved this by connecting the wheels with rods, so that if one pair began to slip it was countered by the other. Another problem was the weight of the locomotive, which, at 8-tons and mounted on four wheels, crushed the track. He redistributed the weight by designing an engine with eight wheels instead of four, although it was rebuilt with four wheels again when tracks improved.

The tracks too were replaced. Where before the rails were 'flanged', the wheels of the rolling stock were flanged instead, as they are today. Hedley's engine, *Puffing Billy*, was the first commercial adhesion steam locomotive in the world. He and his assistants then produced a second locomotive, *Wylam Dilly*, and both engines ran along the 5-mile stretch of the wagonway between Wylam and Lemington for nearly half a century, pulling the coal wagons at about the same speed I would be walking it.

Both engines still exist; *Puffing Billy* can be seen in the Science Museum, London, *Wylam Dilly* at the Royal Museum, Edinburgh. Such a pity they aren't where they belong, on Tyneside.

One occasion stands out in Newburn's history. On 28 August, 1640, when English Royalists suffered an 'irreparable rout' against the Scots. It wasn't so much 'fight' as 'flight'. To paraphrase Shakespeare, it was much ado about bugger-all.

In 1638 Charles I tried to force the religious service of the Church of England on the Scots, which caused a riot in Edinburgh. He ordered the use of troops if necessary; the Scots replied by creating a 'National Covenant', to keep Scotland free of church matters. Thus the Scots were known as the Covenan-ters.

Charles sent an army north. Responding, a Scots army, led by General Leslie, marched south to Newcastle, where they sought permission to cross the Tyne. Lord Conway refused, so the Scots went to Newburn, where they could ford the river, arriving there on 27 August, 1640. Their number was estimated at 20,000 foot soldiers and 2,500 horse. Charles's Royalists, under Conway, numbered at only 3,000 foot and 1,500 horse, gathered at Stella Haugh, a large meadow, on the south side of the river. The Scots, with their considerable advantage in numbers, clearly held the upper hand. They secreted themselves in hedges and lanes and in the houses of Newburn, and turned their guns towards the English, even placing cannon on top of the church tower. You'd wonder how they got them up there.

The following morning Leslie sent a message to Conway, saying he wanted to cross the Tyne to present a petition to the king. Conway said he would allow a few over, not the entire Scots army. With his advantage in numbers, Leslie could have moved forward, but chose not to, probably hoping to avoid bloodshed; but when a Scots officer moved his horse to the water's edge to drink, an English musketeer shot him dead. Leslie responded by charging across the river, at the same time ordering his cannon to open fire. The English fled, leaving about sixty dead.

The Scots took many prisoners, but released them, which seems to indicate there was no real desire to make war on the auld enemy. Meanwhile, fearing the worst, the garrison abandoned Newcastle, leaving all stores and munitions behind. All those who worked in the coal industry, the miners, keelmen, everyone, also fled, believing the Scots would give no quarter. When the Scots entered the now defenceless city 'they possessed themselves of corn, cheese beer, etc'. Meanwhile, the fleeing English army turned up in Durham, whose citizens had also scarpered. Not exactly a grand chapter in England's glittering history, is it?

It was time to head for the old wagonway. But first, a pause by the Boathouse pub, near the end of Newburn bridge, where a series of markers on the wall indicate the flood levels of times gone by, including that of 1771, the highest. The mark is about eight feet from the ground, about 30 feet above the Tyne. The pub wasn't built until about sixty years later, so how they are able to mark the exact level on the wall is uncertain. Nearby is the Tyne Riverside Country Park, redeveloped land from what was probably the site of the Isabella Pit. How things have changed. In the past, standing here, you would have seen and heard the sights and sounds of industry: the winding gear of the pit, the clanging and smoke from Spencer's steelworks, the keels taking coal to waiting lighters, *Puffing Billy* chugging back and forth along the wagonway. Today there is peace, the river no longer serving the needs of man, save his leisure time.

The old wagonway is arguably the most historic stretch of railway in the world. I took to it now, seeing no-one. It led unerringly to an 18th century cottage known as High Street House, at the former trackside. Here, on 9 June, 1781, George Stephenson was born. The cottage is now in the hands of the National Trust and open to the public. Without hesitation I opened the door and stepped inside. Eager as I was to explore the birthplace of the 'Father of the Railways', my attention was instantly diverted by the sound of someone outside locking me in. I was quick, and needed to be. Rattling the door handle and banging loudly, there was a brief pause before the door was unlocked again. When I opened it I found myself staring at a woman with a surprised look on her face. Margaret Starkey announced herself as a guide at the cottage – and admitted that being so late in the day she thought might as well lock up. Time spent in Stephenson's humble home appealed, but not all night. So, after a laugh and a cup of tea with Margaret, I resumed my visit.

The room I was admitted to the entire Stephenson family lived in. That's Robert and Mabel and their five children, including George. The other rooms in the cottage were occupied by three other families. The Stephensons' room was set out as they would have known it, with a bed of straw in the corner, made up now as it would have been, and another below, a 'truckle' bed, that pulled out.

Evidently the cottage is haunted by a ghost, presumably Mabel, who, for reasons best known to her spiritual self, unrolls toilet rolls and leaves them strewn over the floor. The Stephensons lived here in the days of the wooden railway, and George's first job was to chase stray cows off the tracks. George eventually got a job as an engineman, and clearly wanting to make a success of his life he paid for his own education in reading, writing and arithmetic at night school. Just as I broke my journey to explore his birthplace, it's worth spending time on someone of whom Tyneside can be proud.

George Stephenson didn't earn his name 'Father of the Railways' because of his famous engine, *Rocket*. Steam locomotives had been around for years, including *Puffing Billy* and *Wylam Dilly*, as we have seen. Stephenson became 'Father of the Railways' because of the railways themselves.

Stephenson was a colliery engineman, and in 1811, when the pumping engine at Killingworth Colliery broke down, he fixed it and was promoted to enginewright for neighbouring collieries. By then he was an expert on steam-driven machines, so it isn't surprising to find him designing a locomotive of his own, which he called *Blucher*, after a Prussian general. Unfortunately, these new machines were so heavy they crushed the wooden rails, so Stephenson, with others, worked hard on improved designs using cast iron. He realised the only way steam trains would work successfully was to make the tracks as level as possible by constructing tunnels, cuttings and embankments, and building bridges.

In 1821 Parliament sanctioned the building of a new railway from near Bishop Auckland through Darlington to Stockton-on-Tees to serve various collieries. The owner, Edward Pease, and Stephenson himself, used malleable rails, manufactured at Bedlington, and formed a new company, Robert Stephenson and Co (after his son), based in Newcastle.

On 27 September, 1825, huge crowds turned out to watch the opening of the first section of the Stockton to Darlington railway. Stephenson himself drove *Locomotion*, an engine that pulled 36 wagons. The new line reduced the cost of the transportation of coal and another railway company, the Liverpool and Manchester, decided to join in, but before they could build their railway they needed the sanction of Parliament. Not everyone was convinced by the idea of railways; there were many who objected to them. Edward Anderson, counsel representing those opposed to the Liverpool and Manchester Railway, said, 'This railway is the most absurd scheme that ever entered into the head of a man to conceive.'

Despite the opposition, the Liverpool and Manchester Railway won its case, and to decide who would build its locomotives held a competition. It was held at Rainhill, Lancashire, in October, 1829, with each competing locomotive having to haul three times its own weight at a speed of at least 10 mph over a specific distance. Stephenson's engine, *Rocket*, won the day. The railways had arrived, with Stephenson's tunnels, cuttings, embankments and viaducts providing the means by which trains could travel efficiently.

George Stephenson's legacy to the world was, quite simply, the railways, which, in later years, would connect up, so that people could travel from town to town, change trains and go on elsewhere. That he foresaw this is reflected in the standard gauge of 4 ft 8½ inches, which was adopted almost worldwide. *Rocket* still exists, albeit modified. It stands in the Science Museum, London (another historic relic lost to Tyneside).

In 1876, a new railway opened. It ran from Scotswood to Wylam, 'one of the prettiest in the kingdom', the Newcastle *Daily Journal* reported. It was a passenger railway, and was built despite the existence of the Carlisle-Newcastle line, opened in 1838, on the other side of the river. Part of the new railway ran along the route of the old wagonway, right past George Stephenson's cottage. Thus, there were two stations at Wylam, and two railways, running parallel, on opposite sides of the Tyne. It's worth spending a moment at Stephenson's cottage to reflect on the history here: the old wooden rails and the horse-drawn wagons, the early steam locomotives, and the passenger trains running in both directions between Scotswood and Wylam – and beyond, actually, for the new railway went on to link up with the Carlisle-Newcastle line just to the west of the village. That meant a new bridge, but more of that anon.

Today, the old wagonway leads to a car park in Wylam, the site of the former railway station on the north side of the river. It's hard to believe quiet, residential Wylam was once a colliery village, so important that its existence was the reason for the old wagonway and the passenger line that ran until 1966. I stayed at the Black Bull, where, let it be said, two Union Jacks flew proudly outside, upside down, alas.

What is it about the English and the Union Jack? I see it flying upside down so often, everything from public buildings to Wembley Stadium on Cup Final day. As someone who was told how the flag should fly – broad white stripe at the top on the flagpole side – I can only assume those who fly it upside down were never given that information. Does it matter? Yes it does. A national flag represents one's country. Men have died carrying it in battle. During many visits to Scotland I never saw it flying upside down there. The Union Jack incorporates the flags of England, Scotland and Northern Ireland – but not Wales. As the Welsh flag has a dragon on it, maybe it should be incorporated into the Union Jack, if only because then, surely, it would be flown the right way up.

***

The Black Bull was excellent, except it didn't do breakfast. Not even a cup of tea. A small packet of three shortbread biscuits would have to sustain me until I could feast in the fleshpots of Prudhoe. I was long since accustomed to mornings spent on an empty stomach and stopped caring about such trivia. I'm not saying bacon, egg, sausage, mushrooms, fried tomatoes, a generous lump of black pud, some bubble and squeak, two rounds of fried slice and a slice of toast and marmalade wouldn't have gone down a treat. But breathing the fresh Wylam air was just as gratifying. Less fattening too.

It was a damp morning and I am being truthful in saying I couldn't have wished to be in a better place on a better day. I knew just ahead was Wylam Old Bridge, or West Wylam Bridge, or, apparently, Hagg Bank Bridge – take your pick. I had seen the bridge often enough when I was about fifteen and went kayaking on the river. It opened in 1876, enabling the line on the north side of the river to link up with that on the south. It's a Tyne Bridge in miniature – although with a span of 240 feet not that miniature, and constructed of wrought iron. It cost £16,000 and evidently pleased Major-General C. S. Hutchinson, a Board of Trade government inspector who expressed great admiration for it.

As Board of Trade inspector, Hutchinson was responsible for ensuring the safety of the bridge, which was tested rigorously before receiving his sanction.

To 'test' the bridge, a 6 ton locomotive pulled a 25 ton tender across. OK so far, but to be more certain of the bridge's safety the same locomotive pulled a 45 ton tender over it. Fine. But to be even *more* certain they drove a 45 ton heavy 'tank' loco-motive and tender, along with six more locomotives and tenders, each weighing 350 tons, all coupled up, over the bridge on the down line at 'pretty good speed'. And still the bridge was standing. Hutchinson's judgement was that the bridge had passed the test.

The authorities might have wondered about Hutchinson's judgement three years later when the Tay Bridge collapsed on a stormy night in December, 1879, with the loss of sixty lives. The blame was placed firmly on that bridge's designer, Thomas Bouch, but Hutchinson, as inspector, was involved too, devoting 'much anxious care and thought to this important duty' before and after his decision which we can assume was catastrophically wrong. The Tay Bridge collapsed, but Wylam Bridge is still there, long after it closed in 1968. Of course it is; it was built by a W. E. Jackson, a Newcastle company.

The bridge carried twin tracks and has been described as 'ahead of its time'. Spanning the river in one fell swoop was forced on the designers, since the original intention, a bridge of four spans resting on three piers in the river, was unacceptable, due to the possibility that its weight would disturb the shallow mineworkings under the riverbed. Trains using the bridge carried coal from the collieries at Newburn and Walbottle to Carlisle. Bricks, iron and steel, milk and market garden produce were also transported on the railway.

I approached the bridge now (on an empty stomach), just as the trains of old did, chugging along apace. Once, it served the railway, now it serves pedestrians and cyclists, and abseilers, the latter warned off by a sign: 'No abseiling without permits'. There's a great view upriver, where the Tyne flows in a graceful curve. From here, a path to Ovingham follows the river on its south side, through trees: lime, sycamore, beech, today resplendent in autumn gold. Tasty blackberries complemented my now-eaten biscuits. The sun struggled to pierce the grey clouds above and now and again glistened on the slow-flowing river. It was turning into a lovely autumn day.

Half a mile or so upriver was the scene of my kayaking days. I was in the Scouts, 1st Westerhope troop, with our short trousers and Royal Stewart neckerchiefs and badges. Scouts always had badges. They were a means of proving you'd learnt things, like cooking, tracking and identifying trees. Do you remember old pop songs, and identify what you were doing when such-and-such was out? 'Course you do. My kayaking days here remind me of *Handy Man*: 'Come-a come-a come-a-come-come-come-a-come...Oh, yeah, yeah, yeah, yeah, yeah.' Great record. Great lyrics.

Looking across the river now I could see us paddling our canoe, two-up, twisting the paddles to ensure a full blade in the water. We were supposed to turn upside down in the river to see if we could get out. Bugger that, I remember thinking at the time. It was when we were afloat on that calm stretch of the river I used to look up at the miniature Tyne Bridge. I don't recall ever seeing any trains crossing, although it was open then.

We swam in the river too, one side to the other, no problem, despite the sign visible today: 'Warning. The river is dangerous, with strong currents and deep pools'. There may have been warning signs then too, but as young lads we wouldn't have cared. My great pal, Robert Waugh, was usually my companion in the kayak, and in the river, just as he was in so many other places. Robert was one of those guys at scout camp who would readily jump in a river or stream and think nothing of it. I too could swim, but I never could take to jumping into what was inevitably ice-cold water, enough to take one's breath away. Some folk swim in Lakeland tarns, high on the fells. It must be wonderful, but you'd never, never get me in there. Unless you threw me in, of course, which is what happened at scout camp and never mind being fully clothed at the time. Happy days.

He's dead, now, Robert – Bob, as he was called in adulthood, but never by me. As young lads, we did so much together, in the Scouts and later, from hitch-hiking around Northumberland and Scotland, to those first, faltering steps into dance halls and meeting girls, even though in those days that meant cycling to wherever they lived and hanging around, talking and ending the evening with a simple goodnight kiss and fish and chips at last knockings on the way home. Robert was a shy guy, the last person you would expect to stand in front of people and sing, which he did in later life. He had a great voice. He reached a peak when he sang at the Sage, Gateshead. He was a great mate, sadly missed, never forgotten.

Further on I spied Prudhoe Castle, the flag of English Heritage flapping from its slender tower. The castle stands in a great defensive position and has the proud record as the only castle in the north of England the Scots failed to capture, and it wasn't for the want of trying. I would be calling there soon, but first another landmark was looming up: the Saxon tower of Ovingham Church.

The path leads to the Tyne Riverside Country Park, complete with dog poo bins, each with a sticker depicting a dog that has just trodden in some. If a picture paints a thousand words, these images clearly demonstrated the work of a sicko. Anyway, it was time to cross the bridge into Ovingham. I highlight the moment because sight of the bridge makes one wonder if it will stay up long enough to allow you to reach the other side. It looks so fragile, supported on thin-looking steel pylons. However, since it has stood *in situ* since 1883, I considered safe passage a safe bet. It's wide enough for cars only, not lorries, which seems inappropriate in this day and age, but the good people of Ovingham won't be complaining, since this arrangement means 'heavies' can't cross the river and drive through their village. Pedestrians cross by a separate walkway, safe from the traffic. I found it astonishing that traffic approaching the bridge is not controlled by traffic lights, so that drivers must rely on a courteous 'after you' approach. In 21st century England, that's saying something.

Ovingham – the name means *Homestead at Ofa's place* – is worth a detour on anyone's journey. There's the church, a 17th century packhorse bridge and the customary Goose Fair, not that it was taking place when I turned up. It has strong associations with several of Northumberland's favourite sons, including George Stephenson, who was Christened in the church, and Thomas Bewick, who was born at nearby Cherryburn and lies in the churchyard. The church of St Mary the Virgin dates back to 1050, at least the tower does, although the parapet is a 13th addition, as are the walls of the nave and chancel.

Since 1955 Thomas Bewick's headstone has occupied the porch for preservation purposes, marking (as it did) 'the burial place of Thomas Bewick and his wife and sons'. Bewick is Britain's most famous engraver. A self-taught draftsman, in 1797 he was apprenticed to a Newcastle engraver, after which he had his own business at Amen Corner, next to St Nicholas' Cathedral.

His 'charming vignettes' became famous worldwide, especially his *General History of Quadropeds* and two volumes of *British Birds*. Charlotte Bronte had *Jane Eyre* reading one of them in her novel, on Page 2.

In the churchyard stands a 10 feet tall obelisk marking the resting place of Isaac Jackson of Wylam, 'a man of singular integrity and simplicity of character, and of great mechanical ingenuity...Erected by those who loved and respected him while living and who now mourn his loss'. A superb epitaph, don't you think? An inscription on the other side of the obelisk reads, 'Isaac Jackson, original inventor of the double, three-legged gravity escapement, made for a clock for Robert Stephenson in 1857'. I've often wondered who invented that thing.

A notice on the churchyard gate was a reminder of the times we live in – the 'health and safety' era. Posted by the council, it gave notice of its 'intention to make safe any unsafe tombstone or memorial, by either lying the structure flat on the ground, staking and trying the structure or cordoning off the area'. Whilst many, including me, shake their heads at today's health and safety rules, one might see the point. After all some of the old headstones that have stood in the ground since Victorian times and earlier are big and heavy, and would crush anyone unfortunate enough to be standing nearby if one toppled over. Just the same it's a pity that today there are churchyards where headstones have been laid flat or removed completely. After all, weren't they supposed to mark the resting place of the dead forever? They were, but nothing's forever, is it?

Churchyards are quiet, reflective places. However, the peace at Ovingham today was shattered by the ear-splitting roars of a petrol-driven grass cutter and a strimmer, operated by men cutting the grass. Good that the churchyard is being cared for, bad that I happened along when the caring was taking place. I became 'dearly departed' in a different sense, and made my way past the Bridge End inn to Ovingham's 18th century packhorse bridge over the Whittle Burn. Wide enough for packhorses, not for wheeled vehicles.

It was time to cross the river again. I was bound for Prudhoe Castle. I paused in the middle of the bridge to listen to noise of a different kind – music. The music of the Tyne, generated by the water lapping against boulders mid-stream. The water level was low, just right for the symphony the river played especially for me, a tune that blended in perfectly with the view to the extensive wooded banks downstream. The occasional clatter of a vehicle crossing the bridge had no effect; the moment was unspoiled.

The castle stands in a strong position, 150 feet above the Tyne. Two moats ran along the south curtain wall, and between them was a 'pele yard' – pele meaning 'enclosure' (not a tower, although peles usually happen to be towers). A wooden castle was first built here, by Odinel d'Umfraville, a descendant of Robert with the Beard, who came over with the Conqueror. I wonder if there was a Robert with the 'Tash. Or a Robert with the Acne. William the Lion of Scotland besieged the castle in 1173 and 1174, unsuccessfully. On the second occasion, he declared, 'May I be loathed and disgraced, cursed and ex-comm-unicated by a priest if I grant any terms of respite to Odinel's castle.' Frustrated by his failed endeavours, William 'laid waste' to the surrounding area, and even stripped the bark from apple trees. Bully for him. Maybe it should have been William the Spoilt Brat. He wanted Northumberland to be part of Scotland, but Odinel was loyal to the English king.

To the east of the castle is a curious medieval bridge – curious because if you look over the parapet on one side you see the arch is steeply-pointed, whilst if you look over the other side the arch is round. The embankment is too steep to go down to safely explore further.

To enter the castle you cross a millstream bridge and walk up a long, walled passageway that once led to a drawbridge over the inner moat in front of the main gatehouse. A stone curtain wall surrounds the castle, with the 12th century stone keep within. The keep walls are nine feet thick and rise 45 feet to the parapet. The turret at the south-west corner still stands. I explored the castle, noting the contents of the Comments book, by children, who usually tell the truth when it comes to opinions of buildings of antiquity, of anything in fact. 'Brilliant'. 'Amazing'. 'Fab'. 'I've run out of words'. 'I never knew history like this was on the doorstep'. No, they won't unless to tell 'em and take 'em.

Time and hunger obliged me to move on. I hurried through a dene, ending up at some steps leading steeply up to the main street at Prudhoe. Time for food. A bacon butty and a cuppa was all I could find before heading for the nearest bus stop. But first let me tell you, in case you didn't know, that Prudhoe boasts a recipient of the Victoria Cross. He was John Aidan Liddell, who was born in Newcastle in 1888 but lived at Prudhoe Hall until he was sixteen.

Liddell went to Balliol College, Oxford, where he took an Honours degree in Zoology. He joined the army at the outbreak of the Great War, where he served as Captain, spending 43 consecutive days in the trenches, 'a splendid officer in charge of the guns,' as he was described by a serving Private under his command.

In January, 1915, he was awarded the Military Cross, after which he joined the Royal Flying Corps. In July that year he sustained serious wounds when flying over enemy territory, and died as a consequence. An extract from the grounds for the award of his VC reads, '...he was severely wounded, his right thigh broken, which caused momentary unconsciousness...but by great effort he recovered control after his machine had dropped nearly 3,000 feet, and notwithstanding his collapsed state succeeded under fire and brought the aeroplane into our lines'. In a letter to his mother, no doubt urging her not to worry, Liddell wrote, 'I met with an accident which caused me a little inconvenience'.

What happened, and this is much abbreviated, was that Liddell's Beardmore aircraft was engaged over enemy lines, when a spray of bullets shattered his right thigh. He hung on to the controls, although they were damaged, and managed to land in allied territory, 35 miles away, saving the life of his observer as well as ensuring the aircraft remained in British hands. As the *Morning Post* reported, 'He might have been forgiven had he sought a landing, but surrender never occurred to him'.

If my morning's walk had been a joy, so was taking the bus to Corbridge.

***

Like most people today, I'm used to jumping into my car to get from A to B. But a busride changes everything. Driving a car, one's attention must be focused on the road; in a bus one can look at the scenery or do a crossword or even fall asleep. Driving a car, one's position is low; in a bus, even a single-decker, one sits higher with better views.

That's what I had now: views. An autumn sun was beaming down on the lovely Tyne valley, so that the buildings of Stocksfield and Riding Mill were shown at their best from my vantage point on the bus. As someone born in Tynedale, who later moved away before settling in Cumbria, I was pleased and proud to be here, loving every minute. And here I was, fit and free, and due to arrive in one of Northumberland's finest villages: Corbridge.

I alighted in the Market Square. That's what you do when you get off a bus. Alight. 'Passengers must not alight until the bus stops', that's what the notices said when I was a kid. I thought it meant lighting a fag. Anyway, having alighted, I was promptly seated, on a bench outside the church. I wanted to sit awhile and watch the world go by. Plenty of folk about, each with their own lives, their own ambitions. Me, I had no ambition, for a few minutes at least. I just sat there. I was so damned *happy*. And then I got up and went into the church. Outside the church, people; inside, no-one. What they miss!

Most of St Andrew's church is built from Roman stones, taken from *Corstopitum* Roman fort, to the west of the village. The lower parts of the west tower date back to the 8th century, 'the most important Saxon monument in Northumberland, save for the crypt in Hexham Abbey' (Pevsner). Inside, a high arch leading from the former porch, now the Baptistry, to the nave, is one of the most remarkable in England, being a former Roman gateway. Constructed in about AD 150, at some time the stone arch was probably taken from Corstopitum by oxen-pulled carts or by dragging it maybe, and erected here. It probably stood astride the Stanegate.

On the south side of the churchyard is the Vicar's Pele, built circa 1300, where men of God lived as a precaution against being murdered by the Scots. As vicarages go, it's unusual, to say the least. The old oak-boarded door is still in place, bolted onto an iron grill. Inside stone staircases lead to two upper floors.

Next to the pele is the old Market Cross. It stood in the Market Place for 600 years, but was removed to its present location in 1975. Hereabouts, an account of the history of the village is provided by a sign proclaiming Corbridge to be 'the scene of stormy events in the past'. Ethelred, King of Northumbria, was slain here in 796. Regnald the Dane defeated the English and Scots armies here (united for once, it seems). David I of Scotland 'occupied the town' in 1201, and those Scottish stalwarts William Wallace, Robert the Bruce and David II all turned up to burn the town. But Corbridge is still here, and its good citizens have worshipped in its church for 1,300 years.

The basic shape of the village hasn't changed since Saxon times, and streets I walked today would be little different in shape from then. I went back to the Market Place to see the Percy Cross of cast iron, then walked streets I know pretty well anyway. This included sight of Monksholme, an early 17th century house, restored, which never ceases to amaze me every time I see it. Then I came to the Angel Inn. Before the railway, the mail coach used to stop at the Angel, and the landlord read the newspapers, brought from Newcastle, to the locals.

Two hundred and thirty-odd years later I was tasked with finding a sundial in Corbridge. I was fourteen, and the occasion was the beginning of a fifteen mile hike over two days, which I did with Tom Beatty, as the completion of our First Class Scout badge. The hike, over a specified route, included camping out for one night at a location left to us, which meant carrying the inevitable paraffin-fuelled cooking stove, food aplenty – baked beans and corned beef for certain – and tent and sleeping bag. Rucksacks in those days were far from the streamlined sacks that sit so well on one's shoulders today. Instead they were attached to an A-frame, and with a heavy pack one had to bend forward to almost double to counter the weight behind. People hiking in the 50s were like hunchbacks.

Task One was: 'find the sundial'. And there it was, above the door of the Angel, dated 1726. After that we walked to Aydon Castle, Great Whittington and Bingfield, crossing fields and walking along country byways until we (me anyway) were knackered and it was time for tea. We pitched camp, I can reveal, near Low Errington, on a wee patch of grass by a burn, just off the A68.

Next morning we continued to Cocklaw Tower, after which we had to find a tall wooden cross. We found it, right by the side of the B6318, the Military Road – St Oswald's Cross, as it is. After that it was south through Fallowfield and Acomb. To succeed on our mission we had to locate the points mentioned, as well as others, walk the route and camp out. The latter would be only after seeking and getting permission from the owner of the land. Sure enough, I endorsed my log of the walk 'with permission of the farmer'. I believe I can now safely reveal this entry was a falsehood. Sure, we could see the lights of a farm, but after walking all day bent double under the weights of our sacks the last thing two young lads were up for was knocking on a door half a mile away and asking for permission. However, Mr District Commissioner, all the rest was true. Every stooping step of the way.

Corbridge is spoiled, slightly, by parked cars. It seems a pity that they are allowed into the village, that they can't be left across the river so that visitors might walk over the bridge to a car-free zone (disabled visitors excepted). It won't happen, because if you bar the car you lose the visitors. But Corbridge is delightful, nevertheless. Once, it was second only to Newcastle in the county, and even might have been the capital of North-umbria, post Bamburgh. The Roman fort of Corstopitum, half a mile away, was my next objective. As I walked the road, I recalled my one and only previous visit here, through my school, when I was about thirteen. So, they did take us to somewhere of historical significance. Hoo-ray!

Corstopitum existed before Hadrian's Wall, being one of a series of forts on the *Stanegate* (Stone Road), linking it with *Luguvalium* (Carlisle). Corstopitum was a supply base of timber construction. It was abandoned when the Wall was built. About AD 90, after withdrawal from the north (today's Scotland and north Northumberland), the Stanegate was the northernmost Roman frontier. But when the Romans ventured again into the far north the fort was re-constructed, this time of stone. By the 3rd century Corstopitum was a major town, and these are the remains we see today. Where I walked now the Romans walked. After exploring the site I sat on a wooden bench, on the Stanegate, to picture in my mind's eye – it wasn't difficult – the main street, as it would have been, and to take in the moment.

I returned to Corbridge and crossed the Tyne by the seven-arched bridge of 1674, the only one left standing along the entire length of the river after the Great Flood. Across the bridge a path runs over Dilston Haughs. A hundred or so yards along the path I turned to see the magnificent stone bridge bathed in sunshine, with Corbridge on the low hillside to the left. What a picture! I could scarcely stop looking back at the scene. A mile further the path led through nettles and crossed the railway.

I wanted to visit the scout campsite, situated in what was once the deer park of Dilston. The campsite was awash in sun-shine, with several tents pitched. They were nothing like the tents in my day. We had plain brown canvas tents; the ones I saw today were colourful and probably waterproof. I recall camping here only once. There were other troops from the district, against whom we competed in tracking and other scouting activities. Not as enjoyable, to me at any rate, as our troop going off alone, which we usually did.

The story of Dilston is a romantic tale about the Radcliffe family, and in particular James, the 3rd Earl of Derwentwater.

First, the name. *Dyvelston*, as it was, possibly derives from Richard de Dyvelston, who held the barony here; and Devil's Water would derive from the same. But the story really starts nearly 100 miles away, on Derwentwater, in the Lake District. Here, on 'Lord's Island', was a mansion, where lived Sir Francis

Radcliffe, who probably opted to live an isolated existence as a precaution against Scottish invaders. Eventually, through marriage, the names of Derwentwater and Radcliffe were linked with Dilston.

Sir Edward Radcliffe took up residence at Dilston in the 16th century. At the beginning of the 17th century, his son, Sir Francis Radcliffe, built a mansion known as Dilston Hall. A chapel was built, and the Lord's Bridge over the Devil's Water, which was linked to the mansion on top of the hill by a carriageway. Sir Francis's son, Edward, married Lady Mary Tudor, daughter of Charles II, and Sir Francis was created an earl. It seems Edward Radcliffe, the second earl, had no interest in Dilston, and left to live in London. Two of his sons, James and Charles, were educated in France in the exiled Stuart court at St Germain, near Paris, along with James Stuart, their cousin. In 1709, when young James Radcliffe inherited the title 3rd Earl of Derwent-water, he went to live at Dilston, a place he had never seen.

James built a new mansion, which incorporated the present day ruined tower. In 1712, he married Anna Maria Webb. They were the lucky pair, safe and secure in their new home. But that very year the protestant king, George I, was crowned, not the Catholic James Stuart, still in exile in France. Thus was born the Jacobite cause: to install a Roman Catholic on the throne; and thus was born the reason for James Radcliffe's untimely demise, when he decided to support the Jacobite Rebellion of 1715.

That September the Scots marched, raising the Stuart standard as they went. James and Charles, joined other North-umbrian Catholics, including Tom Forster of Bamburgh, who was declared general even though he had no experience as a soldier. For a fortnight they marched around Northumberland, before linking up with the Scots, arriving at Warkworth where they proclaimed the exiled James king.

They marched to Morpeth, only to be told that Newcastle had barricaded its gates and supported King George. On 9 November a depleted Jacobite army, under Forster's command, marched to Preston and proclaimed James king. Three days later the Jacobite army was routed by the Hanoverians. Sixteen hundred prisoners were taken, including James Radcliffe, who was taken to the Tower of London, and Charles Radcliffe and Forster, who were taken to Newgate. Charles and Forster would escape, but on 9 February, 1716, 27-year old James Radcliffe stood trial for treason. He was ordered to be executed by beheading, and on 24 February he was taken to Tower Hill, where four times he was offered his life if he would conform to the established church and accept the House of Hanover. He refused, and paid the ultimate penalty.

James's body was buried in the chapel at Dilston, except for his heart, which was kept by a surgeon. It ended up in France, in the custody of Augustine nuns, then disappeared. His wife, who was pregnant, went to live with her parents in Gloucestershire. She had a daughter, Anna Maria. Earlier, the Radcliffes had had a son, John, who would die unmarried, leaving no heir, after which the Dilston estates fell into neglect.

Charles Radcliffe, meanwhile, living in exile in France, still supported the Stuart cause. He sailed for Scotland in the 1745 rebellion, when Charles Edward Stuart – Bonnie Prince Charlie – led an army as far south as Derby, before turning back to face defeat at Culloden. Charles Radcliffe was captured. This time there would be no escape, and on 8 December, 1746, he was executed. He was buried in London, but his heart was taken to Dilston and placed in a leaded coffin with the body of his brother.

Dilston Hall was demolished in 1768, leaving only the ruined tower, chapel, and a gateway that once led into the courtyard. In 1874 the ruins were plundered, and the body of James Radcliffe and his brother's heart, were removed and interred at Thorndon Hall, Essex.

The present Dilston Hall was built in 1835 and became a maternity hospital where, on a March Friday in 1944, I happened along. According to my dad, he walked to the Hall from Westerhope to visit my mam, and me, only to find himself cut off due to a snowstorm. He occupied himself thereafter by serving tea to pregnant women and new mothers, something that obviously tickled his fancy as he talked of it so often.

Today, I crossed the Devil's Water by Lord's Bridge and climbed the former carriageway, now an overgrown path, to the tower. It stands ruinous and open to the sky. Nearby is the tiny chapel, and a bench with a commemoration plate that reads, simply, 'In memory of James Radcliffe, Third Earl of Derwentwater'. I sat there awhile, in a place I love, where every time I visit a gentle breeze blows as though in acknowledgement of my coming home. Ironically, today my real home is only a couple of miles from Derwentwater, in the Lake District, where the story of the Radcliffe's began.

Why did James Radclife forsake this place to take up arms for a cause he surely could not have won – to unseat the king with a meagre following of men, many of whom weren't even soldiers? Maybe he was fighting for an ideal; he was after all, a Roman Catholic and acquainted with the exiled James. It is said his wife urged him to lead his men against the Protestant army. We cannot know if this is true, but we can respect a man who could have stayed in his mansion, yet chose to fight for what he believed in. It cost him his life, his wife her husband, his children their father:

> How mournful feeble Nature's tone
> When Dilston Hall appears;
> Where none's to wait the orphan's moan,
> Nor dry the widow's tears…

Lord's Bridge dates to around 1621 and spans the Devil's Water in a single, graceful curve. On the Dilston side can be seen the crumbling stone walls of the former hanging gardens, whilst the low-hanging branches of trees are reflected in the clear water below. One can imagine the scene as it was: horse and carriage crossing the bridge on the way to the Hall. Those days are gone, but Dilston retains a charm all of its own, unmatched anywhere. Long may it be so.

I was Hexham-bound and the clock was ticking. The right of way led through Swallowship Woods between overgrown hedgerows. The path was narrow, with ferns, tall weeds, brambles and nettles. Brittle leaves of previous autumns carpeted the floor, crumbling under my feet. I felt as though I was the only person who had come this way for generations.

The way led to Duke's House, with its tall chimneys, reminding me of an Enid Blyton novel I read as a child about some children who went to granny's house, *Tall Chimneys*, and found themselves in a secret passage. I loved the old classics: *Treasure Island, Coral Island, Tom Sawyer, Nicholas Nickelby*. So many more. (I never read *Little Women* although I've often wondered *What Katy Did*). Reading was learning. Reading was fun. Reading was a way of using one's imagination to picture people, scenes, situations. At school we were taught to read early. As a result we could spell and use grammar. Today, alas, there seems to be little reading, even at school. It's far easier to look at a TV screen instead. That's how it seems to me.

After the woods, the path led down the hillside, to Hexham. Since leaving Corbridge I had seen no-one. Now there were people; Hexham is a bustling, busy place. Today had been spent visiting scenes of Northumberland's wonderful history. Tomorrow I was off to the valley of the North Tyne, to visit the scene of the Battle of Heavenfield, where those who fought in the cause of Christianity won such a noble victory, and to renew acquaintance with the Romans.

***

Hexham is a grand place, Northumbrian to the core. Today, I decided to while away an hour here before heading north. It had rained and the morning was dank. But the breeze was fresh and heavy skies were OK by me.

The front of the Abbey faces the Market Place. This part of the church is Victorian, its designer our old friend John Dobson. Pevsner describes it as 'disappointing'. Everyone is entitled to his opinion. Mine is the opposite. The Abbey aside, the dom-inating features of the Market Place for me are The Shambles, built in 1766 as a covered market, which it still is, and the Moot Hall, formerly the castle gatehouse, built about 1400 and fortified against Scottish attacks. The Scots were regular raiders, and in

1296 they burnt the town to the ground, including the 'beautiful church', and not content with that they blocked the doors of the school and set fire to that too, with the children still inside.

Today, outside the Old Gaol, an information panel says the Scots raided England *in response* to bloody English raids, and goes on about the two countries being at war. So they were, sometimes, but more often it was groups of individuals who crossed the border to destroy and kill. The Scots raided England because they were thieves and murderers, not *in response*. The English raided Scotland for the same reason.

On 9 March, 1761, the Market Place was the scene of a riot. It had been the custom for men to be conscripted into the army through being hired to serve by landowners. Then they changed the rules so that men would be selected by ballot. When the ballot at Hexham was to take place, two battalions of the North York Militia were despatched to the town. A crowd of five thousand had gathered in the Market Place, and 240 troops faced them. The Riot Act was read, and when the crowd refused to disperse the soldiers opened fire, killing fifty-one people. There-after the North York Militia was known as the 'Hexham Butchers'. Danes, Scots, the English themselves: they've all inflicted violence on the people of Hexham.

Just off the Market Place is Wetherspoon's pub, formerly the *Forum*, once Hexham's cinema (appropriately named, considering the former presence of the Romans hereabouts). As a primary school pupil at Westerhope I sang here with the school choir. Not because I could sing. Heavens no; I sang here because the school sent a choir and I happened to be in the right class at the right time (or should that be the wrong class at the right time?).

We sang *Nymphs and Shepherds*. The song derives from Thomas Shadwell's poem. For anyone familiar with the words, which I would estimate at about 0.01% of the population, they are very poetic. Shadwell was appointed poet laureate in 1689, so this is not surprising, not that it explains much (to me) about the meaning of his poem. I don't know who (or what) the nymphs and shepherds were, who Flora was and why your flocks could securely rove whilst you expressed your jollity. But I'll tell you this: that having been taught the words at a tender age and never forgotten them, it seems proof to me that the younger the child the better to teach them something. What we learn young is with us forever.

Situated in the middle of the Market Place is the stone column of the former fountain, now sadly dry. It bears a wonder-ful inscription by local poet, Wilfrid Wilson Gibson:

> O you who drink my cooling waters clear,
> Forget not the far hills from whence they flow,
> Where over fell and moor, and year by year
> Spring summer autumn winter come and go...

Hills and fells and moors and cooling waters clear. That's Northumberland!

Hexham's other pride and joy is the Sele and Abbey grounds. I went there now, through the arch 'presented to the town to commemorate the services of the 4th Northumberland Fusiliers in France and Belgium during the War'. The men were from towns and villages in Tynedale, whose battalion mobilised at Hexham on August 4, 1914, went to France on April 20, 1915, and fought at such places as Ypres, Armentiers, the Somme, Passchendael.

I walked between limes to the Priest's Seat, a low hill with wonderful views across the Tyne valley. Moving on, a particularly interesting feature is a mediaeval bridge, unseen to those who cross as it is a bridge beneath a bridge. The bridge spans the Cockshaw or Halgut Burn, which passes through the park in a tunnel. If you clamber down the embankment you can see the lower bridge below. Since no steps or path exists, one assumes you aren't encouraged to do this. They were going to run the Carlisle-Newcastle turnpike through the Sele, but happily the idea was thwarted by Diana Beaumont, the Lady of the Manor, much to the delight of residents then and mine now. There is more to report on Hexham, but now I set out for the day's walk to the North Tyne valley.

Overnight rain had swelled the river, which hurried by in spate below the arches of Mylne's grand bridge. A signpost made it clear there was to be no canoeing at the Country Park in September and October, except here, and no paddling at Bywell Bridge and Prudhoe riverside at weekends. Who's to tell us what to do or what not to do when it comes to paddling and canoeing in our free-flowing rivers? Advice – OK. But to *tell* us?

Signposts are fascinating, don't you think? Especially ones giving us orders. Freedom was the order of the day, for me at any rate, not rules and regulations. And with that in mind I set forth for the bridge. If you ever cross the bridge, do pause and look back to see Hexham, perched on the hillside, a sight that has largely remained unchanged for years, with the Abbey, Moot Hall and the Old Gaol prominent on the skyline. May it ever be so.

On a hill, among trees, is the church of St John Lee, named after St John of Beverley, who lived at Hexham for a time. Happily the church was open. I say 'happily'; so often today churches are closed to the visitor. There was a time most people had little, if anything. Then, churches were open. Today, where almost everyone has material things – TV, DVD, iPods – many are closed. It seems the better off we are the more likely we are to steal. Once, to steal from a church was the crime of sacrilege, which carried greater punishment than 'ordinary' theft, or larceny as it was. We should open the churches and punish those who steal from them accordingly. At the very least make 'em work in the community wearing shirts with 'I stole from a church' emblazoned across the front and back. It would be interesting to keep statistics to see how many stole from a church again.

Inside the church is the Oakwood Stone, a Cup and Ring stone 'characteristic of the Neolithic early Bronze Age carvings found throughout Northumberland'. It dates back to around 2,000 years BC and may have been the capstone of a prehistoric grave. Outside is a memorial, 'To the men of the Parish who fell in the War', meaning the Great War, so called because it was to be the war to end all wars. We now know different.

In the churchyard a headstone marks the resting place of George Frederick Hutchinson, 'killed in action, 1944, aged 19'. 1944 was the year I was born. A young bloke of 19 gave his life so I could live mine. His mother, Isobel, lived until 1968.

Twenty-four years without her son. In the lychgate is a memorial plate dedicated to the men who died in World War II. There are 21 names.

There's a story about St John Lee that's worth recounting. It concerns one Robert Scott, aged 90, and 25-year old Jean Middlemass, who were to marry. Scott had spent the last twenty-six years of his life using crutches to get about, but on his wedding day he cast them aside and walked from his home at Wall to the church and back again without them. Aged 90, his bride 65 years his junior: one might hardly be surprised at his new lease of life. I wonder if he made 91.

Under blue Northumbrian skies, and in a stiff, fresh autumn breeze, I headed for Acomb, crossing a lovely stone bridge across a burn en route. I reached the village square, complete with stone pant and wooden bench with inscription, 'In loving memory of Arty Mews, 1922-1996. He's away to seek the coos'. In the middle of the square is a solid stone edifice with dried-up fountain. Some of the houses date back to 1750. I could have sat here fifty years ago, it would have been little different (except I would have looked slightly younger).

I headed north, along the lane for Fallowfield. The farther I walked, the higher the lane as it climbed from valley and the more exquisite the views. At the top of the hill I stopped and looked back over Tynedale. The view was surprisingly extensive and quite breathtaking. At the scattered buildings of Fallowfield I turned left over a wall stile. Here, at around 600 feet, were tall sycamores, with the wind rustling through their high branches. I had it all to myself. I was in heaven.

The map indicated a 'Settlement' above the village of Wall, my next objective. Lady pheasants abounded, scampering along as they do. No sign of any males. Maybe they were on a motorway somewhere. If I thought navigation hereabouts would be straightforward I was in for a surprise, for here, in the fields above Wall, in clear weather and armed with map and compass, I somehow contrived to get lost. I found myself crossing a huge field occupied by cows, lots of them. At first they ignored me, but they became curious, fascinated even, when the bloke with the rucksack, having walked through their midst, was walking through their midst again. I aimed for a corner of the field. No sign of the path there. I stumbled through nettles, walked alongside a stone wall. But even though Wall itself was close, I could not navigate a way down to it. The Settlement I gave up on.

I checked the map, crossed the field again to the wall and walked alongside it, every step followed by fifty head of cattle. Hither and thither I walked. Hither and thither they followed, until, finally (on a thither bit) there was nothing for it but to make my way as best as I could towards Wall. This meant climbing the wall, which thwarted the cows' endeavours to pursue me further. I trod among brambles before walking down-hill to a field, which I crossed and ended up in someone's garden, where I tip-toed gingerly to a gate through which I passed, unseen, finding myself in Wall, a quiet backwater of stone houses around a large green. No vehicle and no person appeared during my visit, which I spent seated on a bench in the sunshine, relieved after my unexpected ordeal in the fields. Then I took a backroad that led steadily uphill, with a great view of Mylne's bridge at Chollerford.

And so to the Military Road, and St Oswald's Cross, dedicated to the memory of St Oswald and the small army he led in the Battle of Heavenfield, in or around AD 635. Northumbria stretched between Humber and Forth – North-Humber-Land – and was ruled by Edwin. His authority was challenged when two heathen kings, Cadwallon of Gwynedd, and Penda of Mercia, attacked Edwin's army near Doncaster, in 633. Edwin was killed, as were his heirs Osric and Eanfrid. Oswald had had a Christian education on Iona. Now, at 29, he took command of a small army and marched from Bamburgh to face Cadwallon. It seems the night before the battle Oswald held a large wooden cross in a hole in the ground while earth was filled in, and that afterwards he gathered his men to pray for the victory, declaring, 'Let us kneel together and ask God Almighty to protect us from the arrogant savagery of our enemies, since He knows that we fight in a just cause to save our nation.' Oswald and his followers would no doubt say they won because God was on their side. Maybe He was.

The two forces met here, at Heavenfield. A significant feature of the battlefield was Hadrian's Wall, still *in situ* at the time. Although we cannot know what happened exactly, I like to think Oswald and his men were waiting behind the Wall so that the Welsh army, tired from their long march north and the climb from the valley of the North Tyne, found themselves facing – a blank wall. And then, suddenly, Oswald and his men emerged, fresh and determined, and saw the pagans off. The Welsh were routed; Cadwallon was slain. The battle site is known, because bones and sword hilts were found in later years around what is now the Military Road. It was an important battle, insofar as its outcome, a victory for Christianity over heathenism, established a Christian king in Northumbria, after which, soon after his victory, Oswald invited the monks of Iona to set up a monastery on Lindisfarne, which they did under the guidance of Aidan.

A memorial church was erected at Heavenfield, but was replaced in 1737 by the present day building. St Oswald's stands behind tall sycamores, atop the broad ridge. At the back of the church are two benches, one 'in loving memory' of Cecil Ballantyne', the other dedicated to Alexander Mason. Once more Northumbrian breezes rustled the leaves as, alone, I took in the magnificent panorama to the north, where the ground falls sharply away to reveal distant moors and far away hills. This is wild country, a country of space that invokes feelings of freedom. Freedom to roam. Freedom to live. When I returned to the churchyard gate, I saw hikers, probably on Hadrian's Way path, which runs between the cross and the church. They passed by without a glance at either.

I took Hadrian's Way myself, which led to a section of the Wall at Planetrees, where there is a clear join in the Wall, one part being broad, the other narrower. Why did they do this? Were they running short of stones? Were they in a hurry to finish building the Wall? Historians can answer some questions, some they cannot; other questions open up as we know more.

Here I must mention General Wade, who built the so-called Military Road, which runs from Heddon-on-the-Wall to Greenhead. From Heddon to near Planetrees Wade saw fit to use

Hadrian's Wall as a foundation for his road, so that today, as you drive along the B6318 at this (and other) points, you're driving on top of the Wall. The reason for this goes back to the 1745 Jacobite rebellion, when Charles Stuart's army marched south, via Carlisle, with the intention of seizing the throne. An English army was sent from Newcastle to intercept it, but was unable to get there in time because there was no road. Wade's military road was completed too late to do anything about the Jacobites and was never used for military purposes.

At Plantetrees, Wade's road went off half-right, away from the Wall, presumably because the engineers found a better spot to bridge the North Tyne. The Romans, of course, ran their wall down to the river in the usual straight line.

I turned left just before Chollerford bridge, and took the footpath alongside the trackbed of the former Border Counties Railway. The path led to the bridge abutment, where the Roman bridge, or bridges, crossed the North Tyne to *Cilurnum*, today called Chesters, whose excavated remains are visible across the river, the bathhouse so close you could almost touch it. For me, the bridge abutment takes pride of place. Here one can sit and apply one's imagination to the scene as it was nearly two thousand years ago. The first, 'Hadrianic' bridge, built about AD 122, was probably erected just before this section of the Wall was complete, then the Wall ran up to the bridge from either side. The bridge rested on eight hexagonal stone piers. The first pier survives on this, the east side of the river, where it has been incorporated into a larger, 3rd century abutment, part of a second, wider bridge, built about a hundred years later. When building it, huge rectangular stone blocks had to be manoeuvred into position, for which the Romans used a crane, positioned in a hole in the abutment, which can still be seen.

Today, one of the circular stone columns from the second bridge lies on top of the abutment, along with massive stone blocks, all left high and dry due to the river shifting its course over the years. Evidently the Romans considered a phallic symbol to bring good fortune, and I knew there was a carved phallus on one of the blocks. I wandered about, searching for it, to no avail.

The only other company I had was a young woman and her two small children, who were exploring the relics. I wondered if she was local, if she might know of the location of the phallus. But how could I ask? 'Excuse me, do you know where there's a Roman penis hereabouts?' It's not the sort of thing a stranger should ask a woman alone. I sat on one of the blocks, hesitating, not wanting to offend or give her cause to feel threatened. But when she turned to leave, I called out, and asked her directly. She didn't know, but hazarding a guess she pointed to the huge stone column that lay on the abutment. 'Could that be it?' she asked. Size does matter, then. Thanks anyway, I said, and as she turned, I saw it. Right in front of my eyes, a phallus – well, the entire male genitalia – in full view on the side of one of the stone blocks, almost at ground level. I called out to her: 'Found it!' She smiled, either out of politeness, or pity for a bloke who was searching for such an object. The sculpture was unmistakeable but presumably not life size.

Sitting here, one can imagine the scene: the Wall, coming down steeply from the east, crossing the river and running directly to the wall of the fort, then continuing from the west wall, towards Housesteads and Carlisle. What a scene. If only we could step back in time and see it as it was. Instead we must rely on 'artists' impressions' – and our own imaginations.

I returned to the road and crossed the bridge at Chollerford. Mid-bridge I looked upriver to the North Tyne's tree-lined banks, branches hanging right down to the water's edge, on this lovely autumn day a grand sight. There was a distant church tower, Chollerton I supposed; and, sadly, on the far skyline, a wind turbine. Nature gladdens, the wind turbine saddens. I moved on.

Chollerford bridge dates from 1778, replacing the previous one swept away in the Great Flood of 1771. Seen from the path alongside the river it's a magnificent sight. In the years between the old bridge being swept away and its present-day replacement a ferry operated, taking passengers from the nearby Red Lion inn (now gone) across the river.

One of the landlords of the Red Lion was reputedly a poacher whose methods were somewhat unusual, to say the least. He'd soak some barley in rum just before sunset, then spread it around nearby woodlands frequented by pheasants and other game birds. He could then return to the comfort of the inn, safe in the knowledge that he could return later and collect his quarries, by now too drunk to escape.

The B6319 runs past Chesters. I followed it for two miles until a right of way led off, southward, crossing the line of the Stanegate. Here, in the middle of a field, I came across a stone column, 3 feet high, with a metal ring fixed to the back (map ref 896684). Is this a Roman milestone, standing by the Stanegate? High Warden Hill lay ahead. I climbed it without pause, being blessed with stunning views opening up across the South Tyne. At the top another view opened up, eastward to Wall and Hexham, the latter backed by extensive forests. All this I savoured alone on a wonderful autumn day. What more could anyone ask?

A huge Iron Age fort occupies the top of Warden Hill. If they excavated here, what they would find among the many mounds! I moved on, downhill, across a field of a thousand cowpats, taking the bridleway to High Warden and on to Warden church. St Michaels was rebuilt in 1764-65 at a cost of £443-5s-8d. The lower part of the tower may pre-date the Vikings. If so, it could be the oldest in Northumberland.

Much of the church was built from Roman stones, probably from Chesters. In the porch we have 'Warden Man', a split grave cover from a Roman altar. Outside, Warden Cross probably dates back to the 7th century, one of a type raised after the Battle of Heavenfield so that people could come and pray by them, some churches not yet having been built. The lychgate of 1903 has a superb carved timber superstructure. Close to it some graves are protected against body-snatchers by iron bars.

Warden is a peaceful place, 'handsomely situated among the trees near the confluence of the North and South Tynes', as Pevsner describes it. It was not by chance I had chosen to come here on my perambulation of my native county; I had passed this way before, the first time being when my attention was drawn to it by Alfred Wainwright in his *Pennine Journey*, in which he described the church tower as having 'not a single feature to relieve the bare monotony of the plain walls' and likened its appearance to a granary. 'Its expression is blank. It is dumfounded that you, a stranger, should have found your way to it. It hides behind the trees to hide its distress.' I've read much of Wainwright's work and followed in his footsteps over fell and moor (including all his 214 'Wainwrights' several times over), but if he were alive today I would have to challenge him on his description of Warden church. It would not have been difficult to win my case, that Warden, with its church, is a gem in Northumberland's crown. Here is peace, where, as Wainwright himself admits, most strangers pass Warden by. Long may it be so.

It was in a cottage hereabouts, in 1826, that a quiet, inoffensive chap called Joe the Quilter lived. Joe was found dead in his cottage with over forty wounds, the motive for his murder possibly theft, although he was on parish relief:

> His cot secure, his garden neat,
> He loved the lone and still retreat.
> Glad were his neighbours all to meet
> With honest Joe the Quilter.

Joe's assailant was never caught.

I walked down to West Boat, where a ferry once operated. It was replaced by a chain suspension bridge in 1826. This collapsed under the weight of a steam thresher in 1877. It was rebuilt but replaced in 1903 by the present bridge, built by the County Council. The tollhouse still stands on the south side of the river. Beyond, the path led under the railway and to Hexham.

The Carlisle-Newcastle railway is one of the oldest in the country and survived Dr Beeching's cuts. It opened fully on 18 June, 1838. It had been the intention of the railway company to haul carriages by horses, which we may think as quite astonishing now. But by the time the track was laid steam locomotives were established and were used, albeit illegally at first, on a section of this line as early as 1835. Three notable branch lines followed: one from Haltwhistle to Alston along the South Tyne;

the others from Hexham to near Allendale, and the Border Counties Railway from Hexham to Riccarton Junction, Scotland, along the North Tyne. Sadly, they all closed.

So ended the first two parts of my Northumberland expedition (completed over one visit). I looked forward to Part Three with relish, and no wonder; the thought of Hexhamshire, Blanchland, Allendale and the South Tyne valley was mouth-watering in the extreme. I could hardly wait.

Part III

Far Horizons

I returned to Hexham. Of course, I couldn't leave without visiting the abbey.

Hexham Abbey, or priory church as it is, replaced a former church here. The original was built about 675-680 by St Wilfrid. He went to the Continent where he was impressed by the grand, stone churches, and when he returned Queen Etheldreda gave him land upon which he built a monastery church dedicated to St Andrew, 'the grandest house this side of the Alps'. In 681 it was dedicated a cathedral, remaining so until Danish invasions when the See merged with Lindisfarne. In 875, Halfdene the Dane burnt Hexham's church to the ground. Sadly, nothing remains of the original church, save the crypt.

After a period of desolation the church came under the oversight of Durham and later, in 1113, York, when it was re-established as a priory. A new church was built on the site by Augustinian canons, but Hexham's 'abbey' has been a parish church since the Dissolution of the Monasteries. The Augustinian church has been rebuilt in part, and what we see today dates to two main periods: 1180-1250, and 1850-1910.

The Saxon crypt is surely Hexham Abbey's *pièce de résistance*. The crypt lies under the nave, and is reached by a stone staircase. Like the original church, it was built from Roman stones, probably plundered from the abandoned Corstopitum. There are Roman inscriptions on some of the stones, which were laid with the inscriptions outward-facing to help plaster to bind on to them. The crypt was built into a hole dug into the ground before the erection of the original church and was historically used by the monks, and perhaps by pilgrims, who would walk miles to enter its dimly-lit passages, and can be visited today by the likes of me.

It was May, my favourite month. May is spring; May is sunshine and birdsong and bluebells. The May day I resumed my walk was sunny, but cold. Still, it wasn't raining, and that's always a blessing when you're walking England's green and pleasant landscapes. I was southbound, for Blanchland, which meant climbing out of the valley to an ancient bridleway that led uphill, with super views back through the trees over Hexham and the Tyne valley, and the North Tyne valley too, with the abbey taking pride of place. I had looked forward to today for months, to this very view, in fact. I climbed a hillside to heaven.

Cresting the hill I found myself walking down a big, sloping meadow. Here was a bench, with dedication plate dedicated to Jim Hobbs, 'Our friend and secretary for 27 years – Hexham Ramblers' Association'. The bench could not be better placed. I had hardly earned a rest, but I sat there anyway, taking in the view, savouring the peace of a May morn. Daisies abounded all over the meadow, reminding me of childhood days in the 'daisy field' at Westerhope, where Mam made daisy chains by piercing a thumbnail through the narrow stalks and threading the daisies through. It's housing now. That's progress.

I was in Hexhamshire, once a district of the old Northumbria, later part of County Durham. But Henry I decided to weaken the power of the Prince Bishops and made Hexhamshire a separate county, with Hexham its administrative town. It remained so until 1572 when the 'Shire' was incorporated into Northumber-land by Act of Parliament. Today, the parish of Hexhamshire covers 34 square miles, a sparsely populated area mainly of small hamlets and scattered farmsteads and houses.

It was downhill to the Dipton Burn where, on an April day in 1977, I brought my family and parked opposite the Dipton Mill inn. It was our first family walk, the beginning of my own walking 'career'. We did a 12-mile hike around Hexhamshire, the first of many walks that year before we moved away to Hertfordshire. Our children (including twins) were aged from eight to thirteen. I wonder if they remember their dad cooking sausages by the Ham Burn. Today I arrived at the Dipton Mill inn, alone but happy, to re-walk our walk, in part at least, only this time instead of carrying sausages I was carrying thoughts of my family and of happy days spent in Northumberland.

A muddy track leads to Dotland Park, a former hunting lodge for the Priors of Hexham. The right of way crosses the fields towards Smelting Syke. In my 'Ramblers' Tynedale' guide of thirty years before, a 'tiny stream' is mentioned. Today, the course of the stream is no more than a shallow depression in the grass. Where has the water gone? I've noticed dried-out streams in the chalk-based soil of the Chilterns, but here? No doubt 'experts' will put it down to climate change, caused by aerosols, fridges, cars and flatulent cows. D'you know, I once watched a Member of the European Parliament sounding off on TV about getting rid of outside barbecue heaters in the drive to save the planet. What I can never understand is how idiots like this ever get into a position of power to boss normal people around. Save the planet? Save us!

This is grand country: scattered farmsteads, woodland, wide, open fields. And places with lovely, unforgettable names. Like Juniper, where I went down to the Rowley Burn before continuing to Mollersteads, which dates back to the days of the 'Hexham tanners' and is named after the mallows used in the dyeing process (*Maller Steeds*). The path runs near to the burn, which here passes over a rocky riverbed. Water music. Simply wonderful. Further on the music gave way to the screeching of crows. I pressed on, my presence sending panic-stricken rabbits scarpering to their burrows. Kids love 'em, farmers loathe 'em; I feel sorry for them. If humankind isn't shooting them we're running them over. There was a time, at the lane ahead, I could have sought refreshment in the Click 'em In, a pub, now sadly gone (like so many others). Instead I made directly for Whitley Chapel.

St Helen's church of 1742 is simple in design. I love the churchyard with its grand old headstones, some six feet high, with weathered inscriptions. One, at the grave of Robert Stokoe, the inscription is barely legible, but you have the benefit of it here:

> My anvil and hammer he declin'd,
> My bellows have quite lost their wind,
> My fire's extinct, my forge decay'd,
> My vices are in the dust all laid.
> My coals are spent, my iron gone,
> My nails are drove, my work is done,
> My mortal part rests near this stone,
> My soul to heaven I hope is gone.

Your soul is in heaven right here, mate.

Another headstone is 'sacred to the memory of Elizabeth, wife of John Bell, of Aydon Shields, who died January 18, 1836, in the 42nd year of her age'; and 'the said John Bell, who died at Aydon Shields, in 1868, aged 78'. Also 'Hannah, widow of John Bell, who died at Aydon Shields, May 25, 1896, aged 86. John Bell lies with his two wives. Good luck to him. On another, protected by overhanging branches, the inscription, 'Life How Short! Eternity How Long!'. How true, more's the pity. I wondered what difference, if any, St Helen's incumbents would see if they could look around the old churchyard. In this timeless place, none, I would venture. Inside the church, happily unlocked, I checked the visitors' book. It dated back to 1978.

I moved on, making my way to the Devil's Water, further upstream than before, which I crossed and headed south through the woods. Further on the footpath ran between the pines of Slaley Forest and a drystone wall, a narrow corridor the sun barely penetrated. I might have been the only person to come this way since they built the wall or planted the trees. The farther I walked by the wall, the more I appreciated the skill of the men who built it. It was simple but solid, a work of art. Better by far than some of the modern 'art' we find cluttering up our towns and cities.

Suddenly, life! A red squirrel emerged from the forest, took one look at the approaching stranger and vanished. The reds are an endangered species, rarely seen these days, and never at all in England's southern counties. I never thought I would encounter one in a pine forest.

I emerged at the other side of the wall to find myself facing a sea of purple heather: Blanchland Moor. I pressed on, uphill, gratefully leaving the forest behind, climbing the moor towards the summit, War Law. There was a boundary stone, with weathered lettering, 'S H', almost lost in the heather. The ordnance column, my objective, was now clear on the skyline. A thin trod led towards it. I came upon two forlorn stone gateposts, standing in the heather where they have been for years, only the wall or fence that adjoined them, and the gate, have all gone. The rusting iron hinge-pivots remain, testimony to better days.

I struggled on through the heather, presuming I had lawful access in this lonely place. So often I have climbed to ordnance columns, or trigonometrical stations if you will – 'the trig' is what walkers say – and this one was waiting just for me. The hillside was steep, the heather so thick, progress was difficult, but I reached trig S6701 in triumph. There ought to have been a fanfare to greet my arrival, but the only sound was the wind, just a light breeze as I stood in glorious solitude and surveyed the scene.

And what a scene! Far horizons, stretching out before me. Derwent Reservoir, distant fields and forests, endless moorland and, in the distance, I swear, the tall buildings of Newcastle or

Gateshead, along the Tyne valley. To the north, the Border country. There was the drone of a distant aircraft, the singing of a skylark, the wind. Otherwise all was silent, up here, on top of the moor. What a moment. What a place.

Once again I lingered, reluctant to leave. But time is your master, and I headed off, down through the heather where, for some reason I suddenly thought of possible, unseen hazards that might be hidden there: adders, potholes, gin traps. The latter are illegal, but it would be quite possible there were some still *in situ* since whenever. Unscathed, I came to a good path, a six feet wide high 'road' over the moor where I encountered a lone male. We exchanged grunts. The 'road' led to Pennypie house, so called because once, apparently, pies were baked here and sold to miners for a penny each. A plausible explanation, since along the metalled road leading from it is a former lead mine engine house, complete with chimney, known locally as 'Shildon Castle'. Just beyond, Blanchland awaited.

Blanchland, wrote G.W.O. Addleshaw, is 'an Italian village transplanted in Northumberland in an incomparable setting'.

Blanchland didn't develop in the usual sense, but grew from the remains of its medieval abbey, created by the Premonstratensian monks, the White Canons from Premostre, France, who arrived here in the 12th century, their intention being to provide parish clergy for nearby churches. In 1165 Walter de Bolbec 'gave to God and St Mary the Virgin and a house of twelve of the canons of the Order of Premonstre', lands on the north side of the Derwent, and the abbey at Blanchland was founded.

The monks built the first abbey church about a hundred years after they arrived here, and of this church the choir, transept and tower remain. The original nave has gone, although part of it can be seen today as the wall that runs alongside the garden of the Lord Crewe Arms. The row of cottages on the south side was once the canons' refectory, and a room used for curing and storing food is now the lounge of the hotel, once part of the abbot's lodgings.

The abbey was built around a 'second courtyard', now the village square, the present houses being built from the remains of the cannons' offices. Outside the present gateway were the outer precincts of the abbey; here lived the abbey servants and labourers who worked on the estate. The crenellated top of the gate and tower were decorative additions of the 17th or 18th century.

The abbey's days were numbered in 1539 with the dissolution of the monasteries, and the White Canons departed. They were here nearly 400 years. The abbey estates and buildings fell into possession of the Radcliffes (of Dilston), then the Forsters (of Bamburgh), and the abbey fell into ruin. In 1701 the last of the Forsters was murdered, and the estate passed to his co-heirs, his sister Dorothy and her nephew, Thomas, who had a sister, also called Dorothy. Dorothy Forster – the first one – married Lord Crewe, the Bishop of Durham, and they acquired the estate, whilst Thomas Forster, the incompetent general of the 1715 Jacobite uprising, was captured and imprisoned at Newgate for treason. He would have been executed, but Dorothy, his sister, managed to get duplicate keys to him and he escaped and spent the rest of his life in exile in France.

The Crewe Trustees took over the estate, in whose hands it has remained. In 1752, through the Trustees' initiative, Blanchland became a parish with its own parish priest, and they rebuilt the ruined abbey choir as the parish church. When visiting the church at Blanchland, one should remember it was not built that way to begin with, but as a cruciform abbey church. I was too late to visit the abbey today, so I made for my night's lodgings, just a short walk out of the village.

On the way I met Jemima. She was standing in a field, forlorn-looking and in need of company. I've never been one for horses, but I had the impression that if she could have spoken Jemima would have said, 'Hi.' So I said it for her, the only thing I had said all day, actually, apart from the curt greeting I had given to that fellow on the moor, the only person I had seen since leaving Hexham. My host told me that, whilst other horses were brought inside for the night, Jemima stayed out in the field, alone.

My bedroom window gave views of sunlit fields and drystone walls. I might have been in the Yorkshire Dales. I ate in the Lord Crewe, the abbot's house if you will, and retraced steps to my lodgings. Jemima didn't notice me this time. Too busy doing what horses always do. Well, I'd had my supper, it was only right she should have hers.

***

I looked out of the window at 5.30 a.m. The fields were covered in white frost under a pale blue, clear sky. Jemima was stalking about in her field, as though impatiently waiting for someone. 'She gets bored on her own,' my host explained at breakfast. When I leave the farm I tried to engage with my new-found friend, but she isn't interested. Then I see why: two black horses have appeared. I'm miffed that she's waiting for them, not me.

The morning was grand. There was no warmth in the sun, but it didn't matter. Around me all was green, above all was blue. It was barely 9.30 and not a soul was abroad. I went to the abbey. Inside, it was cold but indescribably wonderful. A thousand years ago the White Canons were here; now I had the place to myself. Inside were the names of abbots: 'Alan, 1165', and 'William Spragen, 1537, Surrendered 1539'. That's what they did at the Dissolution: surrendered.

The Visitors' book had some interesting comments: 'Peaceful'. 'Creepy'. 'Beautiful kneelers'. Someone from Arizona had written (of the church), 'Older than my country'. So it is, or parts of it anyway. A notice was more up to date: 'To assist the police the property in this church has been coded with security markings'. What police would that be exactly? I hadn't seen any since leaving Tynemouth. There were jars of blackcurrant jam for sale, £1 each. Ingredients not listed. That's a criminal offence under Euro-law. Tut-tut.

In the churchyard is a 13th century cross, along with lots of old gravestones, including one of Robert Snowball, aged 26 years, 'Cruelly murdered, 1 January 1880'. The crime occurred near Hunstanworth, just across the county boundary in County

Durham. The housekeeper was charged but acquitted. Nine names adorn the war memorial by the gate, 'erected in memory of the men of this parish who gave their lives in the Great War, 1914-1918'. The inscription on the base: 'All they had they gave'. I lingered, taking it all in. Not a sound to be heard. No movement to be seen.

In 1327 Edward III came here in pursuit of the Scots who had been up to their usual gallant deeds in the South Tyne valley, as well as here, where they burned some of the abbey buildings and damaged crops. The king spent the night of 31 July in the abbey. He never caught up with the Scots. They ran too quick. In 1747 John Wesley took a service and preached here, in the churchyard, where local people knelt for prayers on the grass.

I wandered through the old gateway, to the former 'second courtyard'. Here are grey-stone cottages, forming the square, or piazza, the Italian village, as Addleshaw describes it. There's a pant of 1897, commemorating Queen Victoria's Diamond Jubilee. The water pipe is sealed off. How is it the Victorians had water flowing from their fountains but we don't? Never mind, Blanchland is a gem, unmatched in Northumberland or anywhere else. It is timeless, peaceful and quaint. The village sits close to the Derwent, with high moors and woodland all around. It is a secret place, a special place. And this May morning it was my place.

A good hike lay ahead, to Allendale. A path led alongside the Derwent, on the Northumberland side of the river. The river sang just for me as I strolled easily along. So I sang for the river. 'Morning has broken'. It's a religious song, which seemed appropriate, for the monks would have come this way from the abbey. 'Mine is the sunlight, mine is the morning...' So it was – *my* morning.

Half a mile on I came to the road and turned right for Baybridge, where, to my astonishment, I found myself looking at a sign, 'Durham County Council Picnic Area'. Eh? How could this be? Durham's on the *other* side of the river. I checked the map. Would you believe, the county boundary, which runs along the centre of the river at Blanchland, at some point encroaches on to the northern side by about ten yards. So, a few minutes ago I had unwittingly strayed into Durham.

No matter, a few paces along the road I was back in Northumberland, and a few paces more I was passing through the hamlet of Baybridge. Here is, or was, a Wesleyan Providence Chapel of 1867, now vacated, with paint peeling from the door and the iron railings looking as though they might fall over. Beyond, my route was along the valley, to the high moors and beyond that the East Allen. The sun was shining in a blue, blue sky. I was so, so happy.

There comes a point, when writing an account of a long walk, when one simply runs out of adjectives. One village or hamlet may be described as stone-built, so are others; the weather may be sunny and warm one day, so it is on others; I may feel happy, I may be wet, so it will be again. I must, there-fore, ask the reader to be tolerant, for I can only describe how things were, and if, as today, the sun was shining again, and the country I walked was wonderful again, then I must say so again. An earthquake or a hurricane would enable me to break the mould, but would be unlikely in Northumberland. I am not sorry about that, for just as the walking, all of it, every step, every view, every breeze in my face was unexciting, it was wonderful, and that is not too strong a word.

Beyond Newbiggin I contoured Birkside Fell, high above the Beldon Burn. Newborn lambs littered open pastures, enjoying the fun and freedom in their short time on earth. Here and there I paused to look back, along the wooded valley. An observant walker always looks back. Looking back means seeing views you wouldn't otherwise have seen; looking back provides time to reflect on how things were when you visited a certain place. One should look back on life from time to time too. Lessons may be learned for the future. Or even for the present.

Moving on, I came to a stone. It stood by the path, with 'R 2 M' inscribed on it. I calculated the inscription stood for 'Riddlehamhope 2 miles'. The house is marked on the map. Probably derelict, I thought. The track entered a pine forest, where I lost the sun and views of anything except trees. There was a sign:

'Ground Nesting Birds – Dogs on Leads Please. Beware of Adders'. I looked around for adders. These poisonous snakes can be a threat when walking through bracken or undergrowth, but should be easily spotted on the track I walked now. We are lucky in this country to be able to walk without fear of attack from the likes of wolves, which once roamed free throughout Britain. There are moves afoot to bring them back into the wild in Scotland. Should be great fun walking the glens if they do. Whoever is responsible for their introduction, if it happens, should be made to walk a few of the old stalkers' paths first, just to see if it's safe for sane people.

And so to Riddlehamhope. The ruin, as indeed it is, stands above the Beldon Burn, and has been left to its fate. Where once there may have been welcome here, the door now carries a 'Danger Keep Out' notice and the windows are boarded up. On one window, without boarding, I looked in to what may have been the pantry, empty shelves, littered with pieces of plaster from the broken lath and plaster walls. The house might have stood forever, but the roof will fall in one day and the walls will crumble. The nearby outbuildings too are in decay, with old straw lying on the floor of what appear to have been stables. Times change. No longer does anyone wish to live here, to have animals in these fields. Not even to renovate the place, which I found surprising as there are views to die for.

Further along the track was a sign: 'Heatheryburn'. The letters were mounted on the top of a post, with the sky as backdrop. The house lies off to the left, but I turned right for Harwood Shield and crossed the Carriers Way, a track once used for the transportation of lead ore for smelting. Just before Harwood Shield a bridge with unreadable tablet and possibly dated 1832 crossed our old friend, the Devil's Water, here no more than a small brook. I had seen not a soul so far today. Not in Blanchland, not on the trail.

I then encountered two people. I don't know where they came from or where they were going, but they were such a distraction I actually passed the westbound track I needed and walked on a good hundred yards before I realised my mistake. Turning back, I saw the couple looked uncertain about their bearings, and seeing me heading in the opposite direction may have wondered if I knew what I was doing. We exchanged hellos the first time we passed; this time we just smiled.

I was bound for Hangman Hill, high ground atop the moor at about 1,500 feet. This is wide, open country. Why it's called Hangman Hill is unknown to me, unless, as one might guess, folk were hanged here. What for? Sheep stealing? Shooting grouse? On old maps of Northumberland there's nothing marked here. There's nothing in any direction, just broad moorland and the 'road' I now trod, an ancient way from one valley to another. I had the breeze in my face, the sun on my skin. If Northumberland is a land of 'far horizons', then to anyone looking towards this place from afar, I was on a far horizon now. And then suddenly, less distant, about three feet away in fact, I encountered an adder.

He – or she – was minding his or her own business but no doubt not liking too much the sight of the approaching bipod. I whipped my camera out to take a picture; after all, it's not often you see one. Looking back, this may not have been the wisest thing to do, getting close to a snake and stooping down whilst wearing shorts. One swift turn and not even a man with my whip-like reflexes could have got out of the way. I read some-where that a snake can outrun a human. In the event the adder just wriggled away harmlessly into the heather.

There was no shelter from the sun on top of the moor, and by now I was feeling its effects. Still, the odd passing cloud of the fleecy variety provided some respite. Left-right-left. I was in marching mode on easy-going territory, generally flat with little ups and downs, nothing to trouble a man used to climbing the Scafells and Skiddaw. The map indicated a crossroads of footpaths. It was straight on for me, to Stobb Cross, where, would you believe, looking north-east I could clearly make out the smoke from the wood processing plant at Hexham. Ten miles away, surely. I sat on a stone in silence, not even a bird to be heard twittering. Another three miles would bring me to

Allendale. Allendale *Town* I should say, even though it's a village really.

It was an easy march, downhill all the way. In Allendale I found myself outside the school, where children wore smart uniforms of red jumpers, grey flannels or skirts, white shirts. Schoolchildren in uniform suggests discipline and purpose, as opposed to slapdash and shoddy. If we are failing in education today, as we are, we could begin by following the example set at Allendale. Then maybe we could start teaching the three Rs again. From the school I went directly to the church.

St Cuthbert's stands high above the East Allen in a quiet corner of the village. 'A sound, uneventful Gothic edifice', as Pevsner describes it. Uneventful perhaps, but if it's a feeling of being in an historic and special place you want St Cuthbert's fits the bill perfectly. The present church dates back to 1874, although there's been a church on this spot since the 14th century. The church bells date from 1815, the year of the Battle of Waterloo. A sundial on the south wall marks the latitude as 54 degrees 50 minutes north as the geographical centre of Britain. Written across the face are the words (in Latin) *Hora Fugit*: 'The Hour Flies'. Or, if you like, 'Time Flies'.

The lychgate is a war memorial to the fallen of the two World Wars: 1914-1919 (22 names), 1939-45 (2 names). The inscription: 'They whom this lych gate commemorates were numbered amongst those who, at the call of King and Country, left all that was dear to them, endured hardness, faced danger and finally passed out of the sight of men by the path of duty and self-sacrifice, giving up their own lives that others might live in freedom'. Allendale remembers them. We all should.

Robert Patten, a curate of the church, was a participant in the 1715 Jacobite rebellion. He led a company of Newcastle keelmen to join the rebels at Wooler and was made chaplain to General Forster. At the battle of Preston against the Hanoverian troops he had his horse shot from under him, and then saved Forster's life after the surrender by knocking aside a pistol aimed at him. Something of a hero, then, except when Patten was taken to

London he turned King's evidence against his co-conspirators and was spared his life.

In the village is Isaac's Well, where cold, fresh water pours from a pillar. It's named after Isaac Holden (1806-57) who helped improve the water supply. I wandered about the square, admiring the old buildings and taking note of any suitable places to feed my face later. There seemed to be plenty.

Thus satisfied, I made my way down the steep hill known as The Peth, to the bridge over the East Allen. I had over a mile to my night's lodgings. It was late afternoon, and Allendale and the surrounding fields were bathed in sunshine. Deep green was the colour. As I neared Thorney Gate I noticed some silly oik had crossed the two letter 'l's' as you would the letter 't', on the signpost for Cowshill. Whether this was for fun or because Cowshitt, as it had become, is in County Durham wasn't clear. I deplore graffiti and the idiots who write it, usually confirming their lack of education in basic English; but this time I admit to a smile.

Actually, I do think there is a place for some graffiti in our lives. Not the multi-coloured rubbish that adorns the sides of railway carriages and subway walls; not the pornographic words and drawings on the back of doors in public toilets. But if something can make us smile and it's not too outrageous let's have a taste, eh. Like at police headquarters, of all places, where a notice was pinned to the back of the toilet door in the gents: 'Please use the toilet brush when you have finished'. On which someone had carefully written in biro (in his best handwriting): 'But it makes my arse sore'.

The moors of Allenton, as Allendale was called, once provided one-sixth of Britain's lead, peaking in the mid 19th-century. The lead mines have gone, leaving traces of their one-time existence in the form of slagheaps and chimneys that grace the skyline hereabouts. A railway once ran to the town – almost – from Hexham. Work started in 1865, but the railway ran only as far as Catton due to insufficient capital and logistical problems, such as landslips. The railway catered for goods first, then passengers, the latter service being withdrawn in 1930. It closed for goods in 1950. Such a pity.

In his *Romance of Northumberland* (1908), A.G. Bradley, on his arrival in Allendale on a hot day, pictured himself 'in some smug parlour where a foaming tankard might be quaffed in the company of a sheep farmer or two, or some other entertaining native'. Instead he found Allendale 'deplorably fashionable': 'Two or three brakes (wagonettes) were loading or unloading Tynesiders, while individuals in summer suits lounged about, wearing that air of proprietorship which the summer visitor, when he has been more than two seasons to the same place, automatically assumes'. What would he make of today's 4x4s and baseball-capped invaders, I wonder (the latter including me).

Allendale once typified the annual fair and agricultural hirings, where labour was bought, skilled and unskilled men and women working for local families. The fairs coincided with sales of animals, corn, butter and cheese. There was drinking in the taverns, and dancing to the music of fiddles. The drinking's still there, but oh for a return of the fiddles to replace the ghastly piped music we have to endure today. I always think it silly to have piped music in pubs and restaurants, which I regard as places of discourse, somewhere to enjoy a quiet drink and/or a meal. Ordinarily I prefer no music at all, but if we have to have it, why can't it be 'live'? Where are you, fiddlers, jazz musicians and folk singers?

Allendale still celebrates, though, with its annual folk festival, the New Year's Eve 'Tar Barling' ceremony, where locals and visitors assemble in the town's square at 11.30 p.m., and a procession of forty men in costume with flaming tar barrels on their heads marches around the village accompanied by the band, evidently playing 'Wi' a hundred pipers', a Scots song, but which is acceptable, bearing in mind it's hogmanay an' a'. Anyway, just before midnight they throw the barrels on to a bonfire, and as the flames rise and the church bells chime, everyone sings 'Auld Lang Syne'. Fantastic. But considering the sawn-off tar barrels contain sticks and paraffin, and the fire they throw them on sends flames roaring above the heads of the crowd, it's nothing short of a miracle that in these times of health and safety rules, where kids can't have water in their paddling pools in case they slip, they can have the ceremony at all. Long may Tar Barling reign. Long may people enjoy themselves. And let's have those fiddles too.

***

Sunny and fresh. Another good hike ahead today, traversing three high ridges on the way to Alston. Alston is outside the county, but I wanted to go to there for two reasons: to see the clock in the church, which was once housed in the old Dilston Hall, and to catch the train for a mile or so to Kirkhaugh, on the South Tynedale Railway. A third reason is the fact that I like Alston, which is a good enough reason to visit anywhere.

I headed west for a couple of miles to what was indicated on the map as 'Meml'. What would it be? A war memorial, twelve feet high, 'to the memory of the young men of Keenley and Broadside who served in the Great War, 1914-1919'. Keenley I saw from the map, was about a mile away, appearing little more than a farm or two, whilst Broadside wasn't indicated at all. Yet from these two small places six men gave their lives. 'Greater love hath no man than this, that a man lay down his life for his friends'. I have read that so many times. The date, incidentally – 1919 – marks the time when hostilities officially ended, as opposed to when the fighting stopped, in 1918. Sometimes it's 1918, sometimes 1919.

I left the road and climbed to the top of the ridge, at about 1,000 feet, high above the two Allens, West and East, with great views back to the moors of yesterday. Strange-looking birds (to me) flapped and warned of my approach, whilst crows (we all know and love them) pecked at the ground bravely until the last moment before taking off. Near Harlow Bower, descending now, I came upon strange mounds and excavations, possibly the site of an ancient settlement, though none is marked on the map. It would be an ideal site, high on the hillside. Or maybe it was an old quarry, where they just took stone from near the surface. An expert would know. I didn't.

The valley of the West Allen lay ahead, with the tall steeple of Whitfield church coming into view among the trees. This is grand country. Finally I joined the road leading to Blue Back bridge where, unexpectedly, I came upon a simple cross by the roadside. The cross stands under birches, its weatherworn inscription telling the sad story of: 'Lindsay Aulojo Jameson, born Edinburgh, 1870. Killed by Accident near this spot, 16 June 1895'. There is nothing to say how or where exactly the accident happened (and I cannot swear to exact identification of the wording on the cross); but somewhere near here, over a hundred years back, a young fellow was killed. It's nice he's still remembered.

Re-crossing the bridge, I headed through Monk Wood, with views across the river to Whitfield Hall. The wood is a Site of Special Scientific Interest, nearly 50 acres of oak mainly. Waymarker signs indicated I was on Isaac's Tea Trail. Isaac, is none other than Isaac Holden, who helped to improve the water supply to Allendale. Isaac had worked as a miner, and when the mine closed he took to carrying tea, a product becoming more readily available to poor mining families, thanks to reductions in import duty and the ever-increasing quantities of the stuff (I'm drinking tea as I write). He carried it on his back to the farms and cottages hereabouts in the early 19th century. His tea trail is a 36-mile circular route and I was on part of it now.

Isaac was also an early fundraiser, raising money for good causes and paying off debts of local Methodist chapels. Also, in secret, he raised enough money to buy a hearse for the West Allen valley and was possibly among the first to benefit from it when he died in 1857, aged 52. He is buried in St Cuthbert's churchyard, Allendale. A tall obelisk marks the spot.

I'm not sure which way Isaac's Tea Trail goes, but I probably left it a couple miles south of where I joined it, when I climbed steeply out of the valley. I was heading for two chimneys that stand at about 1,500 feet above sea level on my second ridge of the day. The trail sometimes descended into hollows, where the chimneys were unseen, thus necessitating use of the compass, even though they stand tall on the skyline.

It may seem strange, viewing the chimneys from afar, to find them here in this remote place, high atop the moors. But unlike factory chimneys, these two were never connected to any building, but stand remote and aloof three miles away from a smelt mill that operated at Thornley Gate, in the valley of the East Allen. The smoke and fumes created at the mill, instead of polluting the air at valley level, travelled through flues all the way to the chimneys. They weren't built to avoid pollution, but to catch deposits of minerals, such as lead and silver, and the flues were cleaned when the miners were away on holiday.

My inspection of the southern chimney showed two flues leading to it from the valley, whilst one flue served the northern. I entered the latter and looked upward at the hole above and the sky above that. The chimneys are evidence of a bygone age, when men worked the lead mines and corn mills, and are so well built they might stand forever.

If you ever visit this place, do take time to reflect on the history these tall structures represent. Then stand back and cast your eyes further afield, to the far horizons all around you, over deep valleys and wonderful, distant landscapes of course grasses and heathers and low, distant fields in this so-called over-crowded isle, where there is still so much space in places such as this. Then think for a moment about your mortality: that which you see now was here before you were born and will be after you have gone. How insignificant we are in the grand scheme of things. Remember: *Hora Fugit*.

Alston was a long six miles away, across the valley of the West Allen, which I would have to descend into and out of for the second time today. First I headed south to the road across the moor, then north-west towards Mount Pleasant. The footpath on the map was difficult to follow; it led to a lovely stone bridge over a gushing burn. I sat in the sun awhile, listening to the music – you know the music I mean. At Ninebanks I scarcely paused, heading south towards St Mark's church with its spire. I could see the track climbing the third ridge of the day, which loomed ahead. I crossed the West Allen again, heading for the Cumberland border. It was hot and I was thirsty. I felt like one of those cowboys you see staggering across the desert, his horse having bolted when that nasty baddie fired his sixgun into the air for spite. They used to fire about nine or ten bullets from those guns. How did they do that?

The track that crosses into Cumberland is an ancient byway. They might have made it into a motor road. Thankfully they didn't. I could see a motor road, though, one I've driven many times, between Whitfield and Alston. Tiny cars sped along it now in silence: it was as though my ears were blocked. Ah, but they weren't blocked, for I could hear the breeze. Isn't it wond-erful, the breeze? Not that it was strong enough to have much effect in the now hot afternoon sun.

I arrived at the top of White Hill, then Long Cross, names on the map, meaningless on the ground. There was a standing stone, a boundary stone maybe, with 'H' on one side, 1859 on the other. 'H' was probably the initial of the landowning family. A forest lay ahead. The track went straight through it, according to the map. I made a mental note that if it didn't I would sue the Ordnance Survey. It did, and when I passed through the gate at the forest edge I entered Cumberland.

Half a mile further, beyond Clarghyll Hall, which incorp-orates a pele tower, not that I saw it the speed I was going, I arrived at the A686. Here I turned left then right along a country lane that ran through a sort of wasteland before crossing the A686 again. I arrived at a strategically-placed bench, only to find that where the two ends remained standing, the actual seat had disappeared. How uncompromisingly cruel.

Finally a steep hill led down into Alston, where I checked into the Victoria Inn. The broken seat, it would turn out, was merely the forerunner of my misfortunes, for at my lodgings it was the chef's night off, the church was locked, so I couldn't view the clock from Dilston Hall, and a leaflet informed me the trains on the South Tynedale Railway didn't run Fridays, and tomorrow was Friday. On top of all that, although I had a TV in my room, the remote was missing and I actually had to *stand up* to change channels.

***

Alston has a charm of its own, with its Dickensian back alleys, old houses and cobbled main street sloping down the hill. St Augustine's, the church locked to me the previous afternoon, was built in 1870, and the Market Cross just down the hill at a bend in the road evidently dates back to 1764. Pevsner describes it as a reproduction of a former one, but questions whether the 'stubby Tuscan columns' are possibly 17th century.

At over 1,000 feet above sea level, Alston lays claim to being the highest market town in England. The railway came here in 1852, running along the length of the South Tyne valley. It closed in 1976. The present-day line is in miniature, and runs only from Alston to Kirkaugh along the route of the former railway. But wouldn't it be grand to ride the old railway all the way along the valley, across those grand Victorian viaducts. Cost aside, there is no reason I can think of why it couldn't run again, bringing families and children to Alston on great days out, linking up with the main Carlisle-Newcastle line at Haltwhistle. The 2012 Olympics costs God knows what for a three-week event in London, and millions are spent on meaningless statues: can't money be found to reopen some of our old railways? And if it can't, as it won't be, would that perchance have anything to do with the Alston line being in a remote northern valley? I think we as a nation have our priorities wrong.

I stepped from the portals of the Victoria Inn to find Alston quiet, deserted almost. After loitering with intent – intent on enjoying the peace of a fine May morn – I wandered down the hill to the church. It was *open*.

All I knew about Dilston Hall's 17th century clock was how it appeared in a photograph in Frances Dickinson's *Castle on Devil's Water*. It has a see-through face with Roman numerals and only one pointer, and hangs precariously on a frame in the nave of the church. Two ropes reach up to the roof with bricks fastened to each act as counterweights. The clock was rescued from the original Dilston Hall when it was demolished, and presented to St Augustine's, Alston, along with a bell, which is here too, one of ten in the church carillon. Unfortunately the clock was damaged in the process of its removal, and lay unused for 200 years until, in 1977, the parishioners raised the money to pay for a new fibreglass face. The correct numerals for '4' are displayed, IIII, not IV, which is Roman but conventionally does not appear on clock faces bearing Roman numerals.

Haltwhistle is about thirteen miles from Alston, the way I was going anyway. Alas, no lift partway on the train, but no matter: I was fit, the day was glorious and I was in South Tyne-dale. I passed the train-less station and headed for my first objective, Kirkhaugh. A byroad leaves the main A686, after which there's a two-mile walk to Kirkhaugh church.

A long stone wall runs alongside the road on the right, with Kirkside Wood on the other side of it. As I strode along, a red squirrel appeared on top of the wall. Instead of disappearing into the woods, he ran along the top of the wall, a few yards ahead. This went on for quarter of a mile, during which I had continuous sight of his bobbing tail. Every now and then he would pause (as they do), look around then continue, steadfastly refusing to jump off the wall and scarper. Finally he disappeared into the woods.

Immediately afterwards, I had company again, a chap from Cambridge who was cycling around Northumberland. Had a puncture yesterday, he said. It had not been a problem for him, but would've been for me. I couldn't fix punctures. Not even when I was a kid and cycled everywhere. I could locate the hole easily enough by blowing the inner tube up and holding it in a bowl of water till you see bubbles. Hole located, I dried it off, roughed it up with abrasive paper, put some of that chalk stuff on, glued the patch and applied to surface of tube. But no matter how hard I tried the air still hissed out. But I was talking about the Cambridge cyclist. He'd cycled to here, seen me and fancied a chat. So we walked awhile. As we crossed the county boundary into Northumberland he cycled off, bound for Hadrian's Wall or somewhere.

Ahead now low hills rose dramatically from the valley floor, through which the South Tyne heads on its journey towards Halt-whistle and beyond. The hills are bare, save for the occasional scattered farmstead and a patchwork quilt of woodlands. The scene seemed to be saying 'welcome back' after my brief sojourn into another county.

And so to Holy Paraclete Church, Kirkhaugh. A word I'd not come across before, 'Paraclete' means an advocate, or legal helper, in this case the Holy Ghost. The church was built in 1869, its slender spire derided by Alfred Wainwright in his *Pennine Journey*: 'One cannot help feeling that a ghastly archit-ectural error has been committed...it has the same proportions as a tightly-rolled umbrella planted upside down.' Pevsner describes it as 'an absurdly needle-thin spire'.

Well, the spire is thin, but for a reason, that being its designer, Octavius James, had been on holiday in the Black Forest where he was 'so taken' with the churches he decided to build a similar one at Kirkhaugh. Wainwright said the church looked forlorn, but Mee describes it as 'beautifully situated'. It stands a long way from habitations, apart from the former rectory. Inside, by design, the church has no pews, accentuating the lofty interior.

The graveyard has many interesting headstones, many of which have appeared since Wainwright passed this way in 1938, and a magnificent Saxon hammerhead cross. Octavius James is buried by the church door. He was rector here, and died in a fire in 1889 at Clarghyll Hall. The former rectory, now private, was enlarged in the incumbency of Horace Edgar Yorke Breffit just before the Great War. He wore a 'shovel' hat, married at 94 and enjoyed three years of married bliss thereafter.

A few days after his wedding Breffit ordered his grave to be dug in the churchyard at Alwinton, in Coquetdale, where he was then vicar, 'to save time and trouble' when he died. In the three years he went on living after his marriage the grave stood vacant and had to be emptied of water after every storm. I resolved to look out for Horace's grave at Alwinton, which was on the route of my journey, and to pay my respects to the man. Anyone who enjoys 'married bliss' unto death at 97 deserves respect.

Kirkhaugh is a sparsely-populated parish divided in two by the South Tyne. A footbridge 400 yards downstream from the church is the only link between one side of the parish and the other. I went there to find a long, sturdy bridge built on five stone columns. It's long, as the gravely shore has to be bridged too, for the river will be wide when in spate. The bridge is constructed of 'redundant tramlines' spanning stone piers. There's a sort of kink partway along its length, which, as a notice in the church explains, was caused when one of the piers was struck by a tree trunk in a flood a few years ago, accounting for the 'wiggle in the middle'. The pier has been stabilised with two steel piles, visible in the river. Today the level of the river was normal, flowing by without fuss, singing away. Looking back (as ever) Wainwright's 'needle thin-spire' was in view, above the treeline. It may be thin but it cannot be ignored. I sat awhile on the close-cropped grass by the river. What a wonderful way to spend a morning.

I crossed the bridge and followed the right of way under the railway, just yards from Kirkhaugh station, reflecting on the fact that had I taken the train I would have had to cross the bridge and double back, as it were, to visit the church; so no trains Fridays wasn't so bad. At the top of the next field I spied a familiar sight: an acorn sign on a gatepost, marking the route of the Pennine Way. Just here, before heading north, it's worth mentioning John Wallis, Northumberland's first historian, and the nearby Roman auxiliary fort of Whitley Castle.

Wallis was born at nearby Castle Nook farm in 1714. The farm lies close to the fort, now an impressive earthwork in the shape of the distinctive 'playing card' pattern. 'Northumberland being Roman ground,' wrote Wallis, 'I was led by a sort of enthusiasm to an enquiry and search of their towns, their cities and temples, their baths, their altars, their tumuli, their military ways and other remains of splendour and magnificence…and still give pleasure to such as have a gust [taste] for anything Roman'. He could hardly have had a better site so close to hand; at nearly nine acres in size, the fort stood on the open hillside on the Maiden way, which ran north to the Stanegate.

The enthusiastic Wallis would have been dismayed, however, had he been alive in 1826, when the 'proprietor' of Whitley Castle found a large dunghill on the site, which he considered appropriate to use to provide manure for his land. In the 'dung' were Roman shoes, which he cleared away as compost. What else lay there? We will never know, but antiquities that might have been carefully excavated and preserved were lost forever.

After crossing the high moors, walking across the green meadows of the South Tyne valley was a luxury. The views were different too: on the moors heather was everywhere, the horizons distant; but here houses and barns were dotted about the landscape, and I had the river for company. Evidence of the former railway was never far away, in the form of cuttings or straight, grassy strips where the railway ran, and the viaducts. The more I saw these things, the more sad it felt that the trains no longer run, and can no longer, apparently, be made to run again.

I came to Slaggyford, a pretty village named after the slag taken from the ground in the search for lead hereabouts. The inhabitants left to work in the lead mines that sprung up elsewhere. I turned left here and took the course of the former railway, following it for a mile and a half to Knarsdale. Along the railway I encountered a dozen or so sheep. Unusually for sheep, not one moved on my approach. You can bet your life if just one had bottled it and ran off they all would. They didn't even move when I stopped and made threatening glares.

At Knarsdale I went down to the church. St Jude's is constructed of fine, grey Northumbrian stone. In 1777, a rector, Thomas Todhunter, appeared at court for assaulting Walter Batey, and again, the following summer for failing to permit access through the churchyard. There are old lichen-covered headstones in the churchyard, some sinking into the earth. On one, its inscription now eroded, is the epitaph to Robert Baxter, who died on 4 October, 1796. Described as 'doggerel', it reads:

> All those who please these lines to read
> It will cause a tender heart to bleed;
> I murdered was upon the fell
> And by a man I knew full well.
> My bread and butter which he'd lade,
> I, being harmless, was betrayed
> I hope he will rewarded be,
> That laid the poison here for me.

Evidently Robert Baxter quarrelled with a man who left a poisoned sandwich for him, although there is no record of anyone being charged with his murder. There are tombs in the churchyard, with weathered inscriptions, some in a state of collapse. I fancied I could see bones in one, through a gap in the crumbling stonework.

A quiet byroad crosses the river it and continues to Eals. There was an unusual mound hereabouts, clothed in Scots pines. Nothing on the map to betray its secret, if any. Eals turned out to be a tidy place of stone dwellings, straddling a byroad. There was no-one about: no-one walking, no traffic.

Beyond Eals I turned up the hillside, entering a wood where I went astray, and ended up climbing steeply until I reached another byroad just south of a place called Tows Bank. Further on I picked my way downhill again through more woodland on a path that emerged below Lambley viaduct. It's so *high*, a truly amazing spectacle, the railway platform over 100 feet above the river. To think, the Victorians built this, and other viaducts along the valley, for the railway. The thought that screams out loud in one's mind is that it could carry a railway now. Many of today's kids seem always to be staring at a television screen (BBC Children's TV is too dreadful to describe; do they think they are broadcasting to imbeciles?) or using computers or texting on their mobiles: but have you ever seen kids when their parents take them on a train, especially a steam train? Like those we see on the short run from Alston to Kirkhaugh, or maybe a 'full size' version, like the one that crosses the North York Moors on *Heartbeat*. Their faces always tell the same story: that they love it. They'd love a journey all the way along the South Tyne Valley, crossing all those viaducts, seeing the rising hillsides, the cattle and sheep, hearing the train's whistle, listening to the clatter of the wheels on the tracks. So would their mums and dads on what would be a great family outing.

Where was I? Oh, aye: Lambley viaduct. I climbed up the steps to the top, where a plate bears the inscription: 'Designed by Sir Robert Barclay-Bruce, engineer. Newcastle and Carlisle

Railway Company, Haltwhistle-Alston branch. Opened 17 November 1852, closed 1 May 1976. It is now a Grade II listed viaduct, restored 1995-96'. I walked along it, where the railway ran. Looking over the parapet, it seemed even higher than from below.

I headed into Lambley village, to the 19th century church, dedicated to St Mary and St Patrick. It's built of lovely light-grey stones and is exquisite inside, with four painted panels near the altar: St Kentigern holding a fish, St Cuthbert with an otter, St Aidan with a deer and St Ninian restoring the sight of a blind man. There's a tiny turret between the chancel and nave housing a bell from a former Benedictine nunnery. Outside I rested awhile in the sun, a gentle breeze stroking my face, the smell of fresh-cut grass in the churchyard. Fresh-cut grass always takes me back to schooldays, when the grass on the playing field was being cut.

Sadly, it wasn't always peaceful at Lambley. The nunnery was destroyed by the invading Scots led by William Wallace in 1296, the same raid where they burned the school at Hexham with the schoolchildren inside.

A chronicler at Lanercost Abbey wrote: 'They surpassed in cruelty all the fury of the heathen. When they could not catch the strong and young they imbrued their arms with the blood of infirm people, old women, women in childbed and even children two or three years old, proving themselves apt scholars in atrocity insomuch that they raised little children pierced on spikes to expire thus and fly away to the heavens. They burnt consecrated churches, and having herded together a crowd of little scholars in the schools of Hexham, and having blocked the doors, set fire to that fair pile. Three monasteries were destroyed, at Lanercost and Hexham, and that of the nuns at Lambley. The devastation can by no means be attributed to the valour of warriors, but to the dastardly conduct of thieves who attacked a weaker community where they would not be likely to meet with any resistance'.

My visit to Lambley proved that no matter how carefully one studies a map, it is never possible to know exactly what one might find when visiting a place. The map for Lambley shows a cross, denoting a church with no tower or steeple, and a road leading through a village above the river. So it proved, but what the map could not show was how lovely it is. I arrived at Lambley not knowing what to expect. I left with the memory of a lovely place indelible in my mind.

I followed the road, leaving it where a right of way led off across flat meadows, the river significantly wider now. It was a grand afternoon: I might have been the only man in Northumberland. I spied Featherstone Castle on the opposite side of the river, 'beautifully situated in large grounds in the wooded valley of the South Tyne'. The woodland path I walked became rough and stony, with twisted tree roots encroaching over it. Care was needed, holding me up when I wanted to get to Haltwhistle for a bath and to find somewhere to replace lost fluids. There were lots of flowers alongside the path, mostly unknown to me. Finally I emerged on to open meadows and followed the right of way to Haltwhistle.

The meaning of the name, it seems, derives from *Haut-wysel*, meaning 'a meeting of streams', possibly with the French 'haut', meaning high. It has nothing to do with trains halting and whistling. I found myself in a pleasant main street of shops and pubs, along with a park and war memorial. Mee describes the church as 'one of the best in Northumberland', high praise indeed for there's plenty competition.

In the town square was a sign proclaiming Haltwhistle to be 'the Centre of Britain'. Ey-up, I thought Allendale was. But no, there was a post with direction arms pointing to Wallsend 36½ miles, North Orkney 290 miles, Portland Bill, Dorset 290 miles and Bowness-on-Solway 36½ miles. Sadly the best laid plans of mice and well-intentioned worthies had been thwarted by someone who had seen fit to turn one of the semaphore arms to indicate Portland Bill lying in the same direction as Wallsend. Then again it may have been a gesture made by anyone under the age of thirty who went to school in Tony's Britain.

But how can Haltwhistle claim to be centre of Britain when Allendale had claim to it earlier? According to the noticeboard: 'Applied to Britain the longest north-south medium is from Hope Skerries, North Ronaldsway (the Orkneys) to Freshwater Bay,

Portland Bill, in Dorset – mid point, Haltwhistle, from which point there are equidistances to all main compass points, as well as to the centre of England, Wales, Northern Ireland and Scotland and to the extremities of the British Isles'. The extremities? I don't think so. If it's extremities we're talking about, what about the Shetland Islands, well north of the Orkneys and part of Britain, and why Portland Bill, when Lizard Point is the southernmost extremity of the British mainland? But hey, just move the 'extremities' to where you want them, and you can be in the centre, no problem.

It's all in the name of tourism. It's the way it is these days. County Durham signs proclaim it to be 'the Land of the Prince Bishops'; Warwickshire is 'Shakespeare's County'; Nottingham is 'Robin Hood County' (not Hood's, with an apostrophe). So, you're a tourist on the A69 and you see the sign: 'Haltwhistle – Centre of Britain', and, tempted by this exciting and unexpected discovery, you turn your wheels into town. Which you wouldn't have done, go on admit it, if the sign had said: 'Haltwhistle has one of the best churches in Northumberland'.

Holy Cross dates from about 1200. It has no tower, and stands shyly behind the stone buildings of the Market Place, unseen by passers-by, unknown to the stranger. Yet just walk through the gate and in ten paces you are away from people and the Centre of Britain sign. The church is surrounded by lush green lawns and a scattering of headstones. Beyond, one looks across the South Tyne valley to the moors. At the back of the church is an ancient headstone, inscribed, 'Here lyeth the body of Thomas Borr who departed this life August 29, 1742, aged 70'. At the top of the headstone are a skull and crossbones and a coat of arms.

Actually, there *are* signs on the main roads, imploring motorists to visit 'Haltwhistle's 13th century church'. Whether any are persuaded to do so isn't known to me, but let me tell them that if they do they are wasting their time and fuel, for disappointment lies in store as the church is locked to the visitor. It was locked to me, anyway.

Start of a journey:
The end of Tynemouth Pier.

Collingwood Monument.

Arthur Stanley Jefferson, better known as
Stan Laurel. He lived in Dockwray Square,
North Shields.

St George slays the dragon.
War memorial, Eldon Square, Newcastle.

Town Wall, Newcastle (West Walls).

George Stephenson's birthplace.

Tyne bridge, near Wylam.

St Mary's Church, Ovingham.

The Devil's Water at Dilston.

Hexham Abbey.

A corner of Blanchland.

Sundial, Allendale.

Saxon Cross, Kirkhaugh.

Centre of Britain sign, Haltwhistle.

Hadrian's Wall:
Milecastle Gateway, near Housesteads.

Hadrian's Wall, near Walltown.

Stonehaugh.

Hareshaw Linn.

Black Middens.

'The Quarrymen', Kielder Reservoir.

Kielder Reservoir.

Forest road: Kielder to Redesdale.

River Rede.

Part IV

A Frontier of Empire

It was just like one of those old movies. Somewhere in the American mid-West a train rolls into the station. Spencer Tracey or somebody steps down. He's alone, surrounded by sagebrush, hanging on to his hat. Bardon Mill has a station platform but no sagebrush; otherwise I was that man (wearing a baseball cap). As the train rolled off, I hoisted my sack on to my shoulders and enjoyed something Spencer Tracey never got: a smile and a Geordie 'hello' from a young lass pushing her kiddie in his pushchair along the station platform. And, as if that wasn't enough, a man I didn't know from Adam called out 'good afternoon'. He was at least twenty yards away and didn't have to acknowledge me. But he did. They both meant 'Welcome back to Northumberland.' The sun was shining too. Joy of joys!

September is a wonderful month. A time of Indian summers and autumn tapestries. A time to explore Northumberland's great treasure, Hadrian's Wall. Today I was bound for Housesteads, on the Wall. First, though, I had to climb out of the Tyne valley, and my first objective was the Long Stone, situated on high ground next to what is marked on the map as a 'Roman Signal Station'. It would be a good pull up, a great way to get back 'into the groove'.

A signpost pointed to Thorngrafton Common and Cringledykes, such lovely names. A fawn-coloured woollen hat dangled from the semaphore arm of the signpost. If you lost one, that's where it is – or was. A rough stony track led north to wild, open country. Just minutes before I had sat on the train with other passengers, people with individual lives and agendas. They were still there, reading their newspapers and magazines, engaged in meaningless conversations on their mobiles, the sort you hear these days by people who don't seem to be able to sit in silence. But I was free and on the move on an old byway bordered by drystone walls.

Up, up I climbed, forever looking back at the view. I had been looking forward to this moment, a habit I'd got into whenever I plan a walking journey. I'd read the maps at home, studied the contours and the footpaths or lack of them, identified place-names and interesting features. Sometimes what you see is what you get; sometimes there are unexpected surprises.

The track became a thin trod, threading a tenuous route through bracken and heather towards my objective. Thorngrafton Common is wild, its only occupants a few scattered sheep and, today, a solitary walker, the silence punctuated now and then by the sudden roar of low-flying Tornadoes. People complain about them, but they have to practise somewhere. Whenever I am on open fellsides, or here, as today, I wonder if the pilot can see me and wish they could change places. Not on your Nellie, mate. Finally, I saw the Long Stone, on Barcombe Hill.

The walking became rougher. Bracken can loosen one's boot-laces or conceal unseen potholes or adders. Care – and patience – is needed. I had both in abundance. I was aware that potholes and snakes might not be the only things concealed; in the 1830s workmen quarrying stone hereabouts found a bronze purse containing 63 Roman coins, thought to have been hidden when the Romans were quarrying the rock to build the Wall. I calculated I had just about room in my rucksack should I happen to discover any similar treasure.

The man who discovered the coins and the purse was Thomas Robinson. He refused to hand them over to their rightful owner, the Duke of Northumberland, for which misdemeanour he was sentenced to twelve months in prison, but not before he had given the loot to his brother, William. Twenty-one years later John Clayton, who did so much in the way of excavating Roman sites, bought the coins and purse for £50, and saved them for posterity.

Talking of my rucksack, I should mention that on this stage of my journey I was carrying a tent and sleeping bag, necessary for at least one night when I expected to camp out. However, I gave the idea of toting cooking equipment and tons of food up years ago. He who travels quickly travels light said Antoine de St-Exupéry, not that he ever walked around Northumberland so far as I know. But he was right. Even so, what with spare clothing, maps, etc, the sack was weighty. To carry a heavy sack one needs a strong back, strong legs and a sense of masochism. I had all three.

And finally, the Long Stone, dramatically situated on its fractured granite base, atop the ridge. It's about ten feet high and shaped like a witch's finger. Standing by it affords glorious views in all directions, including, below, of the Roman fort of Vindolanda. I could see people strolling about the site. To the north was the dramatic Whin Sill, the location of the Wall and Housesteads fort, and southwards the country I had traversed earlier on my journey. It was a good place to rest, which I did, putting on my jacket to protect against a cutting wind. The stone marked a significant part of my journey: behind was the Tyne valley, ahead was the Wall.

An Ordnance column stands on a separate hilltop near the former Roman Signal Station. Here the ground is 'moundy', which is hardly surprising since it was the site of an Iron Age hillfort. I went down over rough ground to a quiet country road that runs along the line of the Roman Stanegate, the road that linked Carlisle with Corbridge. I followed the Stanegate before turning north for Housesteads and the Wall, which is as good a place as any to include a potted history of Hadrian's Wall, the forts and milecastles, and the Romans themselves.

Not long ago I watched a so-called TV 'celebrity' walking along the top of Hadrian's Wall, declaring for the benefit of the nation that he was walking with 'one foot in Scotland, the other in England'. From that moment on, I thought, millions of people, including children, who hadn't known exactly what or where Hadrian's Wall was, will spend the rest of their lives recalling the moment they saw wotsisname walking with a foot in each country. So much drivel is spoken and written about Hadrian's Wall; none moreso than this, for England and Scotland did not exist as separate countries at the time of the Romans, and, what's more, the Wall in its entirety is situated in what is now England, with no part in Scotland at all.

The Roman Empire stretched from the Rhine-Danube to the Sahara, from Persia to Britain. The Romans built forts, roads, villas, aqueducts and, where necessary, walls and even fences. They arrived in Britain in AD 43 and commenced a steady invasion, reaching what is now mid-Scotland by AD 79. But then they retreated, so that about AD 90 their northern frontier lay across the Tyne Gap. By then they'd built forts, such as at Corbridge and Vindolanda and Carvoran, and roads, such as the Stanegate and Dere Street. Britain then was sparsely populated – it still is along much of the route of the Wall – and the occupying Roman army was constantly under threat from the native Britons, whom they called the barbarians. Then Hadrian took a hand.

Publius Aelius Hadrianus – Hadrian – was Emperor from AD 117 until his death in AD 138. It was probably when he visited Britain that he commissioned the building of the Wall. Work began in AD 122. The Wall would run for 76 miles between the fort at Newcastle (known as *Pons Aelius*, after the bridge there and Hadrian's family name) and Bowness-on-Solway, and would be ten Roman feet wide (9 ft 7 in). From Newcastle to the River Irthing the Wall would be of stone, and westward from there of turf. No-one knows how high the Wall was, but it's generally considered to have been about fifteen feet. The first part of Hadrian's project to be constructed was the bridge across the Tyne at Newcastle. But what was the Wall *for*? We can but speculate, but it was probably to control.

Control movement, that is, allowing people – the barbarians – to pass through the Wall at fortified gateways for reasons of trade and to pay taxes, which, since they had to do so under the control of the Romans, they could only do unarmed. It also enabled the Romans to pass through, and to keep watch. It is important to bear in mind that as time went by the Romans and the natives by and large got along fine, with civilian settlements springing up near Roman forts, Roman soldiers co-habiting with local women and so on. Men and women mix well; it was bound to happen.

But there was more to the new barrier than the Wall itself. First a V-shaped ditch ran the length of the Wall, some six yards north of it. The ditch was eight yards wide and ten feet deep, sometimes dug out of solid rock, although there was no ditch where steep crags fell away in front of the Wall. At every Roman mile there was a milecastle, complete with barracks and gates for access through the Wall. In addition turrets were erected at equal distances between the milecastles. An extension from Newcastle to Wallsend was added to complete the Wall.

The Wall was not built by slave labour, but by the Roman legions. Stone was quarried locally, probably with the help, voluntary or otherwise, of the natives. We see 'artists' impressions' of Roman soldiers on the ramparts, repelling invaders from the north, but there is no evidence that soldiers patrolled along the top of the Wall, which may have been sloped like a roof for all we know. There was no need to walk along ramparts, since observation could be maintained from the look-out towers of milecastles and turrets. Nevertheless, patrolling along the top of the Wall was a possibility. As for repelling invaders, this was never a Roman tactic. Any approaching force would have been spotted and met in the open.

Two years after work began came the decision to build forts along the Wall. These were between six and nine miles apart, and usually straddled the Wall. They had four main gateways, one at the south, the others usually on the north side of the wall, facing west, north and east. It seems the forts were built because without them soldiers, save those few in the milecastles, were stationed too far away from the Wall and would have to march from the old forts to the Wall, becoming fatigued before they reached any field of battle. Being stationed on the Wall meant they could march out through the north-facing gates to engage the enemy.

Another later decision was to provide a flat-bottomed trench known as the Vallum, which ran south of the Wall and broadly parallel to it. The Vallum seems to have been a demarcation line, and the ground between it and the Wall a sort of demilitarisation zone. The upcast soil from the Vallum was piled along each side of it, and set back from the trench, but the earth was left *in situ* at the approaches to the forts, and a gate was placed here through which anyone approaching from the south would have to pass, a sort of check-in point. The Vallum was abandoned before the Wall, and civilian settlements eventually reached up to the forts.

Hadrian was succeeded by Antoninus Pius, who decided the Roman army should return to the land north of the Wall. His military campaign there culminated with the building of the Antonine Wall between the Clyde and Forth, and Hadrian's Wall, although not completely abandoned, was surplus to requirements for a time. About AD 169, when the Romans retreated again, the Antonine Wall was abandoned and Hadrian's Wall once again stood as the northernmost frontier of empire. A new military way was then built just south of the Wall, running parallel with it, to improve communications. So the Wall and its environs remained until the early 5th century; that's about 300 years of Roman occupation along the Wall, a truly remarkable statistic.

Housesteads (*Vercovicium*) is the most dramatically situated and most visited fort on Hadrian's Wall. Constructed in AD 124, it lies on a slope, its northern side reaching almost up to the very edge of the Whin Sill, the dolerite cliff that runs cross country, west to east. It's important to remember, when exploring the site, that the remains are not all of the same period.

Housesteads covered some five acres. There's lots to explore: the South Gate, a double gateway whose east portal was blocked before the civilian settlement was established, known because the civilian houses came right up to the gateway; the Commanding Officer's House, Headquarters building, the Granaries, Hospital, North Gate, Barracks, East Gate, West Gate and the Latrine. The military way led straight up to the East Gate, and continued inside the fort to the entrance of the Headquarters building.

Having explained, above, that the forts along the Wall had three gates opening onto the north side of the Wall, Housesteads was an exception because of the proximity of the Whin Sill. There was a north-facing gate affording access to the top of the cliffs, but soldiers emerging from the fort to venture north passed through another gate specially inserted into the Wall by the Knag Burn, half a mile away. Here, there were two gates in the Wall, with the width of the Wall in between, as at all gateways. This allowed searching and checking anyone passing through the Wall.

The latrine is situated at the south-east corner of the fort at the bottom of the slope. Wooden seats covered a main sewage channel, and there was a small channel on the platform itself in which sponges were washed after use (this was pre-Andrex). Water was fed into the system from header tanks higher up, within the fort. Although the Romans built aqueducts in places, there was evidently none here, so how they got the water to the header tanks is anyone's guess. Mine is that it was carried by barbarians or slaves, either for reward or punishment, or auxiliaries on fatigues. The sewage was flushed away through a drain, onto the hillside below the fort. Artists' impressions of soldiers in the latrine show them seated together, chatting away. There was no privacy, nor would the Romans have expected it.

Aerial photographs show a considerable civilian settlement around the fort, all south of the Wall, of course – Hence 'House Steads'. One of the dwellings is known as the 'Murder House', where two skeletons were found during excavations, a man and a woman, he with a sword point between his ribs. The Romans were strict about burials, and would not have permitted these two to be lawfully buried here. One imagines a soldier was over the side (but not over the Wall) and he and his lover came to grief, possibly at the hands of a jealous husband. Such a pity the remains were removed. They would probably have provided the main attraction to the site, for casual visitors anyway.

But I was more than just a casual visitor. I had walked from the valley bottom to the fort at the edge of the Whin Sill, and now took stock. In all directions lay wild, open country, unpopulated, just as it was when the Romans were here; the only difference was the landscape, then covered in deciduous forests, where wolves roamed free and you travelled at your own risk.

Today, north of the Wall, a few miles distant, lie forests again, millions of conifers that cover the landscape like an enormous blanket, happily far enough away so as not to encroach on the environs and atmosphere of the Wall. Otherwise, east, south and west it is the land of the far horizons, an amazing panorama of emptiness.

But who exactly were the 'Romans'?

Recruitment to the Roman army was, strictly, available to Roman citizens. This is not to say every man-jack was from Rome. The notion that the Roman army across its empire was truly staffed by *Romans* in that sense is inconceivable. A Roman citizen could be from Rome, or elsewhere throughout Italy or even abroad. For example, men from Provence (France) and southern Spain became Roman citizens and thus could join the Roman army. They were well organised long before the invasion of Britain, with length of service (usually 25 years) and pensions. Legions were organised into ten cohorts, each of six centuries, each century comprising 80 men. These were the crack troops, men who fought in the open. It was the legions that built Hadrian's Wall. Their names are found, inscribed on the stones. Then, having built it, they retreated into the background, as it were, leaving the Wall to be patrolled and local battles to be fought by someone else: the auxiliaries.

The auxiliaries were drawn from all parts of the empire. They occupied the forts and milecastles and turrets, they patrolled and fought and scouted and took prisoners. They too served for 25 years, and received 'citizen of Rome' status on retirement. Cavalry units were made up of auxiliaries. The cavalry role was not prominent in battle, but was used for scouting and to kill fleeing enemies after defeat in battle against infantry.

Each civilian settlement – the *vicus* – existed and thrived because of the Wall. The buildings were probably timber-built. Native Britons lived and worked locally, making various implements, and farmed, whilst their children, if male, were potential recruits as auxiliary troops. By and large soldier and civilian got along fine; indeed one cannot imagine how it could be otherwise, considering they lived together for so long, and the longer time went on so soldiers and civilians inter-related, with men and women doing what they do best: producing children. What happened when the Roman army finally left the Wall one can barely imagine: loved ones left behind, babies abandoned, those who consorted with the enemy left to their fate at the hands of the barbarians.

I spent some time exploring Housesteads, abandoning my sack at the museum to allow myself the pleasure without being encumbered. Two features of the site remain engraved in my memory: the amazing feeling I always get when in such an historic place, and Northumberland's wonderful landscapes, seen perfectly from here and which occurred again and again at different parts of my journey. When it was time to go I had no regret, for there was much more to see along the Wall this very afternoon. So I followed the Wall westward. I could have walked on top of the Wall had I so chosen, but there were signs requesting people not to do so 'in the interest of conserving the archaeology'. The Wall here runs close to the edge of the escarpment, with drops of a hundred feet or so on the opposite side. Whatever the lie of the land, the Wall follows unerringly.

Just quarter of a mile west long the Wall is Housesteads milecastle. It may seem strange having a milecastle so close to Housesteads, but, as I have explained, it was built before the decision was taken to build the forts. Bizarrely, a modern wooden gate stands across the gateway to prevent visitors falling to their doom on the other side.

In 1851, John Clayton, who did so much to protect and excavate Roman sites, found roofing tiles, coins and pottery here, and a recessed hearth still black with soot. The Wall continues along the top of the Whin Sill; at Cuddy's Crag, looking back, is one of the classic views of it as it rises and falls all the way to Sewingshields. A steep section leads down to Rapishaw Gap, where the Pennine Way, which runs alongside the Wall from the west, heads north for the Border. Crag Lough loomed up, a cold-looking lake at the foot of the crags. I climbed to where path and Wall run through a wood. I came here with my family in 1977 on a cold day. My daughter, then only eight, remembers it, never ceasing to remind me of the occasion. She hated it!

Today, I walked through the wood in silence, the sun streaming through the branches above. Ancient roots cross the path, defying the boots of walkers, as they have for years. Everything was perfect; the sunshine, the views, the atmosphere. Beyond the wood I had sight of the Twice Brewed Inn, on the Military Road. My night's accommodation was close by. Not much further to go today. Then came the Sycamore Gap, so-called because a magnificent sycamore stands at the foot of the slope, where the Wall goes down then up again. The sycamore has nothing to do with Hadrian's Wall, yet is eagerly sought out by visitors because Kevin Costner climbed it in *Robin Hood, Prince of Thieves*. The sycamore, not the Wall, holds the limelight. It's mentioned in 'Wall' leaflets, and even in respected reference books. What Robin Hood was doing at this lonely outpost is beyond me. If he had wanted to climb a tree, couldn't he have found one in Sherwood Forest?

***

Today was fresh and breezy, typically autumn. I returned to the Wall, bound for Greenhead. Near to the Wall I sat down to enjoy the moment. I'm always doing that: sitting down to enjoy the moment. We should all do it. The moment today was one of utter exhilaration, for wasn't I the lucky one to be here on such a day. A small stone-built edifice caught my eye. It was Peel Bothy, opened by H.R.H. the Queen Mother in June 1989. Might've stayed in it if I'd known it was there.

The Wall led off west, some 4 ft 6 in high here, with long grass on the top as though it needed a haircut. There were wonderful views eastward, along the Whin Sill to Crag Lough, the Wall disappearing into the far distance. I soon had company, seven women carrying packs, heading east. Doing Hadrian's 'path' I supposed. 'Good mornings' all round. As they passed me by I turned to watch their progress as they climbed a steep section. Soon they were spread out, as the strongest went ahead, whilst the least fit struggled to keep up, a principle that applies to us all along life's tortuous journey. Then I had company of another kind, but no-one I could talk to or even exchange a greeting.

Tornadoes. Two of 'em, low-flying and noisy. They were here and gone in an instant, so close and in seconds far away. I saw two more, this time so far off they flew in silence, specs in the distance. What would the Romans have made of them? I pressed on in a stiff breeze, alongside the Wall. Hereabouts the ditch was prominent, but further on, where the Wall runs along the top of steep crags, there is no ditch.

The Whin Sill certainly saved the Romans a lot of digging, providing a natural defensive bastion on which to build the Wall. I reached Windshields Crag, at 1,138 feet, the highest point along the Wall. Not surprisingly there's an Ordnance Survey column here. Perched on top of the crag, column No. S6489 is mounted on a base for the all the world looking a like a lump of Hertfordshire Puddingstone. Here are perhaps the most extensive views along the Wall. It's a natural place to linger, but it was early in the day still and a cold breeze was enough to drive me on.

Ahead was a sign: 'Private Property, Dogs to be on leads at all times (or risk being shot)'. The 'risk being shot' clearly alluded to the owner, not the dog. Fair enough. If I were a farmer, whose living relied on his livestock and saw someone's dog worrying my sheep, I would gladly shoot the dog's owner too. Not the dog, which knows no different.

Further on I encountered a lone fellow. He was 65-ish, and told me he was from British Columbia, Canada. ('The next place you come to is Japan.'). He wasn't carrying a pack and asked where he might eat. I directed him to the Twice Brewed Inn. As we talked meaningfully about the descendants of Scots and Irish emigrants visiting their ancestors' graves, two hikers appeared. My new-found companion terminated our conversation abruptly and took off, keen to have company by the look of it. Unfortunately the feeling wasn't mutual, for the company he desired soon left him in their wake, striding ahead on the next uphill section on the path with my Canadian friend struggling in vain to keep up.

Spots of rain fell as I continued west, the Wall now an impressive shoulder height. I came to a sign: 'Access Land', meaning public access to land, a law introduced to enable those who would explore the right to roam free where before they would be trespassing. I'm cynical about it. Most people just want to walk the footpaths. Considering the empty mineral water bottles and discarded crisps packets and chocolate bar wrappers I come across in the countryside, confining folk to the paths, where rubbish can be seen and picked up more easily by others, is probably for the best. At Caw Gap is a turret, with information board and a superb illustration of a snowbound Carvoran fort in winter, as well as information about the way the soldiers lived their lives in these remote outposts of empire. Full marks for providing information, for adults and children alike.

South of the turret, marked on the map in italics, are the mysterious words 'Mare and Foal'. I left the Wall here, and crossed a big open field towards two standing stones. If the Wall is history, the stones are *pre*-history. They are probably the remains of a stone circle that predates the Wall by centuries. No doubt Hadrian's men, like me, reflected on the people who put them here so long ago. They would be no use in wall building, otherwise the Romans would have had 'em out. Curiosity sated, I returned to the Wall, and continued west, following it to Milecastle 42, a milecastle with a difference.

Well, it's not the milecastle that's different. It's where they put it. In keeping with the lie of the land hereabouts the Wall follows a steep slope down to a depression, then climbs another on its journey west. The bottom of the depression would have been the ideal place for the milecastle. But no: instead, they built it on the slope, a mere fifty paces above the bottom of the depression. Why so? To keep faithfully to the self-imposed rule that there should be one Roman mile between milecastles, presumably. There surely can't be any other logical reason.

But in keeping faith with their own strict rules, the Romans made things difficult for themselves. First, the slope is so steep it's difficult to see how the buildings inside the milecastle could have been arranged, or even how the doors opened; second, one of the purposes of milecastles was to allow soldiers, civilians and livestock to pass through the Wall, but here, they would emerge on to a fairly narrow, sloping strip of land above the cliffs of the Whin Sill, having to then go down to the bottom of the depression anyway to go anywhere.

I pressed on, following the Wall up the slope. But not for long, for at the top a fence barred progress, and just as well, for just beyond the Wall disappears. Gone, it is, through quarrying: the Wall, the entire escarpment in fact. A desecration of an ancient monument, all done before anyone realised its importance (a) for historic reasons, and (b) for the income through tourism the Wall now generates. But it's easy to be wise after the event, as they say.

A footpath led away from the escarpment to a lake with a small crag around it. A notice implores people not to jump into the water, and nearby was a lifebuoy board. At the far side of the lake I found myself looking back at a mini-Matterhorn, showing in detail the different layers of strata formed by the upheaval of the ground at some past time. The layers are of different colours, like a giant, sloping sponge cake: dark red, greeny-grey, light grey. It must be a geologist's dream.

An information tablet gives details of five Roman camps that were dotted about the landscape here: 'Armies on the move make temporary camps to be used for a night, a week, a month. The

Roman army was no different'. The camps were needed for security when the Wall was being built. They consisted of a ditch as first defence against hostile tribes; earth from the ditch was thrown up to form an inner bank which was topped by a fence of wooden stakes. 'In this temporary refuge soldiers pitched tents and awaited orders. In addition to rations, bedding, clothes and weapons, each soldier had to carry digging tools and stakes on the march'. A map on display spells the names of the forts with a 'v', where today we use a 'u', where it appears as the penultimate letter. Hence *Vercovicivm*, (Housesteads), *Cilurvm* (Chesters), *Corstopitvm* (Corstopitum).

Just past Cawfields there is no sign of the Wall, but the ditch is clear enough. Heading west on green meadows I found myself alongside a drystone wall, built of beautifully crafted stones, recycled from the Wall. Having got used to Hadrian's Wall it seemed strange to have a farm wall for company. I almost walked past my next objective without seeing it. The fort of Great Chesters (*Aesica*), like all the forts on the Wall, was added as an afterthought. There's not a lot left of it now. The west wall still stands to a reasonable height, complete with part of the west gate, which was blocked up by the Romans themselves. Along the south wall is a stone with an embossed motif on it, possibly an old altar stone. There were lots of coins on the top – current coins, that is. Nearby is what appears to be a sunken vault – the strongroom, perhaps, where the Romans would have kept soldiers' wages.

Just as interesting lies the answer to where the Romans got their water supply for the fort. After all, on these elevated sites, without rivers, they had to have a good, steady supply of running water to supply their bath houses and latrines. The Ordnance Survey map indicates the route of a six-mile long aqueduct through which water flowed from the upper reaches of the Haltwhistle Burn. It seems the aqueduct was in the form of a channel, three or four feet deep. I have seen Roman aqueducts near Lyon, France, that carry water several feet above ground. One never ceases to wonder at the Romans' ingenuity.

After generously adding a few coins of my own to those on top of the stone (a rash thing to do in days of high taxation to pay for MPs' second mortgages they don't have) I carried on, westbound. The sky was darkening, with a hint of rain. To the north were the dark silhouettes of the Border forests, to the south distant fields and moors faded into obscurity. I followed the escarpment, passing Milecastle 44, with a good section of Wall, and climbed the first of the Nine Nicks of Thirlwall, a series of rugged crags (although there are only seven left due to quarrying).

Milecastle 45 came and went, then I reached Turret 45A. It stands atop a hill and served as a freestanding watchtower shortly before the Wall was built, slightly less than the original planned one-third of Roman mile from Milecastle 45. They were prepared to bend the rules here, then. Then I found myself walking alongside my favourite section of the Wall where, for quarter of a mile, it is six feet high or so, so you can't see over it. Here, more than anywhere, you realise what it meant to have a wall running the entire width of the country; no matter where you stood you could not look northward.

Then, suddenly, the Wall ended again, at Walltown, where they quarried the Wall away as well as the entire hillside. It's ironic that, just where the Wall reaches its greatest present-day glory, it disappears, destroyed by men without vision. As an information tablet explains, 'The rock made an excellent road surface for the fast growing towns of Carlisle and Newcastle. They quarried thousands of tons of stone and part of Hadrian's Wall from the 1870s until 1977, when work ceased'.

Thankfully there has been some reparation in the form of newly-planted trees, and the footpath runs pleasantly to a lake situated in the middle of the quarry 'floor'. As I passed a couple of dozen eider ducks bobbed on the water, the occasional 'quack' suggesting they did so in happy contentment.

The path led to Carvoran Museum, which I visited. There is so much information here, and while there is not the space to include it all it is worth mentioning that Carvoran (*Magna*) was one of the forts that pre-date the Wall. Sadly, the fort has all but been destroyed. It stood on high ground at the junction of the Stanegate and the Maiden Way, which led up from the south, from Whitley Castle. The Vallum runs to the north of the fort here, so the Romans hardly considered the fort part of the Wall.

In 1915 a postman found what appeared to be a bucket here, sticking out of a boggy patch of ground just outside the fort. When he picked it up he found it was a Roman dry-measure of bronze in perfect condition. It bore an inscription, saying it held 17½ sextarii (16 pints). In fact it actually held nearly 20 pints, so maybe the Romans were cheating the natives when buying their corn from them.

A film they show at Carvoran, *The Eagle's Eye*, shows the Wall and fort as they might have appeared from the air. It's a surprise to discover how tall the buildings (probably) were, how busy the streets were. I saw the movie in the company of a group of geriatrics, out on a coach tour. They chatted noisily, some even sitting with their backs to the screen. Their interest lay in each other, not the Romans. They seemed put out when the likes of me, by means of threatening glares, made it clear we wanted to see – and hear – the film. Come on, you guys, it's never too late to learn.

A bright sun and a fresh breeze greeted my emergence from the museum. The way west ran between the Wall and the ditch, the former lying under a grassy mound. A patchwork quilt of fields lay ahead now, across grand country. Ahead I spied the spire of the church at Greenhead, then the ruins of Thirlwall Castle. When I walked the Pennine Way I didn't visit the castle, sparing it no more than a glance as I headed for the Wall. This time it would have my undivided attention.

The castle, what's left of it, is built entirely of recycled Roman stones taken from the Wall, and stands on a rocky outcrop above the Tipalt Burn. The surviving windows suggest a 'gloomy, prison-like fortress', as Pevsner puts it, although it hardly needs an expert to come to this conclusion. With walls almost nine feet thick, it might have been impregnable. It dates back to the 14th century and was built by John Thirlwall as a family stronghold against 'unwelcome visitors' and was abandoned in the 17th century. 'In the 18th century the castle's melancholy appearance, its troubled past and its links with the Wall attracted the first tourists. Historians and artists came to sketch and paint the ruins and humble cottages in the shadow of its towering walls'. Later the castle's stones were recycled again, for the erection of farm buildings and walls. Thankfully, it was rescued from further decay by the Northumberland National Park Authority.

The Wall passed just below the castle's position, through the dell occupied by the Tipalt Burn, but no trace of it here remains. I followed the right of way to Greenhead, with its stone cottages and St Cuthbert's church, designed by John Dobson, and granite war memorial, 'Erected to those who fell in the Great War, 1914-19'. Today, nearly ninety years later, there were fresh flowers at the base of the memorial. Next to the memorial stands a pant, or fountain, of weathered sandstone. No water flowing, of course. The inscription: 'In memory of John Blenkinsop Coulson of Blenkinsop in the County of Northumberland by his widow and family, October, 1865'. Pretty, fresh flowers lay in the water bowls.

Buried in the churchyard is Joseph Alderson, a miner at North Walbottle Colliery, who was killed at the pit on 17 September, 1912, when a stone fell, knocking out a prop. He was twenty-eight years old. Many men, like my granddad, came from the Cumberland-Northumberland border area to work in the pits of the North East coalfield. It was natural enough for them to buried near their homes if they lost their lives down the pit.

I did not locate Joseph Alderson's resting place, but I did locate another. Near to the church wall stands a small black headstone: 'To Dennis, aged 3 years, 1947-1950. Asleep with the angels'. A little lad who died over half a century ago, he is still loved and remembered, his grave tended with fresh flowers. Dennis only had three years of life, but his memory remains precious.

Opposite the church, alongside the Tipalt Burn, is the Millennium Green, with seats and picnic tables and trees. A stone tablet displays various symbols of this area: a Roman soldier's shield and helmet, a double-edged axe and spear crossed with a shepherd's crook, a tractor, a miner's helmet and pickaxe, a ram, a cow, a horse, some pine trees, Hadrian's Wall, a Pennine Way sign, a hiker's boots and woolly hat, the latter a dedication (I like to think) to the likes of me.

I was received at the hotel by a young lass who seized my pack and insisted on carrying it upstairs to my bedroom. Later, as I ate and drank my fill, she waited on me personally and might have even been on hand to assist my (slightly) alcohol-soaked body upstairs. What did I do that was so right? The answer might have manifested itself in my dreams had I had not been rudely awakened by the sound of passing trains at dawn, rattling past about six inches away at the back of the hotel.

***

Scouts. I never seem to see them now, in uniform anyway. Not even in the Lake District, where I live, which arguably is where you'd expect to see them the most – hills to climb, rivers and lakes to swim in, etc. Our troop camped at Stonethwaite once, in the field by the Stonethwaite Beck. There's a tourists' campsite there now, but when we were there the entire area was deserted. We scrambled up the fellsides, swam in the beck, discovered Galleny Force, a wonderful waterfall. I recall sitting there for ages with Robert Waugh, just marvelling at the crashing waters in the narrow ravine close by. 'Scouting for boys' taught me so much, not only about tracking and sleeping out, but life itself. Today's youngsters: what they miss.

Greenhead is a name I always associate with scouting. It was here, in the fifties, that 1st Westerhope, my troop, came for summer camp. I was present on one of those excursions, the last, before going on to new locations. I retain only vague memories of the campsite. But of the experience of camping out my memories are indelible. Eating food, including porridge, cooked in huge dixies. Being cold and damp and hungry, but who cared? Queuing dutifully for a dose of quinine after supper, which, we were assured by caring leaders, was protection against malaria.

Protection against malaria? We were in England! I mention this because swallowing quinine, if you haven't tried it, is an experience so ghastly I wouldn't have wished it on Hitler. A Mars bar would be gobbled up immediately afterwards in a vain attempt to remove the taste. I've often wondered if we were made to take quinine as retribution for not always doing what we were told. But I never, ever did anything wrong, and didn't deserve a dose of quinine. Honest.

The way we got to camp. Whether it was the relatively short distance every Whitsun to Coldcoats, near Ponteland, or summer camp at Greenhead, Stonethwaite or Powburn, it was on the back of a flatback lorry, used, at all other times for carrying coal. The guy who owned it just slung a tarpaulin across the back and on we got, along with our tents and kit. Somehow, I can't imagine this being allowed with today's health and safety laws; but then, we were a group of lads setting out on an adventure. Health and safety? What were they when they were at home?

Camp was four large tents; three for sleeping in, and one the 'cookhouse'. A fifth served as the latrine, covering a hole in the ground which we filled in on departure, sticking a roughly-made wooden cross on the site so whoever followed wouldn't dig theirs in the same place. We roamed the fields on 'wide games' and tracking, or just wandered at will. We wore sandshoes, a sort of forerunner to today's trainers, shorts and singlet and little else. We walked through streams, and some of us swam in them where they were deep enough.

We learned about leaves and trees, and passed tests that earned badges that were sewn on to our shirts by dutiful mothers when we got home. We slept rolled up in old blankets, fastened by huge pins. We sang and shouted, we 'lost' our voices – I did anyway. We had a great time. For years I have walked the hills and moors of this great country, always being confident in navigation and taking care of myself day or night, and it's all thanks to scouting. Halcyon days.

I would be camping tonight, at Stonehaugh, deep in Wark Forest. I'd been there once before, in 1977, with my family, my lingering memory being its remoteness and some totem poles, the latter not what you might expect in the depths of an English county. First, though, it was back to the Wall, which continues to Gilsland, situated on the Northumberland-Cumberland border.

The path, Hadrian's Way, follows the line of the Wall, not visible here. What was visible was cattle, every one staring at my approaching form as though I was the only living thing they had ever seen. This lot were curious or scared or both. After a long, hard look at me, they turned and ran, as if I had suddenly produced a rifle and was about to dispatch them, foot and mouth style. They fled in the direction I was walking, and when they reached a field wall they turned, only to see me approaching still. After a moment's collective thought they charged off again, crossing the ditch to their perceived security at the far side of the field.

In the next field was a dairy herd, lots of cows with calves. The calves stuck close to their mums on the approach of the stranger. I always give cows with calves a wide berth. Y'never know, the protective instincts of cattle might drive them to charge their number one worst enemy. These calves were new-born, one or two barely able to get to their feet, even more reason not to get too close for fear of retribution by mum. It never ceases to amaze me that so-called dumb animals within minutes of being born can stand up, whilst the so-called superior race, *home sapiens*, take about a year. Then again, we do only have two legs.

I passed through a farmyard, where the smell of cow-muck and hen feed brought back nostalgic memories of my uncles' farms in Banffshire. Childhood memories are wonderful, don't you think? To be transported, perhaps suddenly and unexpectedly, to a time when we were young. I lingered briefly, looking back to the crags of the Whin Sill, thinking of times past, Roman or otherwise. Then I thought of time present. It was a wonderful autumn day. I moved on, to Gilsland. It was time to leave Hadrian's Wall and head north for the Border forest. I had walked in the footsteps of the Romans, savoured the delights of the grand monument they have bequeathed to this country and all around I had enjoyed the extensive views of the land of the far horizons. The walking had been wonderful; it was about to take a turn for the worse. But before continuing on my journey I have a story to tell.

It was 1961. I was a sprightly teenager, and when my parents took a week's holiday in a cottage a few miles west of Gilsland I said I said I'd pay them a visit by cycling up to see them from Westerhope. 'It's a long road,' said Mum (I can still hear her saying those words), but youngsters then cycled here, there and everywhere; 40 miles was no problem. The 'long road' was covered mostly under grey skies. At Gilsland the rain fell. I wore one of those yellow plastic capes for the last five miles or so on the quiet B-road where I didn't see a single car. What I did see before my very eyes was a full sized rocketship.

It was fully in view, a few miles off, standing upright, nose pointing skyward. Rockets were in the news then, when the United States and the Soviet Union were threatening each other with annihilation as well as launching human beings into space in the 'space race'. But a rocket in Cumberland? When I arrived at my parents' cottage I asked Dad about it. He shrugged and said he didn't know, clearly thinking I had been watching too many movies. But what I didn't know then, but do know now, is that I looking at Blue Streak, Britain's intended Intermediate Range Ballistic Missile (IRBM), which was standing at its test location at Spadeadam, preparatory to being shipped off to Australia, where it would be launched to test its viability, and, if necessary, to blow the Russians to Kingdom Come and serves them right, they started it.

I had long believed that Britain pulled out of the contest to throw nuclear warheads around because our rocket was useless. In fact, Blue Streak was a success. Evidently we cancelled it due to cost, though since we then paid the Americans millions for theirs I wonder why we didn't keep our own. Anyway, in 1960, after cancelling the nuclear warhead option, Blue Streak was retained as the first stage of a three-stage rocket intended to launch a satellite into space, a European project. Sadly, that, too, was cancelled, and Blue Streak was scrapped.

The Blue Streak rockets were built in Hertfordshire, and I have read amusing accounts of their transportation on the backs of lorries up the old A6, through the middle of Penrith and left parked all night in Carlisle. As for security, I recall the strange signs by the roadside as I cycled towards Gilsland: SPADE-ADAM – STRAIGHT ON. The signs were to guide lorry drivers to the site, as well as any Russian spies with pockets full of dynamite. The rockets were launched in Australia, presumably, where, if they malfunctioned, they would land harmlessly in the desert. Cumbria, remote by British standards, wasn't remote enough. They wouldn't have wanted a malfunctioning IRBM landing in the middle of Carlisle or Newcastle, especially one with a multi-megaton nuclear warhead strapped on. I mean, somebody might have got hurt.

Today, Gilsland served as a sort of watering hole, where I bought a pasty and chocolate before setting off for Stonehaugh. It would be a harder journey than anticipated; in fact in all the years I've trodden Britain's moors and mountains the conditions underfoot would become the worst ever. But first I would visit Wardrew House, one-time spa and place of literary associations. We are talking about two of Britain's greatest writers: Sir Walter Scott and the great bard himself, Robert Burns. Wardrew House stands in isolation above the Irthing, and it was here that Scott, before he was knighted, met Charlotte Carpenter. He must have had Miss Carpenter in mind when he was apparently inspired by the botany of the area:

> *To a Lady, with Flowers from a Roman Wall, 1797...*
>
> Take these flowers which, purple waving,
> On the ruined rampart grew.
> Where, the sons of freedom braving,
> Rome's imperial standard flew...

Burns was born near Ayr in 1759 and died at Dumfries, aged only 37. He is my favourite poet. I say this, even though the meaning of some of the words he used has to be checked to see what he's on about. Burns's poems include, among others, *Tam o'Shanter*, *A Red, Red Rose* (so sweetly sung by Kenneth

McKellar), and one we've all sung, *Auld Lang Syne*. My *Complete Burns' Poems, Songs and Ballads* runs to 629 pages.

In 1797 Burns went on a tour with a man named Ainslie. On 5 May they left Edinburgh and two days later crossed the Tweed at Coldstream, Ainslie having urged him to visit England for the first time. They quickly returned to Scotland, but on 27 May they crossed the Tweed again, visiting Berwick, Alnwick, Warkworth and Newcastle. They went on 'over fine country' to Hexham and on 30 May arrived at Wardrew, the 'celebrated spa,' where they slept. From Wardrew they went to Longtown and Carlisle, before returning to Scotland.

I took a detour now from the country lane I walked, to Wardrew House. Just as I had enjoyed walking in the footsteps of the Romans, now I walked in the footsteps of Scott and Burns. The house stands in private grounds. I got as close as I could without being shot and stood at a gateway of stone columns, the iron hinges *in situ* but the gate missing. A Tornado roared over as I stood there. What would Burns have made of it?

Literary pilgrimage over, I followed the country lane towards Rotheryhaugh, an isolated and possibly ruined dwelling, a must to locate in the forest. The red dotted line on my map indicated the right of way, but once you enter these vast pine forests you're in the hands of the gods. I crossed my fingers, a gesture I've never really believed in, and if I was a doubting Thomas before I'm a total sceptic now. I was destined never to set eyes on Rotheryhaugh.

From Wardrew Farm I took to open pastures. In the middle of nowhere I came upon a high deer fence with high stiles to climb over it, along with a sign with a picture of a bicycle and the word 'Welcome'. There was a small wooden bench, two slats of wood side by side but with no back support. In view of the rough terrain I was uncertain whether it was for sitting on, or lying on after breaking an ankle. I pressed on, conditions underfoot deteriorating, big grassy sods and hidden hollows inviting a foot. 'This is the worst walking territory I have ever encountered,' I told myself, and I didn't argue. But worse was to come.

There was a gate by a stone wall, with bog around it, where the path entered the forest. A mile into the forest I came to a stream in a clearing, a check with the map showing I was entering the Northumberland National Park. The right of way to Rotheryhaugh continued straight ahead, on the map, but I could not locate it among fallen trees, long grass and the inevitable bog. A helicopter hovered overhead somewhere. Was its crew waiting to see if I would emerge from the forest again? In the clearing by the burn I gave up the ghost as far as the right of way was concerned, and headed instead alongside the edge of the forest at a place named on the map as The Wou. Purgatory would be more appropriate.

I am now in the open, the grass so long I can't see where I'm putting my feet. There are holes, trenches really, filled with water, and grassy tussocks everywhere. My feet disappear at every step. The forest edge is on my left, an open wilderness of grass and bog on the right. Each step is into another hole, where I plonk my foot into water and drag the other from the hole it's in, my pack causing me to stumble. It's an indescribable struggle, a living hell. I continue thus for two miles. I swear I stumbled at least fifty times, not headfirst but into long grasses that hide irrigation channels, dragged over by my sack, my feet in never-never land. And then I saw two men.

They were quarter of a mile ahead, two scarecrows in the grass. Who were they? What were they doing here? I made my way, slowly and unsurely, until we met in that great wilderness where they told me this place is a Site of Special Scientific Interest (SSSI) and by the way I was trespassing. One of them had a plan of the site, and provided me with directions to the place where they had parked their car, where, once I'd located it, I would find a forest road and resume a normal life. The men were investigating the ecology and conservation management of the area. And here was me, stumbling across it. Sorry, but a clearly-marked right of way would have made all the difference.

I headed back into the forest, in the hope that I would be able to follow my SSSI friend's directions. It was far from straightforward, what with endless pine trees and the fact that I didn't know where I was exactly. Basically, I had to locate the man's car. And what a wonderful sight it was, a mud-spattered VW Golf standing forlornly on a forest track. It was 2.31 p.m. and I had eight miles of walking to Stonehaugh. I'd have to check every junction of forest road to ensure I didn't disappear without trace.

My immediate destination was Grindon Green, an isolated dwelling about three miles away, where the map indicated a left turn. I followed the forest road, and just before Grindon Green was overtaken by my friends in the VW. 'Are you OK?' asked the kindly Samaritan. When I said I was he said, 'We'd offer you a lift, but I suspect you wouldn't accept.' Of course I wouldn't, I told him. They drove on, with a final call of 'good luck!' With relief I came to Grindon Green. It turned out to be a ruin.

One supposes the likes of Grindon Green were once smallholdings that fell into decay when they created these forests. Names on the map are reminders of times gone by. There aren't many, for this was a sparsely-populated area. This would have been moorland, probably occupied by grazing sheep. Then, there was life: the shepherds, the animals. Today there is nought but silence and millions of trees. I emerged into a clearing, and there was that helicopter again. When I was in the forest I'd heard it from time to time; now suddenly it was in view and very noisy. Its crew would be able to see me now. The chopper reminded me of that Hitchcock movie, with Cary Grant in the middle of a vast prairie when he's buzzed by an aircraft. Maybe this one was buzzing me. Too bad if it was, for the road led back into the forest, so I was out of sigh again.

Every now and then I came upon a signpost, indicating a right of way leading into the forest. The county council fulfilling its obligations, I suppose (or the National Park Authority). An example was one pointing to Hindleysteel, an isolated dwelling two or three miles away, but trees clearly blocked one's passage.

Further on, out in the open again, I had sight of a distant horizon, complete with mountain range. Mountain range? Had the ghastly experience of The Wou and the endless forest affected my senses? Ah, no; the mountain range was simply clouds. Finally, I came to Coldcotes, the first place of habitation since Wardrew

Farm, ten miles ago. It was arrival at an oasis after crossing the Sahara, without the intense heat. Here the rough forest road gave way to smooth tarmacadam. Sheer luxury.

Three more miles led to Stonehaugh, with neat terraced cottages bathed in the evening sun. There was no-one about, not a soul. I located the campsite warden who kindly provided me with the key for the toilet block. I was in for a pleasant surprise, for the campsite had well-manicured grass, and was free of sheep and cattle and the little gifts they leave behind. I had the site to myself: no caravans, no tents, except my wee Saunders Jetpacker. The site was eco-friendly, with a small wind turbine and the roof of the toilet block was fitted with sun panels. The former whirred away, to what effect is uncertain, but I pitched the tent well away from it. I gave the campsite ten out of ten, but none out of ten to Stonehaugh Social Club, which wasn't open on Wednesdays – and guess what day of the week today was.

There's something about camping out under the stars (if you can see them). I suppose in my case it dates back to my scouting days. What I'm talking about here, though, is camping out in a tent you've carried for umpteen miles. One day. Two days. Three. You arrive somewhere where the only choice is to sleep in the home you've carried on your back. You're tired, cold maybe. Wet, usually. But when it comes to turning in there's your sleeping bag, and there's just enough room to crawl into the tent and slide in to it. If you want to know the meaning of 'cosy' or 'snug' you'll find out, especially if it rains through the night.

I've had great times backpacking on the fells of Lakeland, the hills of Scotland, the Yorkshire Dales, Northumberland. And after a good night's rest, there's nothing to match the feeling of the early dawn as you emerge from your sleeping bag, unzip the tent fly and crawl onto the damp, dewy grass. You stand up then, stretch your body and breathe in the air of a new day. It's too wonderful for words. Trust me.

Where was I? At Stonehaugh, where I wandered about on a wonderful September evening, and had a look at the totem poles – not the originals of the seventies but perfect replacements. The year '1992' is etched into the wood. To the west the sky was red.

Red sky at night, walker's delight. Or so I thought. The fields were deep green. The toilet block was shimmering clean. Silence reigned. I crawled into my tent, the happiest man on planet earth.

***

The rain came at 5 a.m., a gentle pitter-patter that would soon turn into a steady drizzle. Nice 'n' cosy in the tent, listening to it. Unfortunately I couldn't stay there. I peered out at a grey sky. It looked as though it was in for the day. Never mind, I had a nice, albeit cold, sausage roll for breakfast, and somewhere to do my ablutions in luxury.

A sandwich last night, a sausage roll this morning. I should explain. Years ago, when backpacking, I carried everything, including the kitchen sink. It felt like it anyway, my pack too heavy to carry and at the same time enjoy the experience. I've seen me set off with tins of baked beans and soup, only to complete the journey without using them. Crazy! So I carry the bare essentials, content to pick up whatever I can to eat. Tent and sleeping bag are essential items. Other stuff I dispensed with: cooking stove along with lots of unnecessary spare food and clothing. Walking is pleasure. Walking is fun. Or should be. There is no point in walking under a relentless, crushing weight. The sausage roll was fine; I could always look forward to a hot lunch in Bellingham in the café there (if it was open).

Today I had to return to the forest, where the right of way – on the map anyway – was clear enough. The rain fell steadily as I broke camp. There's an art to doing this when it's raining…

First, you don't want to be getting dressed in the rain. Instead, you crawl from your sleeping bag and somehow contrive to get your kit on inside the tent. I say 'somehow' because there's barely enough room in a Jetpacker to turn over in your sleep, let alone pull on shirt and pants, etc. 'Kit' here includes waterproofs, jacket and leggings. Second, once dressed, you should pack your sack, again inside the tent; this includes the sleeping bag, which must be kept dry at all costs. Third, you should somehow get your boots on (not necessarily with the laces fastened) and crawl outside, with your gear now inside the sack (and still dry), then release the inner fly and pack that into the sack too. Finally, take the tent down, roll it up and get it into the sack. It should be the only item that's wet. Items such as sausage rolls may be consumed at any stage of the procedure.

I have to admit to some loss of confidence in my navigational skills after the ghastly experience yesterday. I was reassured by the lady warden when returning the keys to the ablutions block. 'Lots of walkers go that way,' she said, probably wondering if I'd walked from Bardon Mill to Stonehaugh what my problem was with the half mile of forest walking I faced this morning. She was the only person I'd seen, let alone talked to, since my arrival at Stonehaugh the previous evening. Naturally, she remarked on the weather. She was bound to. It's part of English culture.

It amazes me that the media, and the BBC in particular, give such broad coverage to the 'weather forecast'. Not because coverage in itself is wrong, which it isn't, although it's far too-often repeated, but because the forecast is often wrong. On *Breakfast*, on the hour, quarter past the hour, half past the hour and quarter to the hour there's someone flapping his or her hands about in front of a disjointed map of Britain with fancy graphics telling sixty million people what the weather is going to do today, tomorrow and next week. Then, as though that isn't enough, there's the 'regional weather forecast', and we get it all again. Britain is a temperate country; failing to successfully predict the weather is no-one's fault. Yet millions of pounds and thousands of hours of airtime (and radio time) is spent on pointless predictions. 'It might be right,' some people say. Well, if you stopped a stranger on the street corner and asked him or her to predict the weather he or she might be right too.

I have stood on Great Gable in sunshine and watched rain sweeping across the Scafells, just across the valley. On this very perambulation of Northumberland, at Embleton, I stood on a beach under grey skies yielding spots of rain, yet the suns rays streamed down on the sea. To be accurate the forecast would have to say this would happen, and it can't. It gives you a 'rough idea' is another argument. A rough idea? For so much money and resources? The best weather forecast is to look out of the window, cross your fingers and hope for the weather you want. Like the 'official' forecast you may be right. Or you may not be. To anyone walking my advice is to put your boots on, pack some waterproofs just in case and enjoy the day. In winter, though, you should check: conditions can be Arctic on Britain's mountains, and the possibility of snow should be considered before setting off.

The rain fell steadily as I took to the trail, the path through the woods slippery and muddy. I emerged into open country, another half mile leading to the Pennine Way. A national trail, it would be waymarked all the way to Bellingham. Acorns on gateposts, and yellow arrows. I followed it north, blundering through bracken and slithering about on muddy stretches (I was enjoying it immensely, or would that be immersely), to the old footbridge across the Warks Burn. The path climbed steeply to Horneystead then to The Ash, names I recalled from when I walked the Way. I was in open country now, green rain-soaked meadows occupied by rain-soaked cattle. I was becoming rain-soaked too. Even modern Gore-tex can't keep persistent rain out forever.

I walked the Pennine Way in its entirety in 1986, 270 miles from Edale, Derbyshire, to Kirk Yetholm, just over the Border in Scotland. It's a tough walk, especially in rain, or just after rain, when the boglands of the Pennines become squelchy, although, let it be said, they've made it easier and better now by concreting some of the worst bits, or laying flagstones down, as I would discover in the Cheviots. In my opinion, the Pennine Way should be walked in one go, not in bits, although I acknowledge that not everyone can take the time required to do this.

If you do complete the walk, and tell your friends and colleagues, I guarantee the first question they will ask you (if they ask you anything) will be, 'How long did it take?' Not, as one might suppose, 'What did you see?' or 'What was the most interesting part of the journey?' No, it's always 'How long?' It's as if speed is of the essence, that the whole point of it is to do it in the shortest possible time.

But if it's speed that matters then reflect on this: a Staffordshire electricity meter reader, Michael Hartley, aged 37, covered the 270-mile route in 2 days, 17 hours, 20 minutes. He had no sleep, and stopped for only nineteen minutes to eat and drink. He went through five pairs of shoes, 27 pairs of socks and lost 10 lb in weight. So, if you can't compete with Mr Hartley, either in time or the cost of footwear, don't bother with the Pennine Way, unless, of course, you undertake the journey to savour the delights of the Pennines, Yorkshire Dales, Northumberland and elsewhere, no matter how long it takes. I recommend it.

I motored on in the rain. I'd intended taking my time on the way to Bellingham, but there was little sense in lingering on such a wet and dismal day. By the time I reached Shitlington Crags – don't blame me for the name – I was wet through and past caring as I traversed the desolate moorland above the North Tyne valley. The path led to the road, with Bellingham just over a mile off. Would the café be open? As I entered the village the little café in Bellingham was my only interest in life. Open or closed? Open or closed? It was OPEN. Oh thank you. Thank you thank you thank you!

Before entering my warm and dry oasis, I quickly checked the bus timetable, which told me I had a couple of hours to kill before the next bus to Hexham was due. In the café I sat in my own private puddle and ordered steak and dumplings, my first meal since breakfast at Greenhead the previous day. It never touched the sides. Still an hour and a half to kill, and I didn't want to spend it outside. I ordered pudding, then tea and a scone, doing my best to make it last as long as I could with great success. During the course of waiting/eating/reordering I was kept entertained by two fat blokes who plonked themselves at a table and ordered steak and kidney pie and a mountain of chips. I wonder how they'd fare on the Wou.

Part V

North Tynedale and Kielder

On Kielder side the wind blaws wide;
There sounds nae hunting horn
That rings sae sweet as the winds that beat
Round banks where Tyne is born.

Algernon Charles Swinburne

It was July. I was outside the railway station at Hexham, waiting for the bus for Bellingham. But when was it due? Fortunately a local woman was on hand to tell me, even the driver's name when it appeared. 'It's Ken', she said, adding, 'he's very good.' How can a bus driver be very good, I wondered? I soon found out. It's just that at Acomb, when an elderly woman alighted, he got out of his seat, and even out of the bus, to help her with her shopping bags, making sure she had them firmly in her hand before getting back behind the wheel. Like the woman said: Ken was good.

Unlike on my previous visits to Bellingham the sun was shining. This pleased me, for today I intended to walk to Hareshaw Linn before setting off for Falstone tomorrow. Happily, unlike my arrival here last autumn, I would have time to explore the village. Or town, as it apparently is. So, having got off Ken's bus I went walkies.

First, to Gingall, the name of a gun with a barrel three-feet long that stands on a stone dais by the roadside. The information plate tells you the gun came from Fort Taku, China, in 1900, and was presented to the town of Bellingham by Commander E. Charlton, RN, of HMS Orlando. Who'd have thought a gun from China would end up in Bellingham? Not that it would be so unusual today, since most other stuff nowadays comes to our septic isle from there. The gun and frame look so flimsy I swear they wouldn't last a day in one of our modern inner-cities, where yobs would wantonly tear it down and reduce it to matchwood before consigning its broken parts to the gutter. That's if they hadn't already smashed the gutter. Call me a cynic. Call me what you want, in Chinese if you like.

In 1597 Bellingham was raided by the Earl of Buccleugh's men in retaliation for raids carried out by the reiving families of North Tynedale. The Scots fired cannonballs into the church, some of which were discovered when the roof was being repaired in the 19th century. Three of them – they are very small, but I wouldn't have wanted to cop one between the eyes – are displayed today in a box near the pulpit.

The church's 17th century stone-vaulted roof was designed as a defence against further raids, and is so heavy it had to be buttressed when the walls started to bulge under its weight. As I wandered about inside I noticed the rope hanging down from the belfry. I'm always tempted to ring church bells when I see dangling ropes. I was privileged to do so once, by invitation, when I called at St Mary's in the Buckinghamshire village of Hedgerley. I was writing about country walks for a magazine at the time, and when I said so to the lady in the church, adding that

I'd always wanted to ring church bells, she kindly invited me to ring the bells of St Mary's. I don't know whether the villagers noticed the unscheduled peel, but it did give me a rather special feeling. Hedgerley, incidentally, was left untouched by the M40 motorway, which passes by not too far away, and the unfortunate sprawl of some towns and villages in the south-east. The Chiltern Hills, where Hedgerley and many other villages still nestle serenely in the English countryside, are threatened with 'development' and a new railway, but remain a glorious landscape of green fields and beechwoods. Long may it be so.

But right now I was in Bellingham, where, in St Cuthbert's churchyard are lots of ancient headstones, some over six feet high and leaning precariously. Solid stone slabs lie on the roof where you'd expect to see slates, all in the cause of defence against the Scots. Close by is the road, but in the churchyard all is peaceful, a typical and quintessentially English scene.

St Cuthbert's Well, a Georgian pant, is situated on lower ground outside the churchyard wall. The spring is supposed to have miraculous healing powers after a young girl, Eda Brown, who had a withered hand, was cured after drinking the water and praying in the church. St Cuthbert, who was evidently an accomplished dowser, reputedly discovered the spring himself. It is said that his body, carried by monks fleeing the Danes who invaded Lindisfarne, rested at Bellingham on its way to its final resting place at Durham. St Cuthbert has deep associations with Northumberland, but his story must wait; first I will recount the story of the Lang Pack.

In 1723, when the rich and retired incumbent of nearby Lee Hall, Colonel Ridley, went off to London with his family, he left his three servants, Alice, Dick and Edward, in charge. Their instructions were precise: fearing theft of his precious silver, under no circumstances was any stranger to be admitted to the house. One can see his point; in the days of lawlessness in Northumberland, the good colonel had every right to be worried.

Sure enough, on a dark winter's night, as snow fell in the valley, young Alice, nodding off by the fire, heard a pounding at the door. 'Whey is't?' she called out. A man's voice was heard in reply. 'A pedlar!' He was carrying a heavy pack, he said, and was hungry and cold after travelling many a weary road. Could she open the door and let him in for a cuppa? When Alice refused he had no choice but to leave, but he asked if she would kindly allow him to leave his pack. She agreed, and accepted it through the door, and he made off into the night.

The pack was about five feet long and two feet wide. Alice dragged it in, laid it on the floor and sat down again by the fire. But as she sat in silence she heard a scratching sound, and when she took a candle and looked at the pack she saw it roll over. One can imagine the scene: Alice alone and snug before the fire – and now, in the flickering candlelight, the pedlar's pack was moving!

Her screams brought Dick and Edward, the latter armed with a gun. When Alice told them she had seen the pack move, Dick said he thought it was the flickering light playing tricks. But even as they looked at the pack they heard a moaning sound come from it and Edward, taking no chances, raised his gun and fired into it. A moment later blood oozed out and trickled across the stone floor. Dick realised there had been a plot to install someone into the house, for the dead man who now lay before them had a horn about his neck to summon accomplices when the time was right. Dick sent Edward for help, and neighbours armed with muskets came to the house. They manned the windows, and when all was still Dick blew three blasts on the horn.

Shortly after, strange men appeared in the moonlight. Their leader blew his horn, and when Dick answered with his they rushed to the door of the house, only to be met with musket fire from those within. Some of the men died where they fell, others ran off into the night. The men in the house waited until they felt certain the men would not return, then went outside where, astonishingly, they found no bodies, just the marks in the snow where they had lain. Colonel Ridley, not surprisingly, was delighted the robbery had been thwarted, and rewarded his servants handsomely. A funeral service was held for the mysterious pedlar, after which his body was interred in the churchyard beneath a stone the same shape as his pack. It can be seen today, a reminder of what happened in North Tynedale that dark winter's night.

You mightn't expect to find a town hall in Bellingham – *Bellinjum*, as they say it – but the town, with a population of only 1,000 or so, is the only sizable place in North Tynedale, so yes, there is a town hall, complete with 'playful lead clock turret, surmounted by a small lead spire and four spirelets' (Pevsner). At the front is the Edwin Johnson Memorial Garden, with a notice: 'This project has been part financed by the European Community'. Was the 'project' the restoration of the town hall or the memorial gardens? Dunno, but hey, good old European Union, eh? We hand over millions so that they can build grand palaces in Brussels and Strasbourg and provide themselves with lucrative pensions, they give us a few bob of our own money back and there's a sign to say they've 'part financed' something. There should be signs around the necks of EU bureaucrats, saying: 'Part financed by English taxpayers'.

But let's focus on the way things used to be in Bellingham. I'm talking about Hareshaw Ironworks, a blast from the past, as the notice by the Hareshaw Burn says. This area was once the scene of industry: 'When local industrialists, Campion and Batson, saw water power, quality iron ore, coal and limestone, all in close proximity at Hareshaw, their eyes sparkled'.

Granted permission by the Duke of Northumberland to mine ironstone and coal, two furnaces were built here in 1838 – there were later three – along with a waterwheel and steam engine. Two dams were constructed, and a waggonway that connected the ironworks with the collieries. There were six rows of workers' cottages for the men who worked here. For ten years Bellingham was the scene of noise and smoke, so typical of those Victorian times; but the scheme was doomed to fail because the pig iron had to be taken to Hexham by cart, a process that was too slow and expensive. The Border Counties Railway arrived too late to save the ironworks.

The industry has gone, but Bellingham and its environs are largely unchanged from Bradley's account, written in the first half of the 20th century: 'A quarter of an hour's walk in either direction will bring you upon the moors, so close that the sound of the sportsman's gun in early autumn is a familiar note in the rural chorus of the valley, the bleat of sheep, the barking of collie dogs, the shout of dusty drovers, the cry of pewits, the sound of rushing waters and at long intervals the rumble of a North British train making for Hawick or Hexham....'. Well, the 'dusty drovers' have gone too, as has the railway. But Bradley's words otherwise ring as true today as when he wrote them.

Today, I was walking to Hareshaw Linn, a wooded ravine with a waterfall over thirty feet high at the far end, 'a place where lovers met, children played, poets sought inspiration and naturalists came to wander'. *Linn*, it seems, derives from the Gaelic, *Linne*, meaning a pool or rushing water. I thought it meant, simply, 'waterfall', but it seems to extend to the entire gorge.

At the start of the walk one passes buildings that once housed the manager's office of the old ironworks, and some of the workers' houses; then the path passes over mounds of spoil, taken from the ground all those years ago. But thoughts of blast furnaces and smoke and noise soon vanish as the path enters the ravine. It was July and the sun was shining, but I walked mainly in the shade, passing through shafts of sunlight that penetrated the thick canopy of the wooded gorge.

I came to a bench, superbly sited above the burn without, unusually these days, a dedication plate. Nearly all benches seem to have a message affixed to them now, in memory of somebody or other. Usually they have the year of birth and death of whoever's name appears, and I can never resist calculating his or her age, at the same time reflecting on whether or not I've outlived them. I wonder what message would appear on a nameplate dedicated to me, however unlikely. Suggestions not welcome, thank you. The gorge is so narrow, the room for a path is restricted and there are six bridges that criss-cross the burn before the waterfall is reached. I walked it alone, soaking up every wonderful step along the way, always to the music of the burn, the singing of the birds and the rustling of unseen creatures darting for cover on my approach.

The Pennine Way visits Bellingham but passes to the east of Hareshaw Linn. This would be a highlight, *the* highlight perhaps, of the entire walk. But the fact is the walk into the gorge is a cul-de-sac, necessitating the retracing of steps before heading north again. What's wrong with that? Only those who have walked the Pennine Way can answer. It's just that having walked from Edale, in Derbyshire, 225 miles away, the last thing you want is a diversion. By now your focus is on the finish, still 45 miles away but close enough to spur you on. Byrness is the next port of call, sixteen miles from Bellingham, all of them over rough terrain; Pennine Wayfarers will have neither the time nor inclination to visit Hareshaw Linn. In one sense it's a pity; in another it's good, for it keeps the gorge quiet and free of hikers, save those on a pilgrimage of love, such as myself.

A striking feature of the gorge is the massive sandstone blocks, from which, in one place, an oak has somehow rooted and thrived. I strolled on, slowly, crossing the bridges. One, the last I think, has lattice-style ramparts, with towering cliffs above and trees clinging to the sides of the gorge. Rich vegetation abounds, and what with the humidity of the day the scene was reminiscent of the scenes from *The Bridge on the River Kwai*. I expected to see Jack Hawkins and William Holden, the latter fulfilling his role as the mandatory American in a British film (to sell it to the US market). Got to have Hollywood stars. The Yanks were always the heroes, the Brits usually bumbling fools or nasties. Robin Hood's a Yank; the Sheriff of Nottingham is a Brit. In the animated *Little Red Riding Hood* you can bet the Big Bad Wolf had an English accent.

The waterfall is quite spectacular. Above and out of sight the Hareshaw Burn has passed quietly over the fields, and now it tumbles suddenly over a natural notch into a deep pool. Wild flowers thrive on the rocky cliffs; the trees cling on to naked rock for dear life; the amphitheatre, rich in colour and blessed with the sound of falling water, is a sublimely lovely place. I made use of a strategically-placed wooden seat and watched the scene awhile. It was a moment to reflect: to think of the Victorians who fashioned the path, of how fortunate I was to be here. Is there really crime and terrorism in the world? You wouldn't think so, sitting here.

The rock that forms the overhanging cliffs will crash down one day as the waterfall recedes through a process of wearing away the mudstone over which it flows. The gorge is a Scene of Special Scientific Interest, which is not surprising, and I had it all to myself on a wonderful summer's day. Ten out of ten to the National Park Authority for maintaining the footpath and bridges; and ten out of ten for Hareshaw Linn.

Back in Bellingham, with time to kill, I wandered on to the bridge across the former railway. Below the bridge grass grows where once trains ran north to Riccarton Junction, south to Hexham. Nearby were derelict buildings, old corrugated iron sheds, discarded cookers, fridges and tyres. The junk of mankind pales against nature's creations, such as Hareshaw Linn.

Ah, yes, I'm on about railways again. It's just that in front of me as I write I have a copy of Bradshaw's Railway Guide, 1922. The railways were privately run then, and the book extends to 911 pages of timetables of every railway in Britain and Ireland at that time. Oh what we have lost! Page 809 lists the 'Riccarton, Reedsmouth and Hexham' timetable for North British Railways. D'you know that on a weekday you could board a train at Hexham at 7.04 a.m. and travel up the North Tyne valley, calling at Wall, Humshaugh, Chollerton, Barrasford, Wark, Reedsmouth, Bellingham, Tarset, Thorneyburn, Falstone, Plashetts, Kielder, Deadwater, Saughtree, Riccarton (in Scotland) and be at Hawick for 9.53, and thence to Edinburgh? What's more, there were three trains per day. This timetable is surrounded by others, all featuring Scottish journeys, suggesting the North Tyne line was primarily of Scottish roots (if there are any enthusiasts who would argue otherwise I willingly cede to your undoubted superior knowledge). The railway, originally the Border Counties line, opened in 1854, and became the North British Railway in 1860. It closed in 1956. That's over 100 years of railway travel along the North Tyne valley. An excellent display in Bellingham's museum shows photographs of the steam locomotives and carriages of the day at remote places in north Northumberland. I recommend a visit.

How I would love to travel the routes of some of the old railways; and yes, at the old speeds. Time to look out of the window and enjoy the view, time to think, with (hopefully) no-one rabbiting aimlessly into a mobile phone. Bradshaw's guide is a fascinating insight into a sadly long-lost part of history, listing, as it does, every route of every railway throughout the land, along with times of trains, how far each station is from the next, details of connections, etc. As it says in the introduction: 'It would make perfect reading on a desert island, there is so much to study'. You could study it on the old railways if we still had them.

***

Saturday morning, Bellingham is a-busy. Delivery vans and lorries manoeuvre for position, there are folk doing early shopping, others await the bus to Hexham (will the driver be the helpful Ken?), shop assistants pile up stuff on the pavement. It's all go, but not for me, content to sit and watch before resuming my journey. Finally I get up and wander off to Cuddy's Well. Yep: the water is still flowing from the pant.

As usual, folk were commenting on the weather. It's an English pastime. I can recall my parents' voices as I lay in bed as a child, as they crossed our back yard to or from the lav, spotting a neighbour, or a passer by. Then, they might have said, 'It looks like we're in for a splash.' Today, in Bellingham, a 'splash' was more than a possibility.

I went down to the North Tyne and headed west along the riverbank, passing below Green's bridge of 1834. It's made of square-shaped sandstone blocks, typical Northumbrian, or it seems so to me. I spot cricket practise going on in a field. They're out their in their whites, and there's the thwack of willow on ball. I always associate cricket with the south, not with Northumberland. We never had it at school, save for a few knockabouts on a concrete pitch, 22 yards long – a chain. We didn't play cricket but we did learn about linear measurements. Surprisingly the sun appeared, giving the morning a September feel. My dad would have said it was champion. So it was.

The path left the river and crossed a field to a road. Thirty yards before the gate I encountered tall stinging nettles. They covered every inch of those thirty yards. Not a popular right of way, obviously. Wearing shorts is not the best raiment for such terrain. At first I gingerly tried to pick my way through, but the nettles were so thickly clumped together I gave up and simply blundered through them. When I emerged onto the road my legs were tingling, and would continue to do so all day. But when spirits were as high as mine that morning nothing matters, not even nettle-rash.

The landscape was changing, green fields giving way to rugged country. I passed under a bridge that once carried the railway, after which a byroad led to a stone house where three black dogs, confined behind a fence, and a yappy Jack Russell, greeted my presence angrily. The Jack Russell was free to approach and did so, but was harmless. The black dogs followed my progress as far as they could, on their side of the fence, barking all the way, until I passed under the railway again, their barking becoming fainter with every step.

Dogs can be a nuisance, especially in farmyards and near isolated houses. My contingency plan in dealing with hostile dogs is to (a) ignore them, sometimes uttering such sentiments as 'Good boy' or 'Take it easy fella', or even 'Piss off, you hairy-faced git' in a friendly voice, at the same time smiling pleasantly, or (b) if that doesn't work and they are getting really nasty, I grip my ruckstrap straps (keeping hands out of the way of snapping jaws, but I can't protect everything) and keep going; or (c) if an attack looks imminent I face the animal and prepare to kick it in the teeth. The latter tactic will not be deployed if the brute looks as though hostilities precipitated on my part will only make things worse for myself, in which case I am without further recourse. If I carried a gun I would shoot any dog in the latter circumstances, along with its owner if he or she appeared.

Half a mile further I arrived at Tarset Castle. It stands – or stood – above the confluence of the North Tyne and the Tarset

Burn. I had looked forward to seeing it, but was disappointed to find nothing more than a series of mounds and a few straggly trees. In fact I never broke stride here, which hardly does justice to a place with such a turbulent history.

The house, as it was, originally belonged to the Comyns, a family of Scottish knights. In 1267 John Comyn was granted a licence by Henry III to fortify it. In 1292, John the Black, as he was known, had claim to the Scottish throne but ended up, in the complicated course of history, being ordered to stay south of the Trent by Edward I. His son, John the Red, fought against Edward and was taken prisoner but released, much to the relief of his wife, Lily the Pink – no, I made that last bit up. Anyway John the Red was elected joint guardian of Scotland in 1299. He later submitted to the king and was pardoned, but his submission cost him his life when he was murdered by followers of Robert the Bruce. Failure to submit to Edward would have cost him his life too. The poor guy couldn't win.

Over two hundred years later, in 1523, the castle was used as a base by Sir Ralph Fenwick and eighty horsemen to 'overawe Tynedale thieves'. It was later attacked by William Charlton of Bellingham and 200 men, who drove Fenwick and his men out. Fenwick re-took the castle, only to be driven out again by a rare alliance of the men of Tynedale and 400 Scots and the castle was destroyed. For their endeavours several Charltons, and Robsons were seized and executed at Bellingham. Just to finish the job of the desecration of Tarset the Victorians drove their railway through the ruins. The castle would have been a great tourist attraction if it hadn't been destroyed. Instead of paying visitors, today only a few disinterested sheep grazed contentedly on the grassy mounds.

I had identified a right of way running off the road, northward, which led over rough country. Just as I left the road I encountered an old boy who clearly wanted a word. Had I taken a wrong turn, perhaps? Was I a trespasser? 'Hey you, get off my land...'. Ah, no, he was just being civil: where was I going, the inevitable comment on the weather. He was a Northumbrian through and through, friendly and plain.

The path led over wild country, towards (on the map) an isolated church over a mile ahead. Hereabouts the path disappeared. I found myself in no-mans land. I wanted to locate the church but couldn't seem to get my bearings. I had all but given up when I found myself at the place I sought: St Aidan's Church, Thorneyburn. Thorney-where? There's no such place indicated on the map, just open country and the church and rectory, isolated and peaceful, on a country lane.

The church was built in 1818 by the Commissioners of Greenwich Hospital, who owned the land, to provide a living for ex-Royal Navy chaplains after the Napoleonic Wars. However, one rector and his wife, 'having passed most of their lives at Portsmouth and Plymouth, were little satisfied with the absolute seclusion'. The parish was and still is thinly populated, drawing its congregation from the scattered farms and houses and the villages of Greenhaugh, Lanehead and Gatehouse. They're hardly villages really, and all in all you'd wonder how the church survives. But survive it does, in its remote location. There are trees around church and rectory, including a magnificent old yew.

Inside the church are windows with meaningful holy messages, and one 'in memory of those who fell in the Great War'. There are five names, even from this tiny parish. Outside was a notice about the wellbeing of red squirrels. It concerned a virus: 'If you see any sick or dead red squirrels with the symptoms, please report them to the red squirrel conservation officer'. The caring society we live in. I digress. St Aidan's is a lovely church in a lovely setting; the sort of place that makes this perambulation worthwhile.

The byroad led to Redheugh, 'a farmhouse with thick walls, suggesting it started life as a bastle' (Pevsner). There were pretty stone cottages here, with manicured lawns and roses, a lovely spot and quite unexpected. There were great views across the Tarset valley, another reminder, if one were needed, of what a wonderful county Northumberland is. A path crossed a field to a dovecote, built circa 1743. It has a slated roof that goes to a point.

As I took the path the sun made it known it was doing its best to make another appearance. A sign at the dovecote read:

'Dovecotes were built to house pigeons as a source of fresh meat, and eggs throughout the winter. The droppings were used as fertiliser on the fields...'. Inside was a row of holes in the walls that once held joists supporting an upper floor; larger holes above were nest boxes. There was a fireplace that provided a heating system through a series of flues. The building is so well constructed it might have served as a lockup, if one were needed here, which is unlikely. The path to the dovecote traverses private land, and the dovecote too is private property, but visitors are encouraged. My chance discovery proves once again that the best way to explore the countryside is on foot. If I'd been in a car I'd have driven right on by.

I entered Kielder Forest at Sidwood, where a sign read, 'Caution. Red squirrels crossing'. As a motorist I'm never quite sure what to do when I see signs about animals such as red squirrels and badgers 'crossing'. Slow down and look out for them I suppose. It's just that there's never another sign further on saying, 'It's OK, the red squirrels and badgers don't cross here, you can speed up again'. Anyway, in the forest I was pleased to see a variation, hereabouts anyway, in the trees I was looking at: Scots pine, conifers, beech, the latter surrounded by the fallen leaves of autumn. Otherwise, for miles and miles, it's tall, regimented pines, Norwegian spruce or whatever.

Further on I emerged into open country, crossed a footbridge and followed a quiet road leading to Black Middens bastle. Which is as good a place as any to look back at the days of lawlessness, of thieving and rustling, of the time when the border counties were the 'forbidden land', when the king's writ did not prevail; the days of the Border Reivers:

> Over the Borderland, wha' will gan wi' us,
> Saddle your horses an' buckle your blades;
> We will bring back wi' us fat Scottish cattle,
> Good Scottish horses and fair Scottish maids.

From the late 13th century till the Union of the Crowns of England and Scotland (1603), and even thereafter, the border country was a lawless place, beyond the effective jurisdiction of either king, where the inhabitants were at the mercy of rustlers and murderers, each side as bad as the other. There were no feudal lords, there was no-one to govern or control, so those who would farm or otherwise eke out a living from the land secured themselves in fortified bastles, or pele towers, such as at Black Middens. Englishman robbed Scot, Scot robbed Englishman. And they robbed their own countrymen too.

They came from all classes: agricultural labourers to gentleman farmers. They rustled cattle, stole property, burned houses. Families demanded and were paid a collection of grain (meal) as 'insurance' against cattle being stolen, the payment being paid at night (black), hence *blackmail*, a word associated with modern-day crime but dating back to the lawlessness of the borders.

On one occasion the men of Tynedale and Redesdale, together with some of their Scots' neighbours, carried out a raid so extensive they reached the gates of Newcastle, killing people and driving off their livestock. The Archbishop of Glasgow excommunicated 'the more enterprising' of these men, his language being 'calculated to congeal the blood of the doughtiest reiver who had any fear of God left in him'. He cursed their heads, the hairs of their heads, their face, their eyes, their mouth, their nose, their tongue, their teeth, their breast, their heart, their stomach, their belly, their back, their arms, their legs, their hands and their feet and 'every part of their body, before and behind, within and without'. One gets the impression the archbishop was none too pleased.

Later, the Charltons and Dodds, in company with the Armstrongs of Scotland, went raiding into Durham. Unhappily for them they were captured and hung in chains at Haydon Bridge, Hexham, Alnwick and Newcastle. They were trapped when the South Tyne flooded and the bridge at Haydon Bridge was chained up.

Another story concerns the Robsons of Falstone and the Grahams of Liddlesdale, Scotland. The Robsons had ridden into Graham territory where they rustled a flock of sheep, which they drove into Northumberland – only to find they had sheepscab. Furious, the Robsons returned to Liddlesdale where they captured seven of the Grahams and hanged them in a row with the warning that 'the neist tyme gentlemen cam to tak ther shepe the war no to be scabbit'.

The reivers' descendants live on, with names like Armstrong, Charlton, Young. No Heslop, though, which might be surprising, since the name derives from just across the border, near Hawick, meaning Hazel-Hope (the valley of the hazelwoods). My ancestors were probably peaceful folk who tilled the soil and reared the odd fatted calf. The tourist guides, ever-eager to cash in on this part of Northumberland's bloody history, suggest well-known latter-day figures are linked to the reivers of old: President Nixon, Bobby and Jack Charlton, the evangelist Billy Graham, Robert Burns and Neil Armstrong, the first man to walk on the moon. I mean, come on…

A notice proclaims Black Middens to be 'a defensible farmhouse in Tarsetburn', and that in 1989 there was 'the first re-enactment of the border raids here, when Greenhaugh First School children were the raiders, helped by staff of Northumberland National Park'. Among the children were Davises, Robsons, Liddles (or Littles) and Taits, 'a reminder that some of the families have lived in this area since the days of the bloody border conflicts'. How refreshing that today's children were being taught history, and were even re-enacting it.

It's hard to believe the bastle was a farmhouse, in the sense we have of a farmhouse today. But its occupants would have been a farming family. It was probably built in the late 16th century. Livestock was kept inside at night, whilst the family lived upstairs. Faced with the perpetual threat of attack from rustlers, one imagines the farmer wouldn't have ventured far to tend his cattle and crops. Those who would attack him and his family and steal his cattle presumably would arrive on horseback, leaving little time for retreat to the comparative safety of the bastle.

The bastle we see today is not quite as it was. Apart from the roof and upper floor being missing, the original gable door – for livestock – has been blocked up, whilst the two ground floor doors and the external stone steps leading up to the first floor are later additions. Access to the first floor of bastle houses was by a ladder, which could be quickly withdrawn. Presumably the stone staircase was added when the reivers ceased to reive. Today it leads to a wooden viewing platform, where one can see walls two feet thick and look down to the ground floor which had two rooms for the livestock. Cattle and goats segregated, perhaps. The windows are square-shaped, narrowing defensively towards the outsides.

Standing on top of the staircase gives one a good insight into how things must have been in the days of the Border Reivers. The bastle was strategically well sited, on a hillside, with good all-round views over country possibly covered by woodland. This is a good moment to pause and think of the people who lived here, and the lives they led over four hundred years ago.

What a contrast in the lifestyles of those who lived then and today. Whilst the former struggled to eke out a living under the threat of having their livestock stolen, their own lives at constant risk, today we have money, whether we earn it or not, food aplenty, washing machines, televisions, computers, healthcare, leisure time and we are free to travel.

Kielder Forest refers collectively to the forests of Kielder, Falstone, Wark and Redesdale and the surrounding hills and moorland, an area of some 250 square miles. First plantings were made in the 1920s, after which the Ministry of Labour supplied unemployed men of the 1930s – there were plenty – many of whom lived in huts in a special camp, and others were provided with specially constructed houses, such as at Stonehaugh. The main conifer is Sitka Spruce. 475,000 cubic metres of timber are harvested annually; newly-cleared areas are now being planted with a mix of conifer and broadleaf trees.

I always think the saddest things about pine forests are the stark, regimentation of rows of trees and the 'dead' ground under the forest canopy, which light and warmth cannot reach so that no vegetation can thrive there, and no animals can live there. There is no beauty in a pine forest, but if we have to have wood it has to be grown somewhere. Kitchen units and laminated flooring don't grow on trees – they *are* the trees. Having said that, how many of Ikea's products are 'Made in England'?

The forest road was stony and deserted, the trees so close together it would be impossible to walk between them for any distance. A ditch runs alongside the 'road', beyond which there are sharp spiky stumps and lots of dead wood strewn about. Between the 'road' and the first trees ferns and grasses thrive, as though in protest at their inability to do so just a few yards away. At Grid Reference 739905 I should have been able to turn left for Falstone, but a bridleway, which on the map leaves the 'road', led straight into a barrier of spruce. This is a right of way blatantly obstructed, and in a National Park too.

No matter, I pressed on along the 'road', which climbed to almost a thousand feet. The 'road' took the shape of a loop, so that I encountered the bridleway further on, or would have if it existed. Here, bizarrely, the right of way was waymarked, not that anyone could follow it. A left turn from the 'road' led to a fire tower perched high above the forest canopy. I was reminded of Colditz. Was I being observed by guards using binoculars, or even CCTV? In today's Big Brother society, where we are covertly observed in city streets and shopping malls, I wouldn't be surprised in the slightest to discover my movements were under scrutiny.

Two miles to Falstone, downhill now. I marched apace along the gritty 'road', easy going, perfect conditions for a sing-song. I sang *The Twelfth of Never*, trying to sound like Johnny Mathis. In vain, but at least I know the words. Somewhere around 'I'll love you till the bluebells forget to bloom' I came unexpectedly upon a huge truck, parked with its engine idling. It was clearly designed for carrying logs. Hardly a surprise. The driver, sitting at the wheel, nodded at my (to him) equally unexpected presence. As I passed by a man carrying a kitchen roll emerged from the depths of the forest. Now, what do you suppose he'd been up to, in the forest with a kitchen roll?

And so to Falstone. The meaning of the name is disputed, but possibly derives from the Anglo-Saxon, meaning 'speckled stone'. Kelly's Trade Directory has it as 'Fast-stone'. The village is tiny, yet there was a station here, on the Border Counties Railway. I went straight to the church. St Peter's burned down at Christmas, 1890, and was rebuilt two years later at a cost of £2,000. In 1832, the Rev Burdon became 'restless, expensive, drunken, embarrassed and eventually insane in retirement'. Some folk just don't take too well to remote Northumbrian outposts.

A notice in the churchyard said that a health and safety survey of memorials had been carried out. 'As a result unstable and potentially unstable memorials will be cordoned off with stakes and ties. Do not approach…'. Some of the headstones are old and mostly leaning, so maybe it's right to prevent anyone getting too close. Then again anyone with common sense wouldn't get too close, you might think. Ah, but some folk haven't any common sense, and then there's kids to consider. A six-foot slab of granite toppling onto a toddler doesn't bear thinking about. Dodgy headstones are the responsibility of local councils, who have the authority to have them cordoned off or laid flat if necessary. One hopes bereaved families are kept informed if any headstone has to be moved.

Falstone's old school has been tastefully converted into a tea room, which I made use of, especially welcome after my forest trek. On the notice board: 'In 1910 Falstone was described in Kelly's Trade Directory as 63,678 acres of wild moor and mountainous land, affording good game and pasture for sheep', and yet another definition of the name, this time said to derive from the Anglo-Saxon, 'Faeston', meaning a stronghold for securing livestock.

Close by is the Jubilee drinking fountain, with the words 'erected by subscription' above the unsmiling features of Queen Victoria. The fountain is made of cast iron and is 'quite elaborate' (Pevsner). No water flowed. I didn't linger long; midges were abroad, so I fled to my night's accommodation, the Black Cock, an ancient inn with modern-day prices. For my money I was provided with a TV with one working channel, a small quantity of shaving cream and a razor, along with an itsy-bitsy tube of toothpaste and itsy-bitsy toothbrush, ideal for folk who carry their homes on their backs.

***

Kielder water is the biggest man-made reservoir in Europe. It holds 200 billions of litres of water. God knows how much that is in English. The shoreline is 27½ miles long. The project cost £167 million and was opened by the Queen on 26 May, 1982. The purpose of the reservoir was to provide water for Tyneside, Wearside and Teesside in anticipation of the requirement of those places that water would be needed for future industrial purposes. To some extent, therefore, it was a white elephant, since successive governments, helped by the trades unions, have contrived to have British industry exported to India, China and anywhere else you can think of. I did buy a pencil eraser once, with 'Made in England' on it, so not everything has been lost.

Nevertheless, Kielder Water is a success, for several reasons. First, its underground springs ensure the level of the lake remains high, so that the outlet of the Derwent Reservoir, on the Northumberland-Durham border, is constantly supplied, even though the level of that reservoir may be low – and that's the source of water for Tyneside; second, they made a damn good job of the dam, which I would find out for myself; and third, Kielder Water is a successful tourist venue, drawing in thousands of visitors who enjoy the various leisure activities here. It always comes down to tourism in the end in Britain now, doesn't it?

In building the reservoir they flooded the upper North Tyne valley, displacing people from their homes in this sparsely-populated area, and they had to build a new road to Kielder village. The North Tyne valley must have once been a lovely place to inspire a chap called Mackenzie to write, in 1825, that 'the banks of Kielder in ancient times have been clothed with wood and the adjoining country, although bleak and barren, has been enriched and beautified with thick groves'.

It was a fine Sunday morn. I had my day's itinerary laid out. First, I would walk to the dam to see Kielder Water for the first time, then visit Tower Knowe visitor centre, before retracing steps to walk alongside the northern side of the lake to Kielder. The dam was a mile and a half away, and on approach I saw the unmistakable straight 'horizon' of the dam wall ahead. Where I walked the infant North Tyne, outflowing from the dam, was low; but on the other side of that wall was enough water to sweep me all the way back to Hexham.

It was one of those mornings when the sun kept popping out and popping in again behind dark clouds. In other words, a chance of rain. At 10.24 precisely I arrived at the top of the sloping wall of the dam to behold an awesome sight, Kielder Water, stark and grey and vast. Here, at the dam, was modern art, with a notice, 'The land around Kielder Water and Forest Park has become the home of a unique collection of visual art and architecture, inspiring artists and architects to create work in response to its vastness ands beauty'. It goes on to describe the reservoir and its environs as an 'open air gallery' with a 'vibrant and challenging' collection of visual art and architecture which will 'surprise and intrigue the visitor, establishing Kielder's national reputation as an essential destination in experiencing contemporary art and architecture in a rural setting'.

Art and architecture; artists and architects. Grand words, but what about the art? The art at the dam was *The Anonymous Quarrymen*, represented by three huge upright stones. Why not stones in the shape of men? Because they wouldn't be anonymous? The stones are cold, unyielding. They fit the scene exactly. But they're nothing like quarrymen, and merit their position without being given a meaningless title.

As I walked along the top of the dam, it was hard to decide which way to look. To the left, the distant green pastures and woodlands of North Tynedale; to the right, the awesome waters of this great lake, now occupying what was once a rich valley, a place of industry, of farmsteads and fields, of people, young and old, going about their work, going to school, where trains ran to and from Scotland.

From 1862 until the General Strike (1926) coal was mined at Plashetts; there was a steam engine for the colliery and a blacksmith's. There were 64 houses, a chapel and a school – and, if you remember the railway timetable, a station. It was all dismantled to produce this great reservoir. There are visitor centres and restaurants, exhibition and education centres, birdlife – the upper part of the lake, Blakethin Reservoir, is a conservation area – camp sites, water activities, forest walks, a youth hostel at Kielder at a time when others are closing, and an abundant water supply. When I started walking over the dam I wasn't quite certain what to make of it all. By the time I got to the far end I was beginning to like it a lot.

The rain came. Nothing heavy, just enough to oblige me to put on my waterproof jacket and pull the hood up. The wind blew spray over the lake surface; mist closed in. It soon passed, enough for me to spot the passenger launch as it was leaving Tower Howe Visitor Centre. I thought it might not sail if the lake was too choppy. So small on the vastness of the lake, it reminded me of *The African Queen*, the movie with Humphrey Bogart and Kathryn Hepburn, when the little boat finally sinks that German gunship. So small, so insignificant. Just like the launch on Kielder Water today.

At Tower Howe were a gift shop, a restaurant and the ferry landing, and a notice posted by Northumbrian Water about the construction of Europe's 'greatest ever man made reservoir in the middle of Europe's largest man made forest', creating a diverse environment supporting numerous species of wildlife, etc. 'The increased planting of broad-leafed trees around Kielder Water has served to enhance the visual appeal of the landscape and encourage a greater variety of natural colonisers…retaining a wilderness quality which attracts occasional rarities such as osprey, hen harrier, montagu's harrier, long-eared owl, great crested grebe, heron, goosander, teal, redshank, crossbill, grey wagtail and tawny owl…Rabbits, hares, weasels, stoats, foxes, toads and frogs…' etc, etc. The Exhibition Centre was showing *The Story of Kielder*. I chose the *Café on the Water* instead. Cappuccino, and a fruit scone made from Northumbrian granite three thousand years ago. I resolved to keep a sharp eye open to see if I could spot a montagu's harrier, not that I would know one even if it stood on one leg and said, 'Hello Paul, who's a cheeky boy, then?'

The café has superb views, almost Alpine. And yet, high on the wall of the café, was a flat screen television. The picture was on, the sound was off. Silent figures were running and falling about meaninglessly, probably to (fortunately) unheard music. In the corner of the café sat a young mum and dad and two small children, the former, along with everyone else, admiring the view, the latter staring vacantly at the silent screen before them. You bring your kids here from miles away and they are watching the telly, even though they can't hear whatever's being broadcast. Oh look at the lake, the trees, the birds, the little boat approaching the jetty! How sad that even Europe's greatest reservoir took second place to something so meaningless.

I went outside to find the sun trying its best to break through. Newly-arrived carloads of folk either proceeded straight to the toilets, hardly surprising since Kielder is miles from anywhere, or to the café; no-one gave the Exhibition Centre a second glance. A young woman with two small kids approached. She was carrying a portable barbecue. Good idea; I bet those kids were loving it. It reminded me of the day I first took my family walking, when I cooked sausages on a stove by the Ham Burn. You don't forget things like that.

The launch, the *Osprey*, was alongside the jetty. I boarded it with half a dozen others. It sailed, despite the lake being choppy and in a stiff wind. I've seen the launches on Derwentwater being kept at the boatlandings in Keswick in better conditions. The skipper – the entire crew, in fact – was Les, who kindly imparted lots of information to me as we sailed anti-clockwise around the lake. If we wanted to know anything, he had to tell us, since the pre-recorded voice on the intercom was drowned out by the combined noise of the engine and the wind. I did catch something about the 'galley', which we could visit if 'hungry or thirsty'. It could only mean the little shop at the stern, which displayed assembled goodies.

There's a whinstone quarry on the far side of the lake, part of the Great Whin Sill. The layers of strata were clearly visible as

Les hove to so we could have a good look. Les said he once worked in the quarry, where much of the stone was taken to build the dam. He explained: 'The people who lived in the valley and had to leave their houses were well compensated, and left without complaint, moving to Kielder, Falstone and Bellingham. The buildings they vacated were demolished or dismantled before the valley was flooded. The timber was burnt and all debris removed.' Any notion I had of ghostly houses now filled with water and occupied by expressionless pike was thus dispelled.

The tannoy cackled again, informing us that Otterstone Lee, now covered with water, was a farm of 9,400 acres, and was the largest farm in England at the turn of the 20th century, and that a bat can swallow 4,000 midges in one night. Why this latter information was imparted to passengers on the *Osprey* wasn't clear to me, although I would have cause to recall it later.

We pulled into Leaplish Visitor Centre where a sign provided the times of opening in the Duke's Pantry in Kielder Castle, which was important as I was wondering where I could get breakfast in the morning. Sadly, the times listed referred to November to February, which was as much use as a chocolate teapot. Another notice warned of adders being 'present in these areas'. The only venomous snake in the UK, it said, for the benefit anyone who didn't know. Back at Tower Howe, visitors returned to their cars and I set off on the nine-mile trek to Kielder.

I retraced steps along the footpath and over the dam, from where the right of way ran through the forest on the north side of the reservoir, Kielder-bound, more or less on the route of the old railway. It led to a stone ruin. The crumbling remains of *Gordon Walls* stand among the conifers, all but engulfed by bracken and undergrowth. Today, it's not far from the lapping waters of the reservoir; in its heyday it stood high on the sides of the valley above the North Tyne. A notice says that it was 'probably occupied by a shepherd'. It's at map reference 703884 if you ever want to locate it. There's little to see but much to reflect on at this little place of history. A shepherd, here! Hard to believe, now that the hillside is clothed with conifers.

Further on the path ran along the floor of the forest. I trod on pine needles and broken twigs and crossed the Belling Burn by a high bridge, the waters of the burn cascading far below on their way to the reservoir, then rejoined the route of the former railway at the former Plashetts Colliery, now lost forever. Around 4.30, and still in the forest, I noticed a few midges in the late afternoon air. They weren't biting – yet: maybe just preparing themselves for their evening onslaught against the human race.

Some of the forest 'roads' north of the reservoir had long, uphill sections. On this terrain I found *rhythm* again. Left, right, left, uninterrupted by any excuse to pause. How long you can keep it up depends on your level of fitness. I was going like a train, the first one to pass this way for years. In places the 'road' emerged from the forest, and here I walked in the sun. The 'road' was metalled alongside Bakethin Reservoir, a sort of extension of Kielder Water. Hereabouts I came upon a fox. He was made of wood and nailed to two posts. Further on, a *seat*. A place to park my bum and rest my legs. Then a sign warned drivers that here they are entering an area used by 'cyclists, walkers and horse-riders'. Of these categories of passer-by there was just one: me.

There have been changes in the short time since I walked along the north shore of the lake. First, the Lakeshore Path, all 27½ miles of it, has been completed, so that now you can walk or cycle around the entire lake on a good surface. The path, all of it, is suitable for wheelchair users and is a superb facility for anyone wishing to enjoy the delights Kielder has to offer.

Another addition has been the 'artwork', dotted here and there about the lakeshore and elsewhere. On a subsequent visit to Kielder I discovered a silver foil-looking viewing shelter that greets you as you step off *Osprey* at the Belvedere landing. Another shelter to the east, known as *55/02*, is bright red. Neither is in keeping with the surroundings, each being 'loud' and constructed of steel or similar material, not eco-friendly at all. Better is *Silvas Capitalis*, a 20-feet high head made of wooden, sculpted tiles. It was designed by artists from Chicago, based, apparently, on their perception of Celtic and Roman mythology.

Haven't we a Northumbrian artist to design something on his or her 'perception'?.

I wonder about this 'artwork'. How much does it all cost? Could the money have been better spent? What is it that makes anyone think the public want to see such things in what, after all, is a magnificent setting? *Silvas Capitalis* I liked, and kids will enjoy clambering up inside to look out of the eyes. But that's not the point. The point is that we see it whether we like it or not. And what will it all look like in twenty or thirty years' time? They've made a great job of Kielder; lets hope they don't spoil it with too much clutter.

Butteryhaugh was lit up superbly in the late evening sunshine. I passed through, seeing no-one. My unerring footsteps led me directly to the Anglers Arms, where I chanced on conversation with a bloke who had spent the day sailing on Kielder Water, and a young German guy who spoke French and declared that Hadrian's Wall had been a big disappointment for him. *Quel dommage!*

Supper eaten, thirst quenched, I made my way to Kielder campsite. It wasn't far, which was just as well for someone who had been walking all day and had just consumed a huge meal and an unknown quantity of booze. The campsite is well-cared for with lots of space, surrounded by trees, the Deadwater Burn close by. The sky was heavy now, and, what's more, I had company. Midges. Millions of 'em, zigging about the way they do. I invented that word for midges: zigging. If you ever see it in a dictionary, which is unlikely, you have me to thank for it.

The campsite warden had a welcome smile and forearms covered in midge-bites. As I made my way to pitch my tent I saw swifts swooping, taking midges on the wing. Good for them. We could have done with a few of those bats the woman's voice on the launch intercom told us about too. The only other occupants on the site, their tents already pitched, were a group of young girls and another lone male, all flapping their arms at the zigging predators. I dived into my tent, zipped up the inner flap with its mosquito net and lay on my back reading *Billy Liar*, at the same time resolving to delay the inevitable visit to the loo. If only I hadn't drank those pints.

***

It comes with age; the need to pee before it's time to get up. It came to me this morning at 5.30 a.m. I was snug in my sleeping bag, dreaming about montagu's harriers and bats catching midges. Talking of which, I didn't want to crawl out on to the damp, dewy grass, especially if Kielder's predators were waiting. But it was no good: I *had* to go.

If I'd been on the Lakeland fells I'd simply have crawled from the tent, do what I had to do and crawled back in again. I could hardly do so here, even at this early hour, not with the girls a mere twenty-five yards away. So I put on shorts and trainers, unzipped the tent flap, emerged into the early morning sunshine and prepared to run the gauntlet of midges to the toilet block, fifty yards away.

To my surprise and relief there was not a midge in sight, not even under the trees by the burn where you'd expect to find them. And so I walked the fifty yards in blissful solitude, soaking up the sunshine of a wonderful Northumbrian daybreak. The midges, like the girls, were still in sweet repose. Duly relieved, I returned to my sleeping bag where I enjoyed a couple of hours' slumber, before emerging again for my morning ablutions. And guess what: the midges were waiting.

It's as if they knew. Maybe the word had got round about the bloke in the shorts and trainers. One or two of the girls had crawled from their tents too, their arms flapping vainly at man's worst enemy. I ran all the way; the midges came with me, zigging around my face, my arms, my legs. I reached the sanctuary of the toilets before emerging to another onslaught. Back in the tent I zipped up the mosquito net, relieved to have reached safety. When I emerged again the midges were still there but seemingly had lost interest. But I knew in a few days the midge-bites would need scratching, leaving angry red blotches and torment that would keep me awake nights.

Culicoides impunctatus – the common midge – is prevalent in northern Britain. They are usually found near water and in glades, and dine at dusk and dawn, feeding off plants and animals, especially red deer in Scotland, which flee to higher ground on the hills. Humans are probably a special delicacy. When breeding, copulation lasts for 2-3 minutes (the midges, that is), and after fertilisation the females require a meal of blood for her eggs to develop. Judging by the amount of blood they sucked out of me, they must have been at it all night.

Kielder lays claim to be the remotest village in England. This may or may not be true, but remote it certainly is, less than two miles from the Scottish border and miles away from anywhere else of sizeable habitation. As though to prove the point, when I called at the Duke's Pantry in Kielder Castle for coffee, two women were discussing the merits or otherwise of Hexham's two supermarkets, Tesco and Waitrose, nearly thirty miles away. Their conversation was hardly inspiring, but I enjoyed listening to their Northumbrian accents, the last voices I would hear until I reached Byrness, in Redesdale.

The 'castle' at Kielder is not a castle at all, but a shooting box, built in 1775 for the first Duke of Northumberland. Sir John Hodgson, the historian, wrote that in 1777 the Duke and Bernard Mitford passed ten days at the castle where 'his lordship entertained the shepherds and girls with a collation of dances, distributing ribbons among the lasses'. Sir Walter Scott reported otherwise: 'The Duke tells me his people in Kielder were all quite wild the first time his father went to shoot there. The women had no other dress than bed-gown and petticoat. The men were savage...and sang a wild tune, "Orina, Orina. Orina". At a certain part of the tune they drew their dirks'. The 'savagery' has gone from Kielder, as has the railway and such industry that thrived. But little imagination is needed to feel the veins of history here.

A forest road crosses the hills from Kielder to Blakehopeburnhaugh, ten miles away. The road is rough and unmetalled, but motorists are nevertheless invited to drive it, paying a toll at the Kielder end. I had planned to take a trail leading across the hills, but abandoned the idea because it leads through the inevitable forest with the possibility, likelihood even, of finding my way obstructed. So I took the forest road, passing the toll booth, Redesdale bound.

The road is long (with many a winding turn) and climbs all the way to Blakehope Nick, the high point on the ridge separating North Tynedale from Redesdale. After three miles of forest walking the road emerges on to open moorland, typical Cheviot country, with distant hills and views to more of Northumberand's far horizons. I pressed on, the only interruption to wonderful solitude being the occasional motorist who had chosen to drive over the hills this way, probably more out of novelty rather than necessity.

The road re-entered the forest, but I had extensive views southward, as the hillside leading down to the Ridge End Burn falls steeply away so that one can see over the tops of the pines. I checked the map for the names of the hills beyond: Wether Law and Berrymoor Edge. North, unseen above the treeline, is the lonely ridge of Oh Me Edge. Now, where did they get that name from?

And so to Blakehope Nick, at 1,500 ft. Beyond the stone marking the summit a heather-clad moor rises to infinity. Wilderness, yes; but there's more to this country than meets the eye, as the information tablets says: 'Kielder Head Conservation Area has been designated a Site of Special Scientific Interest because of its size and the range of moorland habitats represented. Access is limited, partly to avoid disturbing plants and animals, and partly because the terrain of thick vegetation makes walking difficult'.

It was as well I chose the forest road; it would have been a mistake to have trodden another SSSI. As I stood alone at Blakehope Nick a car drove by in a cloud of dust, its driver giving a friendly wave. In Australia they drive out in the bush; in Africa they're on safari; here it's the forest road from Kielder. They'd complain soon enough if the roads back home were unmetalled, but here it's fun. Of the few motorists I saw on the on the 'road' not one stopped to take in the views.

It was downhill now, the forest stretching all the way to Blakehopeburnhaugh and beyond, to a picnic site, where I sat at a table to rest my feet. Not my legs; they were fine. My boots were covered in dust. I looked like John Wayne after driving the herd to Abilene. The silence was unbroken by any sound, save the singing of unseen birds. This will be a popular spot at weekends, mum, dad and the kids having a picnic. A place where you could maybe take your eye off the kids for once. But not today, for the tranquillity was broken by the sudden and noisy appearance of a lorry, driven at speed by a madman, just where your kids might have strayed in blissful ignorance of danger. It was gone as quickly as it appeared, a reminder of the idiots who drive Britain's roads.

I'd long thought Blakehopeburnhaugh, with eighteen letters, to be the longest place-name in Britain, closely followed by the first part of Cottonshopeburn Foot, a mile further up the valley. But I've seen some old maps with the latter spelt Cottonshopeburnfoot – all one word, with nineteen letters. It is remarkable that the two places vying for the title 'Longest Place-name' should be so close together.

I was now in Redesdale, where, higher up the valley on 7 June, 1575, the last battle between England and Scotland took place. Known as the *Raid of the Reidswire*, the skirmish, as it was, seems to have been started by the English. It was customary at the time for the Wardens of the Marches on both sides of the Border to meet to arbitrate over disputes and punish wrongdoers. They must have been busy men. On this occasion the Wardens were Sir John Carmichael, of Liddesdale, for the Scots, and Sir John Forster for the English. The meeting was conducted peacefully, but just when it looked like everyone could go home for tea a dispute arose over an English freebooter with the unlikely name of Farnstein and men being men they started arguing. The upshot was that 'warm conflict ensued' when the English let loose a flight of arrows to the chagrin of the Scots, who chased the auld enemy for three miles, getting the better of them and taking many prisoners. They were later released to prevent full-scale war between the two countries.

Ah, yes: England and Scotland. Long ago they fought one another over many issues; and throughout my lifetime they have been part of a United Kingdom. Now, it seems they are neither one thing nor the other. We have the farcical (and unfair) situation of Scottish MPs voting on English matters in Parliament, whilst the Scots decide on Scottish matters in their own Parliament. Some Scots now call for independence, and I believe if they want it they should have it; and if they don't they should abolish the Scottish Parliament. Me, I'd like us to stay together in a United Kingdom. But whatever I would like is irrelevant; being English, I haven't been asked.

I followed the Rede. The river flows quietly and without fuss and I tarried, watching a frog swimming among the reeds. Its direction was downriver; all he (or she) had to do was go with the flow, with just an occasional kick to steer. The creature eventually disappeared among the reeds. That's what we should all do more often: go with the flow and disappear among the reeds. Just like the frog. The riverside walk was a pleasant change from the stony forest road I'd taken from Kielder.

The path led to Byrness Church.

The church dates back to 1786 and lays claim to be Northumberland's smallest. It was paid for by the Rev. Dutens of Elsdon as a Chapel of Ease and is dedicated to St Francis of Assisi, the patron saint of animals, the environment and Italy. (Not St Francis *is* Assisi). The church served the old village of Byrness, later expanded as a forestry village, constructed to house workers of Redesdale Forest.

You have to be inside to see something unique, a stained glass window of 1903 commemorating those who died during the construction of Catcleugh Reservoir, two miles up the valley. The window depicts workmen labouring with wheelbarrow, pick and shovel, an engine and trucks and a little girl who sits near her father, carrying his dinner in a handkerchief. Underneath an inscription reads: 'To the Glory of God & in Memory of those Men, Women and Children who died during the construction of the reservoir at Catcleugh. Erected by their fellow workmen and friends'. A brass on the wall nearby bears the names of the 64 who died. There is, perhaps, an inference that they died in their endeavours to construct the reservoir, but it seems they died mostly through natural causes. The window is designed in such fashion that the image can only be seen from inside the church; outside there is no clue at all to the pattern.

Catcleugh Reservoir, completed in 1905 for the Newcastle and Gateshead Water Company, was formed by damming the Rede. It took over 600 men fifteen years to build it. They lived in two camps, one either side of the valley known, appropriately, as Newcastle and Gateshead. The thriving community included a hospital, a doctor's surgery, a post office and a police station. The reservoir stretches for nearly two miles by the side of the A68 as it climbs up to the border at Carter Bar, and on a wet day – or even a sunny day – is a stark, inhospitable-looking place.

This stage of the journey was over; its consequences weren't. It's just that in the ensuing days I was constantly reminded of my visit to Kielder through the need to scratch, and the angry red blotches that appeared all over my body – the parts where the midges had got to anyway, which extend to further than you might think. The only other occasion I suffered through midges was at Glen Douglas, Scotland, when I fell victim to their onslaught in the twilight of a wonderful evening. For days after I suffered continuous torment. But let's get things into perspective: the little blighters, henceforth to be known as *Kielderas impunctatus*, made their Scots' cousins look like benign butterflies.

Part VI

Cheviot Landscapes and the Tweed

For years I've walked Britain's so-called 'long distance' paths, either completely or in part, but always alone. Now, for a change, I would walk the next section of my adventure with a partner, Kate, a Welsh lady unused to being away from home with a rucksack for days at a time. Never having previously been to Northumberland, she had to take my word that it was a worthwhile place to visit and walk in, and that it wasn't all pit heaps and whippets as I've heard it described, usually facetiously, by folk who don't belong. We'd start at Otterburn. She was in for a treat, I said.

The Battle of Otterburn, in August, 1388, was born out of a mixture of national and local causes: England was at war with France, to whom Scotland was allied, so it was as good an excuse as any for James, Earl of Douglas, to gather 4,000 men and ravage Northumberland and Durham.

Holystone. Lady's (or 'Ladies') Well.

St Michael's Church, Alwinton.

Cheviot landscape.

Cheviot summit.

College Valley: Cottages at Hethpool.

Church of St Gregory the Great, Kirknewton.   South transept.

Memorial cross at Flodden battlefield.

'To the brave of both nations'.

River Tweed.

Norham Castle.

The Old Bridge, Berwick-upon-Tweed.

Effigy of St Cuthbert, Lindisfarne.

Lindisfarne Castle.

Grace Darling memorial, Bamburgh.

Rock strata, near Howick.

Cowslips, Longhoughton Churchyard.

Alnwick Castle

River Coquet and Castle, Warkworth.

A friendly face.   Wartime relics, Druridge Bay.

Emily Wilding Davison memorial, Morpeth.

'Deeds not words'.

'Janus'.

'Spirit of the Staiths', Blyth.

St Mary's Island.

Spanish City.

Tynemouth Priory.

It was no surprise when the Scots turned up at the gates of Newcastle. The Earl of Northumberland had sent his two sons, Sir Henry Percy (known as Hotspur, after his impetuousness) and Sir Ralph Percy, to defend the town, and we can assume some sort of verbal altercation took place before Douglas and his men rode off with a small pennant, embroidered with pearls and emblazoned with a lion, the *cognisance* of the House of Percy. Percy declared he would have it back before Douglas reached Scotland:

> Gae ye up to Otterbourne
> And wait there days three;
> And if I come not ere three day is end,
> A fause knight call ye me.

Douglas and his men camped that night near Otterburn, presumably to wait the three days to see if Percy would turn up. The impetuous Hotspur might have paused to gather support, but instead marched north directly with an army of 8,000 infantry and 600 archers. The thirty-odd mile hike from Newcastle might have merited a rest before battle, but Hotspur thought otherwise and attacked the Scots at once, in darkness.

Unfortunately, the Northumbrians did not attack the main army camp, and the Scots were thus alerted and able to retaliate. The Northumbrians' ace card was the longbow, but in the darkness such weapons were ineffective against the Scots' infantry and Hotspur's men were routed, losing 1,800 or 3,000 dead (depending upon which account you read) to the Scots' 100. Douglas was killed, and Henry and Ralph Percy were captured and held to ransom, although later freed thanks to payment of £3,000 by the king, no less. All over nothing more than a pointless fight without political or military purpose. The Percies didn't even get their pennant back.

The battle is commemorated by Percy's Cross, a 10-feet high pillar surmounted on a stone base, just off the main road to the west of Otterburn village. It stands in the shade of pines, where streaks of sunlight penetrate the branches, and to me anyway symbolises the futility of the fighting that took place between those who lived on both sides of the border.

Harry Hotspur, was renowned for his campaigns against the Scots and helping to put Henry IV on the throne. But later, aggrieved at the king's refusal to pay monies owed to the Percy family, Hotspur and his brother Thomas joined forces with the Welsh rebel, Glyn Dwr, and tried to overthrow the king and put Hotspur's wife's nephew on the throne. The rebellion was crushed at the Battle of Shewsbury, when Hotspur was killed and Thomas was captured and executed.

Hotspur's body was paraded around Shrewsbury, after which his head was cut off and impaled on the city walls at York. Hot-headed yes, but a brave Northumbrian. The Percies, incidentally, owned lands at Tottenham, north London, and the founders of Tottenham Hotspur FC named their club after Sir Harry when the club was founded in 1882. Their supporters chant, 'Come on you Spurs...'. I wonder how many of them know why.

What was much in my mind as we explored Otterburn was not so much the village itself, but the Otterburn Training Area, 58,000 acres of wild landscape owned by the Ministry of Defence and practised upon by troops of Britain and Nato forces, using live ammunition.

This land has long been the scene of military activity. The Romans were first, building their road, *Dere Street*, and their fort, *Bremenium*, present-day Rochester, just up the road. In 1911 came the Territorial Army, with horse-drawn artillery, and then the regular forces. To those who complain about this I have two things to say: that our armed forces have to practise somewhere, and it's thanks to them the Third Reich didn't get to use the land for target practise. Evidently the idea of a military range was that of Winston Churchill, who visited the area for a spot of shooting around 1900 and remarked that it was a better area to shoot artillery than to shoot game.

Tomorrow we would march to Harbottle, hopefully from Elsdon, the route taking us through some of the land used as a battlefield. Red flags would (hopefully) warn us to keep clear of anywhere where we might be blown to pieces, which could mean inconvenient diversions.

***

> Hae ye ivver been at Elsdon
> The world's unfinished neuk?
> It stands amang the hungry hills
> An' wears a frozen leuk.
> The Elsdon folk, like diein' stags,
> At every stranger stare,
> An' heather broth an' curlew eggs
> Ye'll get for supper there.

We arrived at the 'unfinished neuk' as George Chatt called Elsdon, on a bleak autumnal morn, which somehow seemed to suit this village of grey buildings surrounded by high, grassy moors. There is a feeling of space here, the huge village green criss-crossed by little roads. Elsdon is the sort of place to fall in love with, but only if you're interested in history. Tourists seeking out glitz will be disappointed and will move on. They won't be interested in reading the information tablet welcoming you to the ancient capital of Redesdale: 'Elsdon's importance was due to its strategic position at the junction of the drove roads of England and Scotland'. During the 1830s a new main road, the A696, by-passed Elsdon, ensured that many of the original features of the village survived.

A cooling breeze accompanied us to our first port of call, the church. It seems the present building dates back to the 14th century, and stands on the site of an earlier 11th century church. Rectors go back to William Erito, in 1200. The aisles are narrow, and the church has thick outer walls, probably 16th or 17th century, built that way for defence.

The minute we entered St Cuthbert's I noted it as one of the best, with its arches of Northumbrian stone, the magnificent east window and stone relics lying against the walls. The latter include old gravestones with sundry carvings, one inscribed, 'The family burial place of Robert Laing of Birdhopecraig, Died Feb 4th 1796 aged 63 years, and his son, Edward, who died aged 3 years 3 months, in 1772'.

Against the far wall of the chancel is the Elsdon Stone, found in a field north-east of the Roman fort of *Bremenium* at High Rochester. The Latin inscription reads, 'Julia Lucilla had this stone erected to her very meritorious husband, an inspector under the surveyor of the Flaminian Way, and a pensioner under the surveyor of the public works. He lived 47 years, 6 months, 25 days'. The stone indicates that Roman officers were transferred from one country to another and sometimes served to what was then a relatively advanced age. Around 1720 the bellcote was added to the church. 'It is splendidly wild and rustic', says Pevsner, a description applicable to Elsdon itself. In 1877, when repairs were being carried out in the church spire they found three horses' skulls in a cavity. What was that about, then?

In 1810 a mass grave was uncovered against the north wall of the church, containing about 100 intertwined skeletons. These are presumed to be some of the fallen of the Battle of Otterburn – not many out of the total of over 1,000. Then again, one hundred matches the number of Scots who were killed. Could it be they are buried here? If so, where do the lads of Northumberland lie?

From the church it is but a short walk to the Vicar's Pele, 'One of the finest examples in the Borders of a medieval tower house, and probably the best preserved historic building in the Northumberland National Park'. It was built as a refuge from the Scots and reivers. The walls are eight feet thick, and within one is a spiral staircase. The Coats of Arms of three families adorn the parapet: the Umfravilles, the Howards, the Percies. The pele dates back to the 14th century, although Pevsner points out that 'physical evidence suggests it was rebuilt in the 16th century and is decidedly Scottish'.

The pele looks grand now: safe, solid, comfortable. It wasn't always so. In 1702 the Revd Charles Dodgson, rector, wrote to the Duke of Northumberland about the pele, his home: 'I lay in the parlour between two mattresses to keep me from being frozen to death, for as we keep open house the winds enter from every quarter and are apt to creep into bed with one'. Whilst we must credit Dodgson for keeping 'open house' (bearing in mind Scots' raiders, and reivers from both sides of the Border), the pele is now private property and more is the pity, for I would have liked to have explored.

Dodgson was once addressed by a local chap, Percival Reed, as 'base priest and stinking castrel', and Reed pulled his beard for good measure. Dodgson responded by ordering Reed to appear in the church to acknowledge the error of his ways. The reluctant Reed, obliged to conform to the will of the man of God, feigned illness and sent his wife to appear for him. Where there's a will there's a way, you might say.

Elsdon is a place to wander at will, to look at and admire its old houses and lift one's eyes to the skyline surrounding it. On this breezy, autumnal morn, it was the perfect place to be. But only for a short time, alas, for we had to press on for Harbottle, and our route depended on being able to cross those military firing ranges. Even so, we could hardly ignore Elsdon Castle.

A more fitting description (than castle) is 'Mote Hills', two large, grass-covered mounds, the probable site of an ancient earthwork, used by the Romans, then the Saxons, before the Normans built their wooden fort. A Roman dedication slab to the god Matunus was found here around 1715, although it might have been found elsewhere first and brought here later. Who can say? The name 'mote' here is unclear; it may derive from 'moot', meaning a meeting place from which justice was dispensed by the aforementioned Romans or Saxons; or motte, as in 'motte and bailey', after the castle, which seems more likely.

The castle was built in the 1080s by Robert de Umfraville. The de Umfravilles were the Lords of Redesdale, although they had moved their main seat of defence to Harbottle by 1174. Like many other families hereabouts, they were involved in raids into Scotland. Evidently one member of the family rejoiced in the name Robin-Mend-the-Market. Work out why if you can. I can't.

We accessed the site through a gate and climbed the mounds. To think: the Romans were here, the Saxons were here, the Normans came and built their stockade here. Northumberland has few more historic places. It is a place to linger, to picture the scene as it was. Oh to step back in time! What would the Romans have made of us, carrying rucksacks and wearing shorts and silly hats? Would we have been slaughtered on the spot, or worshipped as gods? Were their ghosts watching us now, so many years later?

The right of way led above the deep valley of the Park Burn. This is rough country, and it's easy to see how vulnerable those who lived here in the days of the marauding Scots and reivers would have been. The landscape is probably little changed since then. The path led to a quiet road, which we followed a short way to an even quieter one, a place with the curious name of Raw. The map indicates several *Bastles* hereabouts, but one in particular was of interest, not because it was different to the others but because it was a murder scene. Raw Bastle, or Pele, was once home to an old woman called Margaret Crozier. She lived here, alone, her home doubling up as a drapery shop visited by locals and travellers who came this way to avoid the turnpike road over Steng Cross.

On the evening of 29 August, 1791 Margaret was seen at her door by her neighbours; the following day she was found dead, strangled and with her throat cut, the motive of the crime being robbery. A 'gully' knife, used for cutting meat, was found among her bedclothes. It had an iron hoop around the shaft. Outside, in the soil, were a number of distinctive footprints, consistent with nailed boots.

On the day before the murder, strangers had been seen. An 11-year boy, Robert Hindmarsh from nearby Whiskershiel, said he had seen a man and two women by a sheepfold near Whitlees Farm, three miles away. They had been eating mutton, which the man had carved with a large 'gully' knife with an iron hoop around the shaft. At least that's what he said, without being prompted one hopes. Robert also noticed nails in the man's boots, as he lay on the grass. The man was of distinctive appearance, with long dark hair, gathered, or 'clubbed', at the back of his head.

Three parish constables set off, on horseback, to hunt Margaret's killers. At Harlow Hill, near Horsley, they arrested a man whose description matched that given by Robert Hindmarsh. He was William Winter, whose boots matched the footprints found in the soil outside Margaret's home. Soon after two sisters were arrested: Jane and Eleanor Clark, who lived near Ryton. The three were said to be members of a 'Faw' gang, renowned for stealing.

They were taken to Morpeth Gaol and held in custody for trial at the county assizes at the Moot Hall, Newcastle. Winter admitted breaking into Margaret Crozier's home and cutting her throat, but said the wound had not been fatal. He said he sent the two women back to prevent her calling for help, thus implying it was they who had murdered Margaret by strangling her, which the women denied. All three were found guilty and sentenced to death. They were incarcerated in the castle keep to await their fate.

On 10 August, 1792, they were taken to the West Gate, Newcastle, on a cart, and hanged. That is to say, strung up: none of your trapdoor stuff; they stood them on the cart, put the nooses around their necks and gave the horse a slap. In keeping with the custom of the time, the bodies of the women were sent for dissection in the name of medical science.

William Winter's body was taken to the high moors at Steng Cross, overlooking the scene of the crime across the valley, and hung in chains from a gibbet. There it was left there until it fell to pieces, a reminder to those who travelled the road of the fate that awaited murderers. A replica of the gallows stands at the site today, with a wooden head dangling from a rope. Whilst it is hardly needed as a 'reminder' of the fate of murderers today, who are usually released after a few years, it serves the needs of tourism, appearing, as it does, in guides and leaflets..

Today, the bastle, or pele, once Margaret Crozier's home, now serves as a store-house and is the haunt of chickens and inquisitive walkers. It is a place to visit discreetly, for it stands on private property, with the risk of being flattened by passing tractors driven by men who have neither the time nor inclination to worry about curious visitors wandering about the farm buildings. Best we move on, then.

We were bound for the valley of the Coquet. And now there were signs: 'Military Firing Range. Keep out when red flags are displayed or barriers closed', and 'Do not touch any military debris. It may explode and kill you'. A narrow metalled road led off eastwards. It was unfenced, with a long line of windswept trees along one side, otherwise the landscape was open moor. No red flags flew to bar progress. The road soon ended, a right of way leading across wild, open country.

We proceeded in the hope that long-since forgotten landmines were never put down here, just waiting for our size nines (in my case anyway) to set one off. Careful navigation was needed, but we came at last to the B6341. Close to the road a red flag fluttered, warning anyone walking in the opposite direction not to proceed across the landscape we had just traversed. So, if you were westbound, you were cautioned against proceeding at the risk of death; eastbound – that's us – no warning flag. D'you think complacency might have set in with the military authorities?

The road passes Swindon Hill, which has an old earthworks, Witchy Neuk Camp, on the top. There were hut-circles and a central paved area. All private land now. Near Harehaugh was born James Allan, celebrated player of the Northumbrian pipes and author of *Salmon Tales up the Water*. 'Pipes' music is usually associated with the bagpipes, but the Northumbrian pipes sound different and are played differently, operated by an arm bellow. I love their distinctive sound. And where once it seemed Northumbrian pipes music was dying out, happily you can now buy it on CD. I recommend it. Allan, incidentally, was sentenced to death for horse stealing. Luckily for him his sentenced was commuted to life imprisonment.

We crossed the Coquet and came to Hepple.

Hepple is a small village, sited above the river. Christ Church stands on well-manicured lawns. It's the sort of place one sometimes finds locked to the visitor nowadays. Happily the door swung open to reveal a lovely interior with a double row of pews.

The font was formerly in Hepple Chapel, which stood on Kirk Hill but was destroyed by the Scots.

There's an interesting memorial tablet on the wall, dedicated to three brothers 'whose bodies lie in Africa, awaiting the Resurrection of the dead'. They are Charles Sidney, Robert George and Henry Edward Buchanan-Riddell. Charles Sidney, died at Magila, in 1886; Robert George, Lieutenant-Colonel in the King's Royal Rifles, was killed in action at Spion Kop, in 1900; and Henry Edward, Major in the King's Royal Rifles, died in March 1900 after being wounded at Lombard's Kop in 1899. Three brothers who died in service abroad. When we emerged from the church a breeze rustled through the trees. I love the sound of the breeze *rustling*. To me it represents freedom and is a symbol of how wonderful life is. I always seem to notice it most in quiet churchyards.

Over the road stands the former Hepple School, closed in 1969. Clumps of grass grow around a building whose purpose was to facilitate the education of children. It is still put to good use today as the village hall. We walked to Hepple Tower, described by Mee as 'a 14th century ruin', one of many strung along the valley in what seems to have been a co-ordinated defensive stratagem. As we looked at it from the road, a helpful motorist pulled up and asked if we needed directions. There was a sticker on the window of his car: 'I love my country; I fear my government'. As this was pre-May, 2010, I for one empathised with his sentiments.

A notice board next to the telephone kiosk attracted our attention. Headed 'Otterburn Training Area. Military Activity Forecast', listed were dates and times, details of the ranges and the 'activity' – artillery and infantry weapons systems. We had heard big bangs today: an artillery day presumably. Mercifully no shells landed on the terrain crossed earlier. Alongside the notice was an advert for oven cleaning.

We left Hepple then, keeping to the high ground above the Coquet. What grand country, the winding river in a wide valley, woodlands dotted here and there. Over to the right, high on the hill, lies Wreighill, a tiny hamlet that has suffered two great tragedies: in 1412 its populace was wiped out by the Scots, and in 1665 everyone who lived here died of the plague. The plague here is hard to comprehend; evidently it was brought here by someone who had come up from London.

We pressed on over fields and meadows and crossed the river to Holystone. In 1291 there were 27 nuns here, along with four lay brothers and a master. They were poor, and would have gone about their business without fuss, but they didn't escape the attention from the brave lads from north of the border. The Bishop of Durham wrote: 'The house, by reason of hostile incursions which daily and continually increase, is frequently despoiled of its goods, and the nuns themselves are often attacked by the marauders, harmed and pursued and put to flight and driven from their home and constrained miserably to experience bitter suffering'. One wonders what, exactly, the 'harm' to the nuns was. The mind recoils from the actions of such men, bent on mischief and malice.

I had been drawn to Holystone in a sort of pilgrimage, having read of St Ninian's Well, or, as it is more commonly known, Lady's Well, or Ladies' Well. The well is a natural pool, contained within a low stone kerb and surrounded by beech trees. The water is always clear and fresh because, unlike a pond, it continually flows through. In the middle of the pool stands a cross.

An 18th century statue, representing St Paulinus, stands at one end of the pool. The statue is engraved thus: 'In this place St Pavlinis the Bishop, baptised 3,000 Northumbrians, Easter, DCXXVII…'. The date, in Roman numerals if you weren't taught them at school, and even if you were you might need reminding, is AD 627. I don't know how we can be certain that St Paulinus baptised 3,000 heathen people over one weekend, but it seems doubtful to me. St P. will feature again in these pages, along with St Cuthbert and others. Northumberland is rich in its Christian roots, as we saw at the Battle of Heavenfield.

But is it Lady's Well, or Ladies' Well? It's important to know which is right, as it seems to me the former, *Lady's Well*, would refer to the person to whom the well is dedicated, St Mary the

Virgin, whilst the latter, *Ladies' Well*, is clearly plural, in which case it would presumably refer to the nuns. This discrepancy – both can't be right – is baffling, although if nothing else it does highlight the importance of punctuation. But never mind the name: this is a peaceful, atmospheric spot, another place to linger and reflect on the events that have taken place here for over a thousand years.

We pressed on for Harbottle. The village not having a pub that provided food, mine host kindly drove us to Alwinton for supper. We ate well at the Rose and Thistle, and drank well there, too, in the knowledge that we had a lift back to base. What a wonderful life.

***

Many people consider the Coquet to be loveliest river in the county. Certainly in its upper reaches, and beyond, the river flows through glorious, wild country, the land of sheep and wild grasses, wide skies and rolling Cheviot hillsides. It rises on the Border and flows for forty miles, reaching the sea at Amble. On its journey it passes through Harbottle, where it separates the village from the skeletal ruins of the castle.

According to Kelly's Directory, 1914, Harbottle was 'much frequented in the summer months by invalids for its pure salubrious air, and the River Coquet is a favourite resort of anglers, the trout fishing being exceedingly good'. Well, it was autumn, and we weren't quite invalids yet but the air was still salubrious; trout fishing concerned us not in the slightest.

We wandered along the street to the fountain, dedicated to Mrs Clennell, who died on 17 November, 1879: 'She devoted the powers of an active mind, the impulses of a generous heart and the industry of a busy life to the welfare and happiness of the inhabitants of Harbottle and neighbourhood'. An active mind, a generous heart, the industry of a busy life. What a wonderful epitaph. It's worth memorising and teaching to others. Especially today, when so many think only of 'self'.

Harbottle may be a remote, sleepy place now, but its history is a turbulent one. The name is a corruption of the Saxon *here botl*, the station or abode of the army. Having taken in the early autumnal air, we crossed the river and walked up to the ruins of the old castle. They stand atop a natural hill, with spectacular views over the village and the surrounding, crag-topped hills, the winding Coquet below. In the sunshine of a wonderful morning we had the place to ourselves. The ruins today are a pathetic remnant of what was, being no more than a few sections of curtain wall, perched precariously on the sides of the mound and looking as though they will tumble down one day, as they surely will. In these times of stringent health and safety rules it is surprising that visitors can walk freely below the walls.

The castle was built about 1160 by the de Umfravilles at the behest of Henry II, presumably as a stronghold against the Scots, who captured it then lost it 1174. Its dungeons were more often ocupied by Northumbrian reivers than Scottish prisoners. Even Thomas Dacre, warden of of Coquetdale and Redesdale, who was supposed to govern the area, was involved in reiving. We wandered awhile around the ruins, soaking up the atmosphere, before moving on.

As so often on this journey around Northumberland, here was a place to linger, but, sadly, had to be left behind. We had a good hike ahead, to remote Uswayford. It wasn't long before our progress was halted, the reason a magnificent lime kiln, set into the hillside with an information tablet close by explaining that burnt lime was used to sweeten acid soil to produce better crops and improve pasture. High operating costs and competition from big commercial kilns forced closure of the Northumbrian kilns, which were built hereabouts around 1827 but had ceased working by 1866. This kiln was constructed against the hillside to allow access at the top of the pot for unloading limestone and coal, a common practice. 'Limestone breaks down at about 1,000 degress celcius and was raked out from the 'eye' at the botom of the arch at 24-hour intervals. The arch provided a draught tunnel into the pot, and access to the 'eye' and shelter for the stored lime and the workers'. I have to admit knowing little about 'liming', and the tablet was so informative. Ten out of ten!

And so to Alwinton church.

St Michaels and All Angels is superbly sited above the meeting of two rivers, the Coquet and Alwin. It stands at the foot of a slope, so that inside ten steps climb from the nave to the chancel. Although the church was restored in the 19th century, the aisles date back to the 13th. The churchyard is neat and of well manicured grass, much looked after and cared for.

But, if you recall, I was on a mission here, to find the resting place of Horace Breffit, former vicar at Kirkhaugh, near Alston. Y'know, the man who wore a shovel hat, married at 94 and had his grave dug three years too early and it kept filling up with water. Find it I did, his headstone engraved: 'Horace Edgar Yorke Breffit, died 24 January, 1962. Vicar of Alwinton 1917-39. Beloved husband of Constance'. Next to his headstone is that of his wife, Ann Eliza Breffit, who died in 1927. He outlived her by 35 years. That's a long time; hardly surprising he married again, even if it wasn't till he was 94, his new wife being Constance, presumably. Here I kept my promise, and paid my respects to a man who, like me, knew Kirkhaugh and Alwinton. He lies in a lovely place.

We made our way now to Alwinton, then took a minor road west, still by the Coquet. There was no-one about, not a soul. We walked in silence punctuated now and again by the distant sound of heavy artlliery and the rat-tat-tat of machine gun fire. They were busy on the Otterburn ranges today. We were well out of it as we approached the lonely Cheviots, sunshine at every step.

The Cheviot Hills – 'these great green bastions', as Mee calls them – straddle the border of England and Scotland, a natural barrier comprising 300 square miles of rolling hills and moorland, where lonely streams, or burns, thread their tortuous way to the valleys of northern England and southern Scotland. Most of the landscape is grass and heather-clad, but there are huge swathes covered in conifers. Otherwise little has changed here over the years; where once there were scattered dwellings and sheep, still there are the same. This is grand tramping country.

I have fond memories of Coquetdale. In 1977, living in the North East then, I took my family to Barrowburn, from where we climbed the four miles to the border fence. This, and other Cheviot rambles, are firmly etched in my mind. I recall later that year, as we prepared to move south to Hertfordshire, wondering about the wisdom of it. Hertfordshire, it would turn out, has charms of its own; but the names of the hills we walked in the Cheviots I took with me: Windy Gyle, the Curr, the Schil, Cushat Law, Hedgehope Hill, Bloodybush Edge and more; and, of course, old Cheviot himself, at 2,674 feet the highest point in Northumberland.

Today we followed the road until it turned north. Hereabouts, on the map, are marked two 'Medieval Villages', neither of which was apparent but nonetheless catch the imagination. People lived here, tilled the land, eked out a living as best they could, probably under constant threat of attack from strangers, and wolves, perhaps. Today there was no-one, save two people of a modern age whose only purpose was one of leisure. How times have changed.

We left the road, and followed the east bank of the winding Coquet – and here came trouble. The path, such as it was, ascended the hillside, where it disappeared in waist-high bracken. The hillside was steep, and progress was difficult, in places impossible. As we struggled uphill, I feared Kate might take a tumble, and felt a growing sense of responsibility. Isn't this what happens when you 'take' someone somewhere? You feel responsible, especially, as in this case, I was, supposedly, the experienced hillwalker and we were off the beaten track. Then, just to cheer me up, I remembered there are adders in Northumberland. Were they hiding, unseen, in the bracken, just waiting for us to step on one?

I climbed up, ahead of Kate, and looked back to see her little white hat in a sea of green as slowly, but steadily, she followed. Complaint came there none, not even when we encountered a nasty barbed-wire fence which we followed higher up the hillside before we descended to the river again, thence to a track that led to Shillmoor.

Shillmoor was a farmstead. Deserted now, it stands in isolation at the confluence of the Coquet and Usway Burn. In 1941 the Ministry of Defence bought the farm and built a pair of semi-detached houses alongside it. Inside we could see unoccupied bunks, which may be used by troops on their military manoeuvres. Here we left the Coquet, and took a wide track by the side of the Usway Burn, northbound for Fairhaugh, This was grand, the track, a rough road, kept close to the burn, avoiding the hillsides, and continued thus for three miles, when it continued for another mile until, at last, we crossed the burn at Fairhaugh.

In May, 1920, Fairhaugh became the eighth and last farm to succumb to Kidland pine forest. A glance at the map shows the names of what were probably some of the others: Whiteburnsbank, Milkhope, Kidlandlee, The Heigh. The contour lines betray what there once was: open hillsides, where sheep grazed and the curlew swooped and thrived. Now forest clothes the entire scene. Fortunately, the Cheviots are so extensive there remains lots of room, where one can walk free. Long may it be so.

For half a mile we walked the forest road, sunshine filtering through the trees and covering the dusty forest floor with streaks of light. Ahead, as if through a tunnel, we could see the exit that would lead us back into the open and the freedom of the hillside beyond; remote Uswayford, backed by the slopes of Bloodybush Edge, now in view, was just over a mile away. The sun beamed on two tired but happy souls approaching their night's lodgings after a grand day's hike. Food and shelter awaited. So did a washing line, which was put to use after Kate washed our sweat-soaked clothes, whilst I sat and plotted tomorrow's route over virtually uncharted country. This may seem the easier task after the trek we'd had, but somebody had to do it.

***

Our first goal this morning was the border ridge, a mile and a half from Uswayford, where we would join the Pennine Way, last seen at Bellingham (in my case anyway). So too a handful of guys, also staying at Uswayford, who were walking the Way; this would be the final day of their 270-mile hike. I remember the border ridge section: all bog and peat hags, tough going all the way to the Schil and the Halterburn Valley beyond. Kate and I would walk about four miles of the ridge, and take in a 2½-mile diversion to Cheviot summit.

The climb through the forest to the border fence was easier than I anticipated, my anxiety about going astray among millions of conifers allayed when we reached the fence at Hexpethgate, just below 2,000 feet. Here we encountered the Pennine Wayfarers, who now had the pleasure of standing back and watching me, standing in England, taking a photograph of Kate, standing on the other side of the fence, in Scotland, her first visit. Exciting stuff. Well, the views were exciting: the rolling hills falling away dramatically north and south, either side of the ridge, here leading off north-east. It was a grey day with high clouds, visibility so-so but at least it wasn't raining.

The path here – the Pennine Way – is now flagged, enabling wayfarers to walk unhindered by peat hags and slimy bog. The Way is easier now, but I'm not being critical; better to walk unhindered than to sink in black glue. It looks good, too, with the heather reaching right along side the path, almost like a fitted carpet in places, and it's better for the environment, since it cuts out erosion – probably the reason they lay the path, rather than for the convenience of walkers.

We bowled along apace, past King's Seat, a high point along the ridge, until we reached a corner in the fence. Here, the ridge turns north-west, whilst a spur runs off to Cheviot summit, not that much higher but meriting a detour nonetheless. The rising ground hardly looked inspiring, but a mile and a quarter would see us on the top. Nearing it we encountered bog, lots of it, necessitating diversions in (usually) vain attempts to keep our feet from being clogged with peat.

At 2,674 feet, Cheviot summit is the highest ground in Northumberland. It's a plateau, 50 acres in girth, and was, and still can be, depending on the weather, a ghastly bog of peat and stagnant pools. The highest point, such as it is, is surmounted by an ordnance column, or trig, which I first visited in 1977 with my family. On that occasion the ground around the trig was ghastly, but notwithstanding this, and being determined to attain the highest point (as walkers and climbers do) we waded through the morass and succeeded in our mission: to climb the hill. One of my sons, David, aged ten, got stuck in the clarts and became quite distressed, and if he's forgotten about it I haven't. Sorry lad. It was up to your thighs, after all. But you did climb Cheviot.

If it's any consolation to him he had a lot more bottle than Daniel Defoe, of Robinson Crusoe fame, who, in 1728, together with a guide and 'five or six country boys' (but not Man Friday presumably), rode up Cheviot on horseback 'till the height looked frightful, and I wished myself down again'. Eventually they dismounted and pressed on, on foot, fearing that they would be in danger of toppling over a precipice. Finally, they sat down, refusing to move another yard, when to their amazement they 'saw a clergyman and another gentleman and two ladies on horseback', who smiled down at them, after which, presumably, Defoe and his party proceeded to the summit.

It's not as though Defoe was a coward. As Bradley points out in his 'Romance of Northumberland', he proved his valour by 'wielding a scythe against Marlborough's regular troops' at the Battle of Sedgemoor. Anyway, I'm pleased Kate didn't find out about Defoe's account of climbing Cheviot before telling her that's where we were going.

Today, despite the path leading to the trig being boggy, the environs of the trig itself were dry. You could have sat down and had tea. The ground immediately around the trig is flagged, and much work has been carried out here to make one's visit an altogether more pleasant experience.

Cheviot summit is a place for views: to the Eildons, the Lammermuirs, the sea, and, of course, the nearby Cheviot Hills themselves – and maybe even Blencathra and the northern Lakeland fells, providing weather conditions allow. Not for us today, though, but it was a fine day to be here nonetheless. Likewise, the whaleback-shape of Cheviot can be seen from afar on a clear day, especially when covered with snow. Although of moderate height really, here one gets a feeling of being on top of the world, away from it all. Alas, the guys on the Pennine Way didn't do it; I saw them heading off along the ridge.

We retraced steps to the ridge, crossed Auchope Cairn and found ourselves above Hen Hole, 'a fearful chasm, so deep that the sun cannot enter it'. There are crags here; you wouldn't want to wander off to spend a penny without being aware. Then we came to a refuge hut, a haven in bad weather. In 1986 an old railway carriage stood here, which, on approach, was a godsend on a day when the wind was blowing gale force. A few minutes respite, to listen to the wind instead of having to walk in it. Unfortunately, the place stank, thanks to abandoned litter, including food, a pile of it left to rot in a corner, along with bottles of plastic and glass.

Today's refuge hut is a worthy replacement for the old railway carriage, but used as a rubbish dump nonetheless. It was erected in 1988 by the National Park Wardens, volunteers and the fell rescue team, assisted by 202 Squadron, RAF Boulmer. 'You are welcome to use the shelter. Please help to keep it in a clean and tidy condition for those that follow'. Some hope! The hut is dedicated to the memory of Stuart Lancaster, a walker who died in a snowstorm near this spot. Some of those who use it hardly show respect.

Not far beyond the hut a path leaves the ridge and heads directly down to the College Valley. I'd walked it years before in the opposite direction on an autumn day, with stooks of corn in yellow fields under blue skies, surrounded by the grassy Cheviots. No blue skies or stooks of corn today, but no matter: I knew we were in for a treat, the path, then the quiet road leading to Hethpool, over five miles away. The valley is accessible to cars, but only up to twelve a day, permits being issued by the landowner, College Valley Estates, who manage the valley 'in a way that increases its value as an environmental, social and economic place of excellence'.

The valley is remote, quiet, unspoiled. Yet for thousands of years it has been occupied by men who have farmed and hunted here. In the Bronze Age men built settlements, known as hillforts, on top of the hillsides – that's 2,500 years ago, give or take. The valley would be well populated then. But were these so-called hillforts places of defence, as the name implies, or settlements built on the hilltops to impress neighbours, or simply places of ceremony? We cannot know. Defence, impression, ceremony: my money's on the former. Men were raiding and killing long after the settlements were abandoned. Fortifications on high ground would have been natural.

We dropped steeply off the ridge and came to the little road that runs the length of the valley. Two miles brought us to Mounthooly, a superbly-sited bunkhouse, 'mattresses and pillows provided'. It even has electricity. Go on, book it for a few days; it will be a magnificent escape from the oft-grim realities of modern life. You can't buy any newspapers here to be reminded about today's Britain, or the current situation concerning our so-called celebrities and their boring, irrelevant lives.

Another couple of miles and we arrived at something that is far from irrelevant, a memorial 'in memory of the allied airmen who lost their lives on the Cheviots, 1939-1945'. The memorial stands on a stone base, surrounded by a wall with a small bench, where one can sit and reflect, perhaps on the Britain those men died for. A tablet bears the names of thirteen aircraft that came down: Wellingtons (2), Spitfire, B17 (Flying Fortress), Hawker Hart (trainer), Lancaster, Stirling, Warwick, Hampden, Mosquito, Halifax, Beaufighter, Hurricane. Thirteen aircraft, but how many men? The monument is a tribute to those who gave their lives then so that we can walk in the likes of the College Valley today.

Two of the aircraft, the Lancaster and the Flying Fortress, came down in December, 1944. The Lancaster was returning from bombing submarine pens in Norway. Off-route and in a rainstorm, it crashed with the loss of all crew, seven Canadians. The Flying Fortress was returning to RAF Kirmington (now Humberside Airport), with a crew of nine Americans. Their mission was to bomb a railway marshalling yard at Ulm, Germany, but the formation was recalled due to bad weather. The pilot of the B17, 2nd Lieutenant George A. Kyle, was misled by

German transmitters and flew too far north. Over the sea they would have jettisoned their bombs, but believing they might be over land they retained them. At 1.15 p.m. on 16 December the aircraft, flying in cloud, crashed into the side of snow-covered Cheviot. Two of the crew were killed, Lt Kyle was seriously injured.

Fire broke out, but mercifully the bombs did not explode. Lt Kyle was pulled from the burning wreckage, and with two others went down the hillside where they found a farmhouse. They were taken to a first aid shelter near Berwick. The remaining four, some injured, escaped, some being dragged out in actions of heroism. After some hours one of them felt a dog licking his face; it was Sheila, a collie. Her barking had alerted two shepherds, John Dagg and Frank Moscrop, who had been searching for the men in the storm. Dagg's daughter ran two miles to a telephone to summon assistance, and the four crewmen were taken to the first aid shelter.

Lt Kyle was invalided back to the US. James Hardy, who pulled him from the cockpit, resumed flying duties and completed a further 30 missions. The mother of one of the men who was killed wrote to Dagg, thanking him for his efforts and requesting one of Sheila's puppies. A few months later, one was flown to her in the States by the RAF. Lt Kyle, who recovered, thereafter became a frequent visitor to the crash site. When he died in 2006 his ashes were scattered there.

I mention this to highlight two things: that not all wartime aircraft were shot down, that many crashed on British territory; and the fact that so many who fought for freedom were foreign, based in Britain to fight a common enemy on behalf of all of us. How many other stories are there to tell of crashed aircraft and their crews? And if war is evil, which it is, doesn't it bring out the best in people, who show courage and unselfishness on bleak hillsides like old Cheviot?

Two more miles led to Hethpool, with its row of fine cottages, and nearby Hethpool House, built for a Tyneside industrialist, Sir Arthur Munro Sutherland. Close by are the Collingwood Oaks, planted by none other than Lord Collingwood, anxious about lack of wood to build more ships for the British fleet. But future ships were built of iron, and the wood was never needed.

***

It was a grand morning. A perfect morning to be walking, for sure. Autumn provides such colour, such freshness. One cannot imagine the College Valley looking lovelier.

We took St Cuthbert's Way. The Way is a 62-mile hike from Melrose, where St Cuthbert started his ministry, to Holy Island, where he became Bishop of Lindisfane. It was opened in 1996, another 'long distance' footpath, one of many following the opening of the Pennine Way (1965) and others.

Alfred Wainwight said he 'wondered' about long distance paths, since their repeated use causes erosion (even though he wrote a guidebook on the Pennine Way and created the Coast to Coast walk from St Bees to Robin Hood's Bay). I wonder about them too, although I've used them often enough. As far as St Cuthbert's Way is concerned, a glance at the map shows it traverses grand country, including the Cheviots, as well as, presumably, satisfying an interest in religious history. Kate and I would enjoy it for only two miles; we left it near Torleehouse, resolving to 'do it one day'. Today, our interest was focused on history easily pre-dating St Cuthbert: Yeavering Bell hillfort.

Perched on the twin summits of Yeavering Bell, 1,182 feet above sea level, this hillfort was an Iron Age town. The ruins of a massive wall, over a thousand yards long, enclosed an area of 13½ acres. Within were about 130 timber dwellings, whose occupants were the Votadini tribe. We had not the time to climb up today, alas, but we were conscious of being in a place of ancient history, moreso at the roadside ahead, where a monument marks the site of Ad Gefrin, 'Royal Township of the Seventh Century Anglo-Saxon Kings of Northumbria', discovered in 1949, when the foundation trenches of the buildings were seen from the air. The site was a royal centre in the kingdom of

Bernicia, which would become part of Northumbria, said to have been visited by St Paulinus, whom we encountered at Holystone.

In 625 Paulinus, a Roman monk, accompanied Ethelburga, King Eadbald of Kent's sister, to York, where she was to marry Northumbria's king, Edwin – a pagan. Paulinus converted Edwin to Christianity. It was here, in Glendale, he allegedly stood from morning till night for 36 days, baptising converts to the faith, 'washing them with the water of absolution in the River Glen'. Bede described Paulinus as 'tall and thin, a slightly stooping figure with black hair, an aquiline nose and of venerable and awe-inspiring aspect'. He would be stooping if he'd baptised folk for 36 days, non-stop. Paulinus died in AD 644.

We took the main road for Kirknewton, to the church. 'There is more to the church than meets the eye', wrote Pevsner, presumably meaning when first sighted. I find this to be the case with most churches, but I take his point. St Gregory the Great's Church dates back to the 13th century, or earlier. Much renovation has been carried out, notably by Dobson in 1860. It's the chancel and south transept that catch the eye, for both have pointed tunnel vaults, with hardly any vertical wall at all. This feature is unusual, proving that it's not until you look closely at something you find what you could never have imagined would be there.

Set in a wall near the chancel arch is a relief portraying the Adoration of Magi, possibly 12th-century; Madonna and child are seated on a trough, the Wise Men, clad in *kilts*, offer their gifts. Joseph stands behind, one arm around her, his right arm raised. 'Very rude workmanship', observes Pevsner.

There's a window dedicated to and erected by 'officers of RAF Milfield to keep alive the memory of the men who died for their country whilst flying from Milfield RAF station', together with a framed Roll of Honour nearby. They are buried in the churchyard. On a wall near the door is a picture of Josephine Elizabeth Butler (1828-1906), the social reformer, who is also buried here. There is not, sadly, the space in these pages to satisfactorily give full account of her work, but that below will, hopefully, serve to highlight the life and work of a woman of whom Northumberland should be proud.

Josephine Grey, as she was, was born in 1828 at Milfield, the daughter of John and Hannah Grey. In 1833 John Grey was appointed agent for Greenwich Hospital's Northern Estates, the land sequestrated to the Crown after the abortive attempt by James Radcliffe to unseat the king in 1715. As a result, the Grey family moved into Dilston House, later known as Dilston Hall. Like his cousin, Earl Grey, John Grey was passionate about social reform; he despised injustice and encouraged his children to take an interest in such issues.

In 1852 Josephine married George Butler at St Andrew's Church, Corbridge. Soon after, he was appointed Examiner of Schools at Oxford University. On moving to Oxford Josephine found herself in an institution 'pervaded by a strong atmosphere of misogyny', her husband's colleagues taking it for granted that 'a woman's ideas were not worth hearing'. Her political views they held in scorn.

Later, George took the post as Vice-Principal of Cheltenham College, a boys' school. Tragically, at Cheltenham their only daughter, 5-year old Eva, fell to her death over the staircase banisters as she ran to greet her parents. Eighteen months later the family moved to Liverpool, where George had been offered the job as principal at another school. Josephine, taking up charity work to help her get over the loss of her daughter (which she never did), visited the workhouse. In an extract from her *Autobiographical Memoir*, she described 'huge cellars, bare and unfurnished with damp stone floors' – these were the oakum sheds, where women came, driven by hunger, destitution, vice, begging for shelter and bread, in return for picking oakum – ships' tarred ropes. Many were or had been prostitutes, whom Josephine invited to her home for shelter.

But it was through her ceaseless campaign on behalf of women relating to the Contagious Diseases Acts that Josephine Butler cemented her name forever as a champion of women's rights.

The Contagious Diseases Acts of 1864, 1866 and 1869 were designed to control the spread of venereal disease among servicemen in designated garrison towns and seaports. The law promoted the doctrine that men had to have sex, and the medical profession was convinced that the way to prevent soldiers and sailors getting VD was to prevent them getting it off women who sold their bodies. Consequently Parliament passed laws designed to enforce women, suspected of being prostitutes, to forcible genital examination, often on the say-so of individual policemen.

On New Year's Day, 1870, 124 women, including Josephine Butler, signed a manifesto condemning the Acts, drawing attention to the unequal treatment and degradation of women: 'It is unjust to punish the sex who are the victims of a vice and leave unpunished the sex who are the main cause...We consider arrest, forced surgical examination, or, where resisted, imprisonment with hard labour to which the Acts subject women, are most degrading'.

The women's campaign was long and difficult – and successful. The Contagious Diseases Acts were repealed in 1886. But Josephine Butler wasn't finished. She went to Europe and campaigned, again successfully, against the trafficking of young girls who were sent abroad as sexual slaves. Her efforts, over thirty years, on behalf of women and girls were untiring. As the notice in the church at Kirknewton says, 'Her life's work was to change society's attitude to women, man's double standards and women's own view of themselves...She fought for equality between men and women in all respects: moral, legal, economic and social'.

Josephine Butler is largely unsung, her name unknown to most people, even within her native country. There may be a reason for this: if the names of Florence Nightingale and Grace Darling are 'famous', and Josephine Butler's isn't, it may be because it wasn't – and isn't – easy to tell people, especially children, that she was a campaigner on behalf of the welfare of prostitutes and sexually exploited women and children. No matter. I feel privileged to have been born in Dilston Hall, the house where she lived as a child.

There are times when it is good to look back, and so it was here, to the Cheviots, behind us now, and the twin summits of

Yeavering Bell. Crossing the Glen, we followed a byroad to Milfield, and had lunch in a roadside café reminiscent of an American diner: tea and a sarnie. Then we were off again, for Flodden. You could hardly say you were 'walking around Northumberland' without visiting the Flodden battlefield. Fought on 9 September, 1513, this was the final major battle between England and Scotland, save for the odd skirmish afterwards.

James IV of Scotland was a good king, under whom Scotland thrived. In 1502 he married Margaret Tudor, daughter of Henry VII, and a stable alliance between England and Scotland prevailed. Unfortunately, another alliance was in force, that between Scotland and France, whereby if either country should be attacked by England, the other would take up arms in support of its ally. When James's brother-in-law, Henry VIII, invaded France in 1513, the French asked James for his promised support. A man of honour, he would have considered he had no choice but to give it.

That August James gathered an army and marched into England. James's army, it seems, numbered anything from 40,000 to 100,000, but before crossing the border many clan chiefs had deserted, taking their men with them. Nevertheless, at least 30,000 strong, the Scots captured several English castles, including Norham, before marching unopposed to Ford Castle, which James made his headquarters. The Scots' army included James himself, 15 earls, 20 barons, as well as bishops, abbots, hundreds of knights and even fifty French who had brought money, wine and weapons, their main purpose being to train the Scots in the use of the long pike, a weapon not familiar to them. The Scots also boasted some heavy cannon.

Ford Castle was occupied by the owner's wife, Lady Heron, whose husband had been seized by the Scots as hostage for his bastard son, John. It is said she allowed herself to be seduced by James, in order to slow his advance. Whether this is true is doubtful, but when James finally left Ford he burned the castle anyway. A man of honour, did I say?

In any event the Scots had advanced a mere four miles into England. Hardly the behaviour of an invading army, but James had fulfilled, to some extent, his obligation to the French. Henry VIII, being in France, had left the defence of the northern part of his realm to the Earl of Surrey. 'I trust not the Scots,' said Henry. Surrey gathered an army, moved north through Newcastle and Alnwick, and with a force of some 26,000 marched on to Wooler.

James was still ensconced at Ford Castle, detained there either through the charms of his hostess or by tactical design. Surrey sent him a message: come and fight. James accepted Surrey's challenge and said he would wait for him. His army had rested for a week, whilst Surrey's had marched for miles, 'with little or no wine or beer and had to drink water'. Passed through Newcastle without a drink? That must have been a first.

James's army waited on Flodden Hill, but Surrey didn't come that way. Instead, he continued north on the other side of the Till, which his army crossed in two different places. Due to the lie of the land, the Scots did not have sight of Surrey's men until they unexpectedly appeared to the north. At dawn Surrey's army marched for battle. To maintain his high position, James moved his army and his heavy cannon 1½ miles north-west, to Branxton ridge, and waited. Then the English too occupied high ground. Between the two armies was a wide hollow, at the bottom of which was a ghastly bog, known to Surrey, but not, to his cost, James.

On the Scots' left were the Earl of Home and his Borderers. They normally fought on horseback, but today they were armed with pikes. In the centre were thousands of Scots; on their right Highlanders. The Scots artillery opened up first, but the English guns, though smaller, were more accurate and more manoeuvrable. The Scots had the better of it at first, which may have been the reason they left the high ground and ran to the advancing English, only to find themselves knee-deep in bog.

At that point, for reasons best known to himself, the Earl of Home withdrew, or fled if you will. The centres of each side then engaged, James himself taking part in the fight. The Highlanders were decimated by English archers, then the main Scots' force, with their unfamiliar long pikes, were cut to pieces by Englishmen carrying billhooks, hacking at hapless men who found themselves holding useless splinters of wood. Scott:

> The English shafts in volleys hail'd,
> In headlong charge their horse assailed;
> Front, flank and rear, their squadrons sweep
> To break the Scottish circle deep,
> That fought around their king...

In just two hours the greatest Scots army ever to fight the English lost around 10,000 men, including James IV himself, along with almost the entire ruling class of his country. So much conflict had gone before between the two countries, but none was greater than this. But for the disaster they suffered at Flodden – or Branxton as it was – the Scots have themselves to blame. They were an invading force, and the English were entitled to defend their own soil.

Today, a tall granite Celtic cross stands on the site of the battle. It was erected in 1910 by the Berwickshire Naturalists Club, and is inscribed, simply, 'Flodden 1513. To the brave of both nations'.

Geographically, the site has changed. In 1513 it would have been wooded, and there was that awful bog. Today it is open, with fertile fields, the land drained and cultivated and open to the visitor, along with strategically-placed information panels.

One thing hasn't changed, though: Branxton Church, although largely rebuilt, still stands sentinel over the valley, just as it did when men were killing each other within sight of it. It too played its part in history, for the hacked body of James IV, wrapped in his Royal Standard, was taken to the church before being taken to Berwick and thence, under escort of the Earl of Surrey himself, to London for burial.

What was it all about though? Yes, we know why politically. But imagine it: 50,000 men, give or take – Scots, English and a handful of Frenchmen – here, in the fields of north Northumberland, fighting with billhooks and pikes and bows and arrows, and discharging cannon. Thousands dead, the ruling class of Scotland wiped out. One side won, one side lost. Looking at it now, did it matter? Would the Scots army have gone on to conquer England? I doubt it; there would be many more Englishmen waiting if James and his men, what was left of them, had headed south. Such futility. Such waste. Just like all wars, then and now.

A few miles along country lanes brought us to Cornhill on Tweed and our night's accommodation, a 19th century former coaching inn, the Collingwood Arms.

***

On the face of it, today's walk of 15 miles to Berwick looked grand, mainly along the south bank of the Tweed, visiting the old bridge at Twizel – in 1513 crossed by Surrey's forces on their way to engage the Scots at Flodden – as well as Norham church and castle, and Horncliffe Glen, if there was time. Sadly our plans were thwarted by the dreadful weather awaiting us when we emerged from the Collingwood Arms, the worst on this entire Northumberland venture.

Rain. The bucketing kind. The sort that drives into you and soaks you through. A strategic decision: we'd catch the bus to Norham and continue from there, hell or high water. High water, as it turned out. Still, having to wait for the bus – they are few and far between everywhere these days – we wandered into Cornhill churchyard. St Helen's is Victorian, Gothic in appearance with tilted gravestones. It was a plate on a bench that caught my eye: 'In memory of Susan Maxwell, aged 11, of Cornhill, August 1982'.

As a former detective, I remembered Susan's name. She lived at Cornhill. On 30 July, 1982, she walked across the Tweed bridge towards Coldstream to play tennis. She never reached her destination, for she was abducted by a monster called Robert Black, who sexually assaulted and murdered her, then dumped her by the roadside near Uttoxeter. Black went on to murder more little girls before he was caught in the act of abducting another near Galashiels. He was sentenced to life imprisonment, with the recommendation that he serve at least 35 years. Why such a person should ever be considered to have his liberty again is beyond me.

And so, the busride to Norham.

It may be difficult to imagine, but Norham was, until quite recent times, the northernmost outpost of Durham, and the castle was built and maintained by the Prince Bishops. They, not the kings of England, held sway in Norhamshire. Most of the time, anyway. A wooden castle of the motte and bailey type was built first, by Bishop Flambard, in 1121. Henry II built the stone keep, but the Scots captured it twice, and Northumberland too, but the county was retaken, after which alterations to the castle were ongoing until it was abandoned in the 16th century. Kings visited, including Edward I, who held audience in Norham church, or in the castle grounds (accounts vary), with thirteen candidates vying for the Scottish throne. He chose John Balliol, who later allied himself with the French, causing Edward to sack Berwick and crush Balliol's army at Dunbar, after which Balliol was stripped of his crown and thrown into the Tower of London. This was the decade when William Wallace, Scots' hero and scourge of the English, repeatedly raided Northumberland before he was captured and executed in gruesome circumstances.

Today, Norham castle stands ruinous above the Tweed, the topmost of its four stories having crumbled away. On our journey the ruined keep was no more than a blur in the rain, and instead of exploring we turned down to the river for the march to Berwick. But if the weather thwarted exploration of Norham then, it was kinder by far when we returned on a spring day afterwards to see the sights I had read about and which I was determined to see: the old market cross on its base of 13th century steps on the village green, St Cuthbert's Church and, of course, the castle.

The church is big and quite magnificent. It stands on the site of an earlier building, where they buried the remains of St Ceolwulf, a Northumbrian king. The oak pulpit, vicar's stall and organ screen were brought here from Durham Cathedral; in a recess lies a reclining stone figure of a knight, dating back to circa 1310, his hands clasped in prayer.

As usual I noted the names of vicars, in this case dating back to Robert de Clifford, 1220. It occurred to me that of all the churches I've visited, and there have been plenty on my travels over the years, I've never seen the name Heslop listed as vicar. It's probably too late for me to change things in that regard, so I wouldn't bother looking out for my surname if you visit a church, wherever it might be.

The castle is approached by crossing a wooden footbridge and passing through 'Marmion's Arch', named after a Lincolnshire knight who came to Norham wearing a gold-crested helmet given to him by a lady who demanded he seek the 'daungerest place in England' to make the helmet famous – in other words, prove his love.

One can hardly imagine a more 'daungerous place' than north Northumberland in those days, so Marmion chose Norham. His judgement was sound, for just four days after his arrival, a Scots force turned up at the castle gates. Brave Marmion donned the helmet, mounted his steed and, alone, rode directly at the Scots. Not surprisingly he ended up on the ground, wounded, so the governor of the castle, Sir Thomas Grey, 'with al the hole garison he lette prik among the Scottes and so woundid them that they were overthrowen, and Marmion, sore beaten, was horsid again and with Gray pursewid the Scottes yn chace'. Whether Marmion's courageous if futile attempt to defeat the Scotties single-handed was sufficient to win the heart of his lady back in Lincolnshire isn't known, to me anyway, but his endeavours seem to be the reason Scott, albeit setting the scene at the time of Flodden, wrote his immortal lines:

> Day set on Norham's castle steep
> And Tweed's fair river, broad and deep
> And Cheviots mountains lone:
> The battled towers, the donjon keep,
> The loop-holed walls where captives weep,
> In yellow lustre shone.

Robert Bruce besieged Norham castle for nearly a year, using the church as his headquarters; in fact, he failed to take Norham three times. As we have seen, James IV's invading army succeeded in capturing the castle on his way to defeat at Flodden, when the castle walls were battered remorselessly by 'Mons Meg', a huge cannon (so-named because it was cast at Mons, France). Today the castle stands somewhat forlorn-looking, the holes in its walls like sightless eyes staring blankly over the Northumbrian countryside. There is access to an upper floor, where one can look down on the outer bailey, but sight of the Tweed is blocked by trees. Our revisit to Norham over, it is time to return to that rain-sodden day when we were bound for Berwick, which, let me say, we could once have done by train.

According to Bradley's Railway Guide of 1922, we could have caught the Kelso-Berwick train at Norham for a 21-minute ride to Berwick. Another railway that is no more, alas. But if you're wondering if we'd have taken the train on the day the rains came, I can assure you we would. Might've even taken the train if it had been fine, and thus savoured another of Britain's great railway journeys.

No train meant Shanks's pony. Eight miles to Berwick, along the south bank of the Tweed. Straightforward enough, but what was clear on the map was different on the ground, thanks to the rain. We were about to embark on a nightmare journey: three miles to Horncliffe. Alighting from the bus, we pulled up our hoods and battened down the hatches, ready for a walk of attrition.

The Tweed, swollen from the rain, was in an angry mood, moving swiftly just below the muddy path we trod, the scene a bleak one under leaden skies and driving rain. We walked slowly and carefully, dreading a slip that could have meant sliding into the river and being swept away. Walking alone, one is responsible for oneself; with a companion, there comes responsibility for another person. I dreaded the thought: Kate slipping, fingers clawing vainly at something, anything, to prevent entering the heaving river. Me, struggling to maintain balance, reaching down to grasp muddied hands, only to see her being swept away.

I'd have gone after her, but it wouldn't have done any good: wearing waterproofs and walking boots, I'd have been swept away too. It doesn't bear thinking about, yet from time to time my thoughts wander back to those few miles by the Tweed that day.

The path led below the castle, not that we could see it or even tell it was there, and followed the river, always muddy and perilous, One mile. Two miles. No-one else about, needless to say. Finally we came to a footbridge over a burn, where, mercifully, a path left the river and we followed it up to Horncliffe. We wanted shelter and found it in the Fisher's Arms. We had soup and hot drinks and took our time with it, I can tell you. But then we had to return to the delights the British weather had to offer.

I considered walking the road all the way to Berwick, but a local chap, seeing me poring over the map, had a better idea. Walk the path, he said, on the *other* side of the river. Take the road out of Horncliffe to a bridge across the Tweed, after which a better path follows the north bank. Slight problem: the first mile and a half would be in Scotland, and this was a Northumberland walk. Still, it was better than walking all the way to Berwick on tarmacadam.

A mile from Horncliffe we came to the Union Suspension Bridge. Designed by Sir Samuel Brown, a Royal Navy captain, and opened in 1820, it was the first suspension bridge in Britain to carry wheeled traffic and replaced a ford over the Tweed near here. A ford over the Tweed! Looking at the river today, you could scarcely have imagined it. It reminded me of the Mississippi in *Showboat*, Paul Robeson singing *Ol' Man River*. It's the sort of film you see as a kid and never forget. What a voice that man had, singing of the strife of black people and the uncaring river, the Mississippi. And there was the Mississippi now, alias the Tweed: cold, grey, uncaring, as in the movie. Rollin' along...

Four miles to Berwick. We kept by the grey waters of the river, so wide here. At one point we found we had walked along a peninsula, only to find ourselves at a dead end. We retraced steps, a good half mile, then walked half a mile again to end up just feet away from where we'd been standing half an hour earlier. The rain eased, then stopped. At some point we re-entered England, as the national border, hitherto following the centre of the river, diverts north just west of Berwick.

I checked the map; the Whiteadder Water, a river in miniature, ran into the Tweed a mile ahead. A footbridge was indicated, but with no right of way leading up to it. I hoped we could locate it and cross. We did, continuing again by the river and crossing the A1, the buildings of Berwick now in sight. We passed through a wood, after which the path crossed meadowland, all under water. There was a footbridge over a stream, a perfect crossing, except the water was higher than the platform of the bridge. We plodged merrily through it.

Further on we found ourselves under the Royal Border Bridge. Designed by Robert Stephenson for the new railway, it was the final link between Newcastle and Edinburgh. It has 28 arches, each 61 feet 6 inches in span, is 717 yards long and stands 126 feet above the Mississippi – sorry, Tweed. It has been described as 'a wonder of the railways'. So it is. It was completed on 26 March, 1850 and opened by Queen Victoria that August. She kindly gave ten minutes of her time before leaving town, much to the chagrin of the natives who had gone out of the their way to suitably prepare for her visit.

As we passed beneath the towering arches I thought the bridge must be unchanged since it was built, except there is a change: what would Stephenson, and Queen Victoria for that matter (if she'd bothered to look) have made of those strange gantries on the top. Electrification: but the gantries take nothing away from the grandeur of the bridge. It's too big and proud.

We left the river at last and climbed into the town, our feet squelching in our boots. In fact, we were both pretty well sodden and eager to get out of wet clothes. We quickly located our lodgings, and prepared to shower, but not until I flicked the telly on to catch the news. It was BBC *Scotland*. How does that work out, for a town in England? Doesn't the normally politically-correct Beeb know its geography?

Part VII

A Glorious Coast

According to the Lanercost Chronicles, in the 13th century Berwick-upon-Tweed was 'so populous and of such trade that it might justly be called another Alexandria, whose riches was the sea and the water its wall'. More recently, Pevsner described it as 'Red roofs on grey houses with hardly any irritating buildings anywhere'. I wouldn't argue. But I want to focus on Berwick's history, although I can't cover it all.

The Battle of Carham, in 1018, was fought between Malcolm, King of Scotland, and Uchtred, Earl of Northumberland. Details are scant, but its outcome, victory for the Scots, may have established the Tweed as the border between England and Scotland. If so, Berwick, on the north bank of the river, would have then been in Scotland. Despite this, Berwick is now in England. This is because nowadays the national border loops around Berwick, setting it firmly in Northumberland.

The town has long been disputed between the two countries, and was once independent of both. 'Ownership' of Berwick has changed hands no less than thirteen times over the years. In 1174, William the Lion of Scotland, captured at Alnwick after invading Northumberland, was taken to Berwick where he stood in chains before Henry II and surrendered the town as part of his ransom. Richard I – the Lionheart – sold Berwick back to the Scots to finance his Crusades. In 1216, his brother, King John, annoyed because his northern barons were paying homage to Alexander of Scotland, brought an army to Berwick and took it back, 'executing the most barbarous cruelty on the inhabitants' before burning the town. When Berwick recovered it fell into Scottish hands again.

Edward I was bent on the unification of England, Scotland and Wales, with him as king, we can assume. So, in 1296 he led an army into Berwick, where his forces of 30,000 foot soldiers, 4,000 horse and a fleet of ships, easily took the town, allegedly slaughtering 7,000 of the inhabitants. When Edward left for London, William Wallace recaptured Berwick for Scotland, after which Edward marched north again and conquered Wallace's army, thus returning Berwick to English hands. After Edward died Edward II lost to Bruce at Bannockburn, and Berwick returned once more to Scotland.

In April 1333, Edward III laid siege to Berwick, but the Scottish garrison resisted. So Edward's army desolated south-east Scotland and captured Edinburgh castle, whilst Douglas's Scots' army ravaged Northumberland (which is a perfect example of both sides being as bad as the other). A sort of stalemate prevailed until the Scots garrison at Berwick said it would surrender in five days, and handed over the son of the deputy governor, Sir Alexander Seton, in good faith. Another of Seton's sons was already in English hands. King Edward, fearful that Douglas's army might appear, insisted on an immediate surrender or he would execute them both. The Setons refused, and watched in horror as both boys were hanged on a knoll, known as Hang-a-Dyke Neuk, near to where the present-day Royal Border Bridge stands. William Seton had nothing to say before he was hanged;

but Richard Seton declared, 'It was hard to die for nae crime ava, while his feyther and mither looked on.'

Douglas, with a 'mighty army', then crossed the Tweed to the west, and met the English at Halidon Hill. As at Flodden, nearly two hundred years later, the Scots were routed, first by English archers, then spearmen, then men-at-arms at close quarters who cut the kilties to pieces in a 'dreadful slaughter'. Berwick surrendered and Edward, foreseeing a need for loyalty by its townspeople, encouraged English merchants to settle in the town. Despite this, bitter strife continued here for two more centuries until, at last, in 1482, Berwick was settled under the English crown.

It was ironic, therefore, following the death of Elizabeth I, that James VI, of Scotland, should pass through the town on his way to London, to be crowned James I of Great Britain. A union of crowns (but not political union) at last.

The bridge James would have crossed on his journey south was an old and dilapidated wooden one, causing him to declare (so it is said), 'Is there nae man in the toon who can build a brig?' The townsfolk were so impressed, or maybe depressed, by this remark they built a new sandstone bridge, which opened in 1624. It's there today, a wonderful sight. Costing £15,000, the 'Jacobean' bridge has fifteen arches, is 388 yards long, and 45 feet high at its highest point, designed that way to allow shipping through at the deepest channel in the river. James would have been pleased, although it is doubtful that he saw it; he died in 1625.

It was April. Kate had again agreed to accompany me on my journey, having been assured there would be no more walks along muddy riverbanks and that, instead, there would be glorious sandy beaches and castles to see (having not seen the one at Norham due to the weather).

Having wandered the streets of Berwick, it was only natural to make our way to the Jacobean bridge. The bridge provides a grand crossing over the Tweed estuary. Incredibly, it carried the A1 until 1928, after which the Royal Tweed Bridge took the burden, although the present-day A1 by-passes the town. Once across the Tweed – into what was north Durham (I know it's hard to imagine, but we've the Prince Bishops to thank again) – we followed the road to St Bartholomew's Church, Tweedmouth. Here were lots of ancient headstones, some dating back to the 18th century, many over six feet high. Should they be left alone, as they have been for generations? Or laid flat, in the interests of health and safety? It's a dilemma: leave things alone versus the safety of anyone wandering the churchyard, as we did now.

One huge headstone was inscribed, 'Here lyeth the body of Mary, daughter of Charles Lambert, died on 22 January, 1759, aged 2 years'. Next to it, another marks the resting place of 'The children of John and Eleanor Dickson. Mary, died 26 Sept 1793, aged 2; John, died 2 November, aged 1'. Small bodies marked by huge headstones in times of high infant mortality.

Nearby, we came upon an information tablet, marking the Lowry Trail in Berwick and Tweedmouth. Y'know, L.S. Lowry, who painted matchstalk men and matchstalk cats and dogs (and kids on the corner of the street with their sparking clogs). 'Britain's best-loved painter was especially fond of Berwick-upon-Tweed', said the inscription. 'He visited the town many times from the mid 1930s until the summer before he died. He thought about buying a house on the Elizabethan walls…'. That's a first: an epitaph to someone who *thought* about doing something without actually doing it.

Lowry produced over thirty drawings and paintings of Berwick, but was he really Britain's best-loved painter? Near the lifeboat station was another Lowry notice, this time with a photograph of the great man standing on nearby Carr Rock in 1969. 'He had friends to drive him places'. Lucky him.

The lifeboat station dates back to a shipwreck in 1834, when hundreds of people watched as the *Christiana* was wrecked off Berwick. All eight crew drowned. Voluntary subscription raised money to buy a lifeboat, which was stationed here from 1835. It was voluntary then, it's voluntary now; the lifeboats (and mountain rescue teams) in this country are paid for by money contributed in the cause of saving lives. It's money well spent, unlike taxpayers' money, much of which is wasted on pointless quangos, the BBC, MPs' duckhouses and the like. To those who sail the seas and climb mountains I say: contribute generously to those who are prepared to come to the rescue you may need, and do it before the need arises.

Spittal lies 'around the corner' from the mouth of the Tweed. The name derives from a leper hospital dating back to the 12th century. It closed with the dissolution of the monasteries. Until the 1950s a ferry, the *Border Chief*, ran between Spittal and Berwick. If only it still did; such a lovely way to arrive (then walk back across the Jacobean bridge for the best view of Berwick). A notice proclaimed Lowry to be 'fascinated by such craft, and he painted ferries'.

To me, Spittal is reminiscent of some Scottish towns, with its grey sandstone terraced houses, unchanged for generations. Spittal Community School has a concrete yard, a scene from the fifties. Takes one back, just looking at it. I wonder if they teach the three Rs. Bet they do. We came to the promenade. It was clean, with a nice beach alongside. Today, the Pavilion Family Fun Centre, with amusements, pool table and snack bar, was almost deserted.

'There's more to Spittal than meets the eye', said a notice. 'It began life as a salmon fishing village. The fishing waters were in the Diocese of Durham and were known as the Bishop's Water. In 1097 King Edgar of Scotland granted a fishing charter to the monks of Holy Island, who received one fish for every ten caught'. In the 19th century came herring fishing, with smoking sheds for kippers, barrel making (for pickling and salting fish), a processing shed employing local people.

Other industries moved in: gas, a chemical works, an iron foundry. 'In the late 18th century the reputation of Spittal mineral spring became widely known. People came from far and wide to partake of waters "rich in iron and sea bathing". By the late 19th century Spittal was *the* spar resort...the bracing, seaside air and sporting pursuits: boating, tennis, golf, bowls and walking. People came from London and Europe, but mainly from the border towns: Hawick, Jedburgh, Selkirk, Galashiels, Kelso. In the first half of the 20th century it was common to see Spittal sea front jammed with charabancs, containing church and Sunday school outings. Special rail fares further developed Spittal's popularity. But visitors' tastes changed; a holiday camp was opened in 1945, followed by a caravan park in 1950. The closure of the Kelso branch railway in 1968 was the beginning of the end'.

Nothing is forever. But if Spittal's 'popularity' has waned, its quality as a coastal village and its calm, peaceful atmosphere, makes it today a special place to be, 'a place rich in local culture and vitality'. Oh, there's another picture by Britain's best-loved painter: *Girl in a red hat on a promenade*. Forget Lowry: Spittal has artwork all of its own. Better than matchstalk men any day.

You can't say you've been to Berwick unless you walk the Elizabethan wall that circumnavigates the town centre, 'the best surviving example of its sort in Europe'. The wall seen today superseded the previous wall, begun by Edward I when he captured Berwick in 1296, although some of the defences remain.

The ramparts of the Elizabethan wall were designed by the English engineer, Sir Richard Lee, based on a system developed in Italy. It consisted of bastions, or gun platforms, that projected from the wall so that a wide field of fire was possible. The bastions were built of stone and were connected to the curtain wall, which was heavily buttressed internally. The strength of the wall lay in the thickness of the soft earthwork behind it, designed to absorb the force of gunshot. In front of the wall was a water-filled ditch.

Whether these defences would have proved sound enough to repel attack is not known, for Berwick, despite being the subject of attacks for centuries, was never attacked after the construction of the Elizabethan wall. It may be significant that during the risings of 1715 and 1745, the Jacobite armies gave Berwick a miss by by-passing it. Kate and I walked the wall now, anti-clockwise, enjoying the views and special atmosphere. I took note of much information, but there is far too much to impart here. Suffice to say if you ever go to Berwick, walk the wall.

That night we wandered the town again, noting that Charles Dickens stayed at the Kings Hotel on 26 September, 1858 and 25 November, 1861. I wonder if there will ever be a sign to commemorate where Kate and I stayed, the Cobbled Yard Hotel. Have a look if you like, but I wouldn't hold your breath.

***

We were bound for Holy Island. And we were going to walk there, across the famous causeway. Our journey was dictated by the tide, so we took the bus to West Mains, eight miles down the A1; it was vital to set off from the mainland when the tide was out and nowhere near coming in. I didn't want us to become an unwelcome headline about irresponsible hikers being trapped, having to be rescued by helicopter. Or not rescued, which was more likely.

It was a bitterly cold morning. Alighting at West Mains it felt like getting off a train in Siberia, but brisk walking soon warmed us up. The quiet road led east, an uneventful plod, except it's worth mentioning the flowers, weeds more like, at the roadside, so pretty, as though defying the temperature. We crested the hill at Beal, for a great view of the sea, with Holy Island and Bamburgh Castle prominent. Another mile led to the causeway, where a sign confirmed the times of the tides. The sign is big, and clearly indicates the times when it's safe to cross to the island. Yet one reads of motorists being trapped by the sea. True, it doesn't look far, and in a car it appears there'll be no problem making the crossing. But the tide rises swiftly, and once it's up to your hubcaps…

The causeway was constructed in 1954. Before that a row of stakes led the way along a 'wet track', as Bradley puts it. Writing of his crossing to the island around 1900, he describes being transported in a 'two-wheeled dogcart…progress taken at a walk…the heaviness of the draught made us feel how hopeless would be a race with the in-coming sea'. For the return, he writes, condescendingly, 'The ladies of our party thought it would be fine fun to drive back through the in-flowing tide, a prospect I admit I did not hail with particular enthusiasm...'. He concludes, 'I noted with a qualified measure of relief a roomy box on a platform supported far aloft on stout stakes, whence a ladder descended...'. He meant, of course, a refuge hut. I don't know if it's the same one, but one matching that description stands today by the side of the causeway.

The refuge is a box-like edifice, mounted on four thick wooden posts, with a row of steps leading up to a door. Anyone with the sea lapping at their ankles would be mightily glad to reach it. Kate and I climbed to this lofty perch to find a view over a landscape of mudflats, wet grasses and rocks, a nature reserve, in fact. A telephone for emergency use only was provided, and a notice regarding same, written by a semi-literate, or maybe a Chinese, read: 'In emergency this telephone can only be used conact [*sic*] local police Dia 999'. Much graffiti had been obliterated, although since it was visitors have scribbled 'Feyenoord Rotterdam – the boys from Holland', and 'Jesus Christ 2000'. A business card was tucked behind the sign: 'Border Cabs. 24-hour service available'. Not at high tide, surely.

The causeway isn't the only crossing to the island. A line of stakes clearly marks the Pilgrims Way, where pilgrims crossed a thousand years ago, and present-day pilgrims do the same thing, bare feet and all. The Pilgrims Way runs to the south of the causeway, and is about three miles long. Anyway, as Kate and I walk the causeway, here's a potted history of this *Holy* Island. We will be concerned primarily with three saints: Oswald, Aidan and Cuthbert.

Christianity came to Britain courtesy of the Romans. When they departed, around AD 410, Christianity went with them, replaced by the pagan beliefs of new immigrants from northern Europe: Angles, Saxons and Jutes. Then an Englishman, Patrick, went to Ireland as a missionary, and by the time he died Christianity was firmly established in that country. The Venerable Bede (673-735) wrote his *Ecclesiastical History of the English People*, a great work through which we know so much of this period, including the events that took place on Lindisfarne, or Holy Island.

Early Northumbria comprised two kingdoms, Bernicia and Deira. Bernicia stretched northwards from the Tyne or Tees to the Firth of Forth; Deira southwards to the Humber. Although Bernicia and Deira were separated for a time, they joined to form Northumbria. Christianity came when Edwin was baptised by Paulinus in 627.

It was a Christian king, Oswald, who did much to promote the spread of Christianity in Northumbria by sending word to the Irish to send a bishop. One was sent from Iona, off the west coast of what is now Scotland. He was Corman, who failed in his mission, reporting that Northumbrians were 'too stubborn'.

Another followed, Aidan, who, with twelve other monks, founded the first monastery on Lindisfarne in 635. Aidan and his monks, Irishmen all, did not speak English at first, and it is said that Oswald translated for them. The monks converted many Northumbrians to the faith by travelling on foot between villages. They belonged to the Irish branch of Christianity, as opposed to the Latin, under the Pope in Rome. When Aidan died in 651 he was buried on Lindisfarne.

Cuthbert (c.634-687) was a shepherd boy who, it is said, had a vision of Aidan being carried to heaven by angels, and went to a monastery at Melrose where he became prior. From there he would travel for weeks on end, living and preaching among the border hills. When the Synod of Whitby decreed that Christianity at Lindisfarne should convert to Roman Catholicism, Cuthbert was sent there at the behest of the abbot to 'ease the transition'.

In 676 Cuthbert went to live in a cave, then settled on one of the Farne Islands, where he lived as a hermit. Eight years later he was elected Bishop of Lindisfarne, but served there only two years before moving to a cell on Inner Farne, where he died on 20 March, 687. His body was placed in a stone coffin and he was buried under the floor of the church on Lindisfarne.

About a hundred years later the Vikings came and plundered Lindisfarne, along with everywhere else they landed. Many of the monks on the island were murdered, others fled. The monks returned, but the Vikings returned too and this time the fleeing monks took Cuthbert's remains with them, along with the head of

Oswald, which had been brought to Lindisfarne, and the bones of Aidan, which were all placed into the coffin. The monks left in 'sorrowful procession', and carried the coffin for seven years, guarding it wherever they went throughout the northern counties of England and parts of Scotland until, in AD 883, they arrived at Chester-le-Street where the coffin and its contents rested, undisturbed, for about 100 years. Yet more Viking incursions drove the monks south to Ripon, again carrying the coffin, until, at last, it was taken to Durham. Scott:

> How, when the rude Danes burned their pile,
> The monks fled north from Holy Isle;
> O'er northern mountain, marsh and moor,
> From sea to sea, from shore to shore,
> Seven years St Cuthbert's corpse they bore.

A church was built at Durham, and made ready for the internment of the coffin. By now the Normans had arrived, and William the Conqueror sent an army to deal with problems in Durham. Once again the monks took the coffin away, and it was returned to Lindisfarne. But in 1104 St Cuthbert's remains were taken back to Durham to a final resting place in the grandest of cathedrals.

Approaching the village on Lindisfarne, a line of guide posts marks the Pilgrims Way, 'Erected by the Community Task Force as part of the Manpower Services Commission Community Programme by the Rt Hon John Selwyn Gummer, MP, Minister of State (Agriculture, Fisheries and Food), 24 September, 1987'. To think: a member of HM Government came all the way up here from London and erected these stakes. A grand chap. Mind you, he did charge us for clearing out moles and jackdaw nests from his country estate. Unlike Aidan and Cuthbert, and many others whose purpose was to serve others over many generations, today our so-called public servants serve themselves. I digress; but then I said I would.

The village has a market place with village cross. I spied Bra Cottage, with a sign, beside a nesting box, saying, 'Tits only'. Just offshore was a rocky outcrop (an island when the tide's in), with a wooden cross. We crossed slippery rocks to reach it, keeping an eye on the sea just in case it crept in when our backs were turned. St Cuthbert reputedly prayed in a monastic cell here. The low remains of a chapel seen today are medieval, according to Pevsner. Kate and I explored the remains, the bitter cold of the North East coast seeping into our bones. I've known warmer days on top of Skiddaw in January.

Back in the village, St Mary's Church is built of wonderful Northumbrian stone. The chancel is 13th century, but some of the building is of Saxon origin. Inside is a sculpture, in wood, of six monks carrying St Cuthbert's body. On the list of 'Bishops, Priors and Vicars', Aidan is first (653); Cuthbert is at number six (685).

It was good to find the church open. It wasn't when Bradley called, circa 1900. 'This church, of all churches in the kingdom, where there are neither vagabonds, tramps or ruffians, and whence come a small but steady stream of respectable and intelligent pilgrims, is kept securely locked, the key lurking somewhere in the village'. By 'of all churches' he meant that here, more than anywhere, one needs access without having to track down the key because by the time you locate it you're liable to be cut off from the mainland. Why should the keys to churches in Herefordshire, for example (he asks), be in the grip of job gardeners or wandering washerwomen? So, locked churches are nothing new, only the thieves are of a different type: in Bradley's day they were tramps, vagabonds and ruffians, as he describes them; today it's anyone with a car and light fingers. Another difference is that in Bradley's day tramps and vagabonds had nowt, whilst today's thieves are already pocketing dosh on a regular basis, thanks to the taxes those who work for a living pay.

There was lots of information in the church, including of the name Lindisfarne, said to derive from 'Lindis', a tidal stream, and the Celtic word 'Fahren', meaning a place of retreat. Lindisfarne was established as a centre of learning, covering a 'golden age, where the vitality of the Anglo-Saxons welded with Christian scholarship to produce an important cultural flowering, the centre of religious learning in western Europe for 100 years'.

There's also mention of the Lindisfarne Gospels, 'a masterpiece of 7th century art, illuminated by Eadfrith', who became Bishop after Cuthbert's death. The Lindisfarne Gospels were created to honour St Cuthbert. They were carried off with Cuthbert's body, but fell into the sea off Scotland, yet astonishingly the manuscript was saved. You can see it in Durham Cathedral, or rather a facsimile of it; the original is in the British Library, London, though why it can't be where it rightly belongs, on Lindisfarne, or maybe Durham, is a mystery to me. Bring it home, I say!

Close to the church are the magnificent priory ruins. Not of the original monastery, of which nothing remains, but the Benedictine Priory, built around the same time as Durham Cathedral (1093) and modelled on it. A sculpture, Cuthbert of Farne, by Fenwick Lawson, fits the scene perfectly, in my opinion anyway.

If Kate and I were cold when we crossed to St Cuthbert's Isle, we were freezing by the time we left it. A brisk if short walk would warm us up a little. There was one in the offing: to the castle. Lots of people have seen the castle, mostly from afar and in many cases not knowing what they were looking at. The castle sits on the rock so closely it's as though nature herself fashioned it that way. It was built by Henry VIII as a defence against the Scots and French, using recycled stone from the priory. It was attacked by neither, but was occupied alternatively by the Royalists then the Roundheads in the Civil War, and a garrison was stationed here until 1819.

Edward Hudson, owner of *Country Life*, bought the castle in 1902, and employed Sir Edwin Lutyens, the architect, to convert it into a private home. It was given to the National Trust in 1944 and can be visited today. The approach is by way of a ramp, and inside are passages hewn into solid rock and ancient rooms. We explored at our leisure, and took our time about it, not least because it provided shelter from the bitter cold outside.

There's a canny story about the castle. It concerns Lancelot Errington, a Jacobite, who captured it during the 1715 rising. Errington and his nephew arrived off Lindisfarne and kindly invited twelve of the castle's garrison of fifteen men on to their ship for a feast, which naturally included alcohol. Having got them drunk the pair went to the castle armed with pistols and succeeded in turning out the three remaining occupants, upon which they entered, locked the door and hoisted the Jacobite flag. The flag, white in colour, was espied by the folk of Berwick and a detachment was sent to investigate.

One can imagine the situation: open the gates or we're coming in – although they might have wondered why the gates weren't already open, as they were looking at a white flag. Maybe the Jacobites failed because their enemies thought they were continually surrendering. Anyway, Errington and his nephew refused to surrender, despite being fired upon. They escaped, and hid among the rocks outside, only to be forced out by the rising tide and captured. Both men were taken to Berwick, where the feelings of the citizens were mixed, depending on one's loyalties. It mattered not, as both escaped and fled to Bamburgh where they hid in the castle for nine days, helped by a friend, even though there was £500 on Errington's head. They ultimately moved to Newcastle where Errington ran a pub for thirty years.

***

Today was the day, I told Kate, that she would see for herself Northumberland's glorious beaches and a great castle. We were Bamburgh-bound and, beyond, to Seahouses. First, though, we went for a walk on the links, before returning to the village to look at the cross in the market place, rebuilt by John Dobson. Newcastle Central Station, countless houses in city and country, churches, even a cross on Holy Island. What a busy man he was. Here too was a mine, big and red. This one's a money-box now, collecting for the Shipwrecked Mariners Society: 'a naval mine of the type used in the Second World War in defence of our coasts'. As Kate and I contributed to this worthy cause, I wondered how often they empty it.

A small minibus conveyed us to the mainland. Now, how shall I put this: the driver, being Northumbrian and naturally helpful, kindly drove us a little way off his route down the A1, and dropped us at the entrance to a field. No names, no pack-drill. Don't anyone contact me asking about him or her, or the date or even to confirm this. He or she was a great help, as we didn't want to walk the A1 and there were no obvious rights of way across the flat landscape in the hinterland of Budle Bay. I had thought about crossing the bay, but reference to Ian Smith's *Northumbrian Coastline* is more than enough to focus minds: 'Lives have been lost here'. The bus it was, and we were happy to stroll the country road to Waren Mill.

The tide was still out as we approached Budle Bay, an extensive panorama of mudflats, not pretty to look at, despite the sign: 'Area of Outstanding Natural Beauty'. The bay is a nature reserve, the haunt of thousands of seabirds, a twitcher's delight I imagine. And if it doesn't look pretty when the tide is out, I imagine it's a fine sight when it's in. Waren Mill is situated at the southern extremity of the bay. There was a harbour once, used by boats to collect flour from the water-powered mill built in the 12th century and developed during the Napoleonic wars, when coal was brought in by sea to supply a steam engine. We passed it by and climbed the hill, which is an appropriate place to recount the story of the Laidley Worm.

Knowledgeable readers will have heard of the legendary Lambton Worm, of Durham. Well, Northumberland had a worm too, on Spindlestone Heughs, crags near Waren Mill. It seems that a king who lived in Bamburgh castle had a beautiful daughter. The king was widowed but he re-married, and his new wife's stepmother, who was a witch, was jealous of her stepdaughter's beauty so changed her into a loathsome serpent – the Laidley Worm – so that nothing could restore her to human form again save the appearance of her brother, who was abroad, unfortunately.

The Laidley Worm took herself off to Spindlestone Heughs, where she consumed the milk of seven cows and poisoned the land:

> For seven miles east and seven miles west,
> And seven miles north and south;
> No blade of grass or corn could grow,
> So venomous was her mouth.

In time the brother heard of events, and with the help of his mates built a ship, with masts of the rowan tree, making it resistant to witchcraft, so that when he set sail for Bamburgh and his wicked stepmother saw it she wouldn't be able to cast a spell on it. When he reached Budle Bay he saw the Laidley Worm wriggling on the beach. With sword in hand he approached the worm, which addressed him thus:

> Oh quit thy sword, and bend thy bow,
> And give me kisses three;
> For though I am a poisonous worm,
> No hurt I'll do to thee.

And so, right then and there, her brother stepped forward and kissed the Laidley Worm, which crawled into its nest to emerge, as if you hadn't guessed, as his beautiful sister. They then went to Bamburgh castle, where the brother turned his stepmother into a toad. Served her right, don't you think?

At the top of the hill we took the right of way across fields. Soon we reached the sea and followed the path along the clifftops, Bamburgh barely two miles away. We reached the beach at a strategically-placed pillbox, one of many throughout England, leftovers from the war. Inside was a gun emplacement, with a gap on the seaward side though which missiles could be fired at Gerry. Great swaths of the Northumbrian coast would have made ideal landing beaches, which is why pillboxes, huge cube-shaped concrete blocks, and coils of wire adorned miles of this coastline. Concrete is difficult (and expensive) to move, so we see the pillboxes and concrete cubes today, a reminder of the perilous situation Britain was in then.

We stood in the pillbox awhile, looking seaward. It was easy to imagine landing craft, front doors opening, enemy soldiers pouring out, cannon-fodder for machine gunners in the pillbox, until, of course, enough of them got ashore when the defenders in the pillbox would have been overrun.

Our route led alongside a golf course. There can be few better sited in Britain. I've never had any interest in golf, but it must be wonderful to play here. Tee off, then take a look around as you walk the fairways: in splendid view are Bamburgh – village and castle, the sea, Holy Island, the Farnes, even the Cheviots on a clear day. 'Golf is a good walk spoiled,' wrote Mark Twain. Ordinarily I wouldn't argue, but here I happily make an exception.

We continued along the coast, with wonderful views all the way to Bamburgh. Two flags fluttered proudly in the village, each bearing the distinctive red and gold stripes of Northumberland. I say proudly because, if you recall, there were moves to abolish Northumberland as a county altogether. This was happily thwarted by the natives who voted overwhelmingly to keep things as they are instead of creating a North East 'region' to suit EU requirements. The Northumberland emblem appeared on my school exercise books and on scout badges. History and heritage mean a lot to people. It meant a lot to Northumbrians when they were asked to vote in Prescott's spurious ballet.

Church Street has lovely stone buildings, one of which, the Copper Kettle tearoom, served our needs. Y'can't beat a cuppa, especially when it's taken in such a lovely place. Suitably refreshed, we wandered the streets until, inevitably, we arrived at a little cottage bearing the sign: 'Grace Darling died here, 20 October, 1842'.

Grace Horsley Darling was a true heroine. She was born at Bamburgh in 1815, one of nine children of William and Thomasin Darling. Her father was lighthouse keeper on Brownsman island, one of the Farnes, where Grace spent the first ten years of her life, until, in 1826, the family moved to nearby

Longstone island, a barren outpost of the Farnes, where her father would be keeper at the newly-built lighthouse. From her birth until her early twenties, living on two islands off the Northumberland coast was the only life Grace knew.

History was made here on the morning of 7 September, 1838, when the steam packet, *Forfarshire*, sailing from Hull to Dundee in stormy seas, foundered on one of the Farnes known as Big Harkar. She carried a cargo of hardware and other goods, and approximately 60 passengers and crew.

At a quarter to five Grace saw the wreck from her bedroom window. At first there was no sign of life, but then movement was seen: survivors, though it wasn't possible to say how many. William Darling's opinion, incorrect as it turned out, was that neither of the lifeboats at Bamburgh or North Sunderland could be launched in such heavy seas, but nonetheless he, together with Grace, put out in his 21-feet long coble.

Although the distance to the wreck was 400 yards, it was necessary to approach it on the leeward side of the island, which meant rowing for a distance double that amount. They knew that when they reached the wreck, they alone could not possibly row back in such heavy seas; they would have to rely on those they hoped to rescue to help. They found nine survivors on the reef, one a woman holding her two dead babies in her arms. They took her and four others, and rowed back to Longstone.

William Darling, together with two of the rescued men, then rowed back to the wreck and rescued the others. Nine more were picked up off Tynemouth. The North Sunderland lifeboat did, in fact, reach the wreck, only to find three bodies, their crew heroes nonetheless.

Grace Darling became a national heroine. She sat for portraits. The Adelphi Theatre in London offered her £10 a week for her to appear on stage, 'rowing' her boat. Books and poems were written. There were offers of marriage. £1,000 was raised by public subscription for Grace and her father, including £50 by Queen Victoria. She received several awards, including one from the Royal Humane Society. Despite the accolades and the money, Grace continued to live with her parents on Longstone. Alas, she lived only four more years, passing away on 20 October, 1842 through tuberculosis. She was buried in Bamburgh churchyard, whilst near her grave the Grace Darling Memorial stands proudly behind iron railings, put there to be visible to those at sea. The memorial is a copy of the original, which was moved into the church.

The Times asked the question, 'Is there in the whole field of history one instance of female heroism to compare with this?' Perhaps not, yet I feel it is appropriate to remember, too, the actions of her father. He had been involved in rescues before, including one in 1834 when he and his three sons went to the aid of a vessel that had struck the Knivestone, in the Outer Farnes. Two of the crew perished, the third was rescued. Two oars were lost and the Darlings were fortunate to survive. William Darling spent his life manning lighthouses and rescuing people at sea. A memorial to him in the churchyard is merited, surely.

St Aidan's is one of the largest parish churches in Northumberland, and one of the best. It stands on the site of the original church, with the sea a magnificent backdrop. The chancel dates back to c.1230. Inside is a 13th century crypt, discovered in 1837, when five coffins were found containing the remains of the Forster family, including Tom Forster, leader of the ill-fated 1715 Jacobite Rebellion, and Dorothy Forster, his sister, who reputedly rescued him from Newgate prison, London.

Inside a notice gives a potted history: 'It is reported that Aidan died leaning against a beam outside this church. The beam has survived fires on two occasions when the church burnt down and can now be seen in the ceiling, above the font'. The original Grace Darling memorial graces the north aisle.

It seems reasonable to assume that as long as man has needed to defend himself against attack he would have built some sort of fortification on top of the Whin Sill crag that stands next to the sea at Bamburgh. We know that in AD 547 the Northumbrian King Ida the Flamebearer built a wooden fort here (although with a name like that he was taking a risk), a Saxon settlement known as *Dinguardi*. Later, his grandson, Ethelfrith, bequeathed it to his widow, Queen Bebba, and it is from her that the castle takes its name: *Bebbanburgh*, hence Bamburgh. Northumbrian kings were crowned here, including Edwin, who gave his name, *Edwin's Burgh*, to an outpost at the northern extremity of Northumbria – Edinburgh. Bamburgh was a royal palace as well as a castle.

It was from Bamburgh that Christianity spread to northern England. Oswald, the first Christian king, we have seen defeated the heathen, Penda, at Heavenfield. Penda had seen fit to visit Bamburgh, where he set fire to the outworks of the castle. It is said that the prayers of Aidan, retreating to the Farnes, caused the wind to change direction, thus thwarting Penda's intentions. In 933 the Vikings sacked the castle.

When the Normans came they probably built a wooden fortification here, and they certainly built a stone one, for there it is now, albeit much restored with modern apartments within its walls. The outer walls of the keep, 10-feet thick, are original, however, and Bamburgh Castle is an unmistakable and grand sight from whichever direction it is seen.

In 1095 William Rufus, for William II, the Conqueror's son, besieged the castle, demanding the rebellious Robert de Mowbray surrender himself on a charge of plundering Norwegian ships. In fact, Mowbray had escaped, but was betrayed and captured at Tynemouth and, threatened with having his eyes put out, forced to surrender the castle. Mowbray was not executed as one might have expected, although he was sentenced to 30 years' imprisonment. Many kings came to Bamburgh, including Edward I. The castle fell during the Wars of the Roses, when it became the first castle to succumb to artillery. Thereafter all castles were rendered useless, although many have since been put to good use as museums.

Kate and I arrived at the foot of the whinstone base on which the castle stands. Here, hewn into the rock, is a huge cross, a war memorial to the fallen of 'two world wars'. We then made our way up the slope to the eastern gatehouse. Bamburgh Castle is magnificent, and so are Northumberland's beaches, 'The ones I was telling you about,' I told Kate. And so we made our way through grassy sand dunes to the beach, with great views of the

Farnes, the red and white striped Longstone lighthouse 4 miles away.

It was time to take a walk for three miles on sand, to Seahouses. Clean, natural sand, unchanged and unspoiled in over forty years since I had last stood here with my mate, Robert Waugh. We'd hitch-hiked (as youngsters did then) along the coast from Newbiggin. If we remember where we were – as we do – when a certain, major event takes place, so it is here. It was August, 1962, and the event was Marilyn Monroe's death. I thought she was quite beautiful, and now she was dead. Suicide, they said. Murder, many suspected. We'll never know. Goodbye, Norma Jean.

The beach was typically perishing. They say Northumberland can never have holiday resorts on her beaches because it's so cold. Long may it be so. Already wearing boots and carrying rucksacks, we now donned windproof jackets against the bracing wind – even as two small children, wearing only swimming trunks, played with buckets and spades not ten feet away. We walked close to the sea, which made for easier walking. It was so good to *hear* the sea, the low rush of the waves breaking gently on the shore.

The walk to Seahouses, every step, was a joy. I always find proximity to the sea an invigorating experience. So it was here. My thoughts of Robert lingered. He was a great friend, someone who was part of my life when we were young. He came here with me. Now he's gone. Looking around now at this wonderful landscape reminded me of our immortality, of how we should always make the most of what we have and do things when we can.

We didn't hurry. Rather we dallied, breathing in Northumberland's fresh, bracing air, gazing out to sea, looking back at the receding form of the castle and the Farnes. Eventually we made our way to the road, and thence to Seahouses, a place of ice cream and fish and chips, gift shops and cafes. And a harbour, where you can take trips out to the Farnes. But that was for tomorrow.

***

The Whin Sill of hard, dolerite rock runs for approximately eighty miles from High Force, in Teesdale, through County Durham and Northumberland and ends as a group of rocky islands off Bamburgh. These are the Farne Islands, between 15 and 28 of them, depending on the tide. The Farnes are treeless and virtually uninhabited – by humans. But they very much inhabited by seabirds: puffin, cormorant, shag, guillemot, tern, kittiwake and more, nesting in their thousands on the rocky clifftops and, in the case of the puffins, laying their eggs in the shallow earth. Until I went to the Farnes with Kate I never knew that last bit.

Seahouses Harbour. That's where we went directly on this breezy April morning. A handful of passengers, including us, embarked on our ocean-going voyage, during which, on the sight of puffins, Kate demonstrated their flying style by bending her elbows to right angles, and flapping her arms quickly up and down. Actions speak louder than words. She said she would try and spot a dolphin. My eyes were fixed firmly on the scenery: the sea, the far-away Cheviots, the skeletal ruins of Dunstanburgh Castle to the south. Proud of Northumberland? You can bet I was.

We embarked on Inner Farne, the largest of the islands, and followed the path to the clifftops, where seabirds, thousands of them, sat, swooped, sang and did anything else you can think of beginning with 's'. They were all there, living happily together, with, it seemed to me, puffins, shags and cormorants in the greater number. We were up really close, at the edge of the cliffs, the birds occupying rocky ground just feet away. The islands are owned by the National Trust, and if you aren't already a member but have wondered if you should be then I would urge you to join, if only to contribute to the protection given to the wonderful birdlife here.

For centuries, until the dissolution of the monasteries, monks and religious hermits lived on Inner Farne. Most famous were Aidan, who left Lindisfarne from time to time to pray and meditate here, and Cuthbert, who built a windowless dwelling of stone with an opening in the roof to afford only a view of heaven.

He lived here for six years (678-684), before he went to Lindisfarne, but returned in 686, where he lived until his death, here, on Inner Farne in 687.

St Cuthbert's Church stands today, although it's no more than a chapel. The building is simple, about 50 ft by 16 ft, with a galilee (vestibule) at one end and dates back to the 14th century. It was restored by Archdeacon Charles Thorp, who bought the islands in 1861, and who furnished the chapel with carved oak furnishings brought here from Durham Cathedral. The chapel was abandoned after the dissolution, and occupied by an elderly couple, who, before the lighthouse was built, tended the beacon fire which was lit nightly on top of Prior Castell's pele tower. It would have been a lonely life, but one with much responsibility. Today, puffins flew through the open windows of the public lavatories. What amazing creatures they are.

Resuming our trip, we sailed out to Longstone Island, with its distinctive red and white striped lighthouse. It was from here, their home, on the night the *Forfarshire* foundered, that Grace Darling and her father rowed to the rescue. Pause awhile to reflect on the fact that Grace spent her entire life on two of these islands: little, if any, communication with the mainland, no radio or television, no internet, no e-mail. Here she lived with her parents, long after her brothers and sisters had left, before her dramatic rescue and early death.

Ashore again, the day seemed colder, although that could be down to cruising the North Sea in April. We took the road out of Seahouses and got on to the beach, a mere two miles from Beadnell, and pressed on for the little harbour there. A cuppa would have been appreciated. Alas, there was nowhere. Despite being situated on the east coast, Beadnell's harbour is situated 'around the corner' of a headland and consequently faces west. It's a sheltered spot, which is probably one reason why it was once reputedly used by smugglers.

Just by the harbour wall are some limekilns, built in 1798. They were expected to produce at least 1,000 cartloads of lime every year, coal and stone burning slowly for weeks to produce quicklime. Imagine the black smoke that must have belched continuously. The kilns are now a convenient place for storing lobster pots, and seats are tucked away inside, out of the now-cold wind but today occupied, with everyone looking as though they could do with a cup of tea.

South of the harbour Beadnell Bay sweeps away in a graceful curve, the beach marred by seaweed. Here I was, expounding the virtues of Northumberland, only to find this beach festooned by blackened, dead matter. Can't the council or somebody remove it? Or is it washed ashore daily by the tide? We walked the beach anyway, at one point having to cross a stream by a footbridge, unusual to say the least. After an outcrop of rocks we came to the unusually-named Football Hole, a small bay with a glorious beach sadly strewn with more seaweed. I suppose it might be argued that this is its 'natural' state.

The path crossed meadowland, climbing to a headland with great views seaward. Nothing at all graced the blue waters of the deep. In his *Northumbrian Coastline* guidebook, Ian Smith indicates 'Cowslips in spring' at Newton Point. This was spring; would they still be there? They were, familiar yet rare yellow flowers snuggled in the grass. There are numerous tales about them, my favourite being one from Norse mythology, that cowslips were dedicated to Odin's wife, Frega, a goddess who held the keys to happiness and sexual love. Not ordinary love, *sexual* love. I always thought sex was taboo in the past, but not to Scandinavians, apparently. Do you have a favourite wild flower? I love bluebells, poppies and cowslips. Each has its place, with the common denominator being sunshine. They all belong in England's green and pleasant landscapes. To me, they all mean life and happiness. And now, in the case of the latter, sexual love.

We cut inland, crossing more green meadows, occupied by sleepy cows. The sun was struggling to get through as ahead lay the broad sweep of Embleton Bay, the remains of Dunstanburgh Castle prominent on the headland beyond, now only three miles away. Our footsteps led us directly to Low Newton-by-the Sea. I was pleasantly surprised when we reached this 18th century hamlet of fishermen's cottages, grouped around a village green, the Ship Inn tucked away in one corner. The village is only accessible by a dead-end road, so no through traffic disturbs the place. Today, although the sun had appeared, it was still on the cold side, and we were glad of a cup of coffee at The Ship. No, not a pint. If I drink alcohol through the day it reduces my legs to jelly and renders me pretty useless – for anything (even sexual love).

We took the coast path again, crossing more meadows with more sleepy cows and cowslips (and cowpats), to a lane where we cut inland to Embleton. The village lies over a low whinstone ridge. It was bathed in sunshine and was deserted. Its name evidently derives from 'A hill infested by caterpillars', or maybe it's because the whinstone ridge resembles a caterpillar; then again it might derive from 'The hill of a man called Aemele'. I wouldn't worry about it.

With time to spare and on a wonderful late afternoon we wandered down to the church. Holy Trinity is unusual in that the chancel is offset slightly to the left as you look along the nave. The oldest part of the church is the tower, with parts of the lower level dating back to 12th century. Rectors of Embleton date back to Adam, circa 1220-45. Close by, the Old Vicarage is sometimes described as a Vicar's Pele – like the one at Corbridge – but there is dispute about this; it seems it may have been built as a conventional house in the 14th century, then remodelled as a tower later as a defence against the border reivers and Scots. Later work, by John Dobson – him again – converted the 'tower' to a house again.

We sat awhile, the sun at last bearing a degree of warmth, before making our way to our night's accommodation, the Bluebell Inn. Later, we dined well in the Dunstanburgh Castle Hotel.

***

Although the sun shone on a shimmering sea, Embleton was under grey skies. We returned to the beach, which we had to ourselves. So bracing, so invigorating: it felt great to be alive.

Dunstanburgh Castle, just over a mile off now, looked splendid, just inviting us to call.

It was St George's Day. How many English people can name the date? How many care? I do. St George is our patron saint, whose emblem, a red cross on white, the English flag, was brought to England by Richard I, *Coeur de lion*, in the 12th century. Yet, far from showing pride, I have read of English magistrates refusing to grant an extension to licensing hours on St George's Day, yet allowing an extension for the Irish on St Patrick's! This could only happen in England, kow-towing to minority groups and politically-correct nonsense. Give England back to the English – you idiots!

Dunstanburgh Castle stands on a high whinstone promontory. It is, or was, the largest castle in Northumberland. To the north, facing the curve of Embleton Bay, it was naturally defended by high cliffs, and the east and west sides were also well protected; only the south side was vulnerable, approached by a slope.

The castle was built in the 14th century by Thomas, Earl of Lancaster, who lived in the time of Edward II, with whom Thomas was constantly at loggerheads, especially over the favouritism the king showed to Piers Gaveston, his alleged homosexual lover. When Thomas had Gaveston captured and executed it didn't go down too well with Edward, and what with constant Scots' incursions and incurring the king's wrath Thomas decided to build the castle at Dunstanburgh. Sadly for him, his castle wasn't much good when he decided to venture out of it, for he was captured at Boroughbridge and executed in 1312.

During the Wars of the Roses the castle changed hands five times. The ruins visible today are scant, but the Lilburn tower and 3-storeyed gateway remain impressive. Another good thing about the castle is that it is not accessible by road. One has to either walk from Embleton, as we did, or Craster, to reach it. No cars, no clutter and fewer visitors, since few people walk anywhere.

It was a pity Kate and I didn't pass this way at on a dark, wintry night, when we may have seen the ghost of the White Lady of Dunstanburgh, a beautiful woman who took the fancy of Sir Guy, the Wandering Knight, who passed this way 'when the moon was overcast and Dunstanburgh's castellated turrets stood out against a sullen sky'. As Sir Guy rode close to the castle, he espied a light shining from a window. To his surprise the drawbridge was down, and as he crossed it the castle door swung open.

He rode on to the sound of a mysterious voice, with bells and shrieks and screams 'like unto those of an abandoned soul', and arrived at a magnificent chamber with glistening marble pillars, interspersed with statues of knights who sat on bronze horses; and there, reclining and encased as a prisoner in a crystal globe, lay the White Lady. Sir Guy did what any man would do, and feasted his eyes on the sight of a beautiful woman with 'long raven tresses and breasts like perfect peaches'.

The voice spoke again as a phosphorescent arm appeared holding a golden horn and a curved sword. He was implored to choose one of them and so release the White Lady. He chose the horn. Mistake! For this proved he was lacking in personal valour, since it meant he was summoning assistance. He should have selected the sword to prove his bravery and thus free the maiden. (That's what I would have done). It seems he then found himself outside the castle walls, soaked to the skin and freezing cold. And so it is the White Lady seeks release to this day.

We passed the castle on the landward side – as you must – and walked by the south curtain wall. A wire perimeter fence runs alongside, and comes to an abrupt end above a rocky inlet where the sea rushes in dramatically. The fence was rather rickety. One wouldn't want to fall over the cliffs here; it wouldn't do at all. So we moved on for Craster, a walk on grass above the high whinstone cliffs, over more green meadows with sprightly lambs and with a southerly breeze in our faces. We were eager for a morning cuppa and maybe a snack, but Craster, like Beadnell, disappointed. We couldn't even smell any kippers, for which Craster is renowned.

I have read that the name Craster derives from the Roman fort of Crawchester, or from the Craster family, of whom mention is made of William de Craucetr in the 13th century, or 'an old fortification or earthwork haunted by crows'. The Craster family certainly built the harbour, in memory of Captain John Craster who was killed on active service abroad. Craster kippers have been supplied to the royal family, and also to my parents on occasion.

I mustn't press on without mention of Craster being the alleged birthplace, in 1265, of Duns Scrotum – sorry, Scrotus – scholastic theologian and Member of the Franciscan Order. I won't dwell on this except to say his 'Scotist System' was ridiculed by humanists and reformers of the 16th century, who coined the term 'dunce' after his name. Scholastic theologian to dunce; it's hardly how he would like to be remembered. Maxton, in Roxburghshire, Scotland, also lays claim to his birthplace. I don't think the good people of Craster will mind.

Southbound again, on the clifftops, two wonderful miles to Howick, where the cliffs are formed by layers of sandstone and dolerite, like a giant sponge cake with a topping of grass. Our route was south, but first a short detour to the row of estate cottages of Howick village, with their lovely gardens, today picturesque with spring flowers and blossom. On a central gable is displayed the Grey crest and motto: *De Bon Vouloir Servir Le Roi* (Goodwill in Service to the King). The Grey family built nearby Howick Hall in 1728.

Charles, Earl Grey, lived here. As well as his political achievements in political reform, we have something else to thank him for. When, as Prime Minister, he sent a diplomatic mission to China, by chance his envoy saved the life of a Chinese Mandarin, who, to show his gratitude, sent the earl some 'delightfully scented tea'. You've guessed the rest: Earl Grey asked his tea merchant thereafter for that blend of tea, which was later sold to the public bearing his name.

We had decided to visit Alnwick. You can hardly perambulate around Northumberland without visiting what is, or was, the county town. I notice Morpeth also lays claim; Morpeth is where county hall is so maybe that qualifies it for 'county town' status. But maybe Alnwick should be county town, not least because this is the seat of the Percies. So, at a car park by Howdiemont Sands, we took a byroad for Longhoughton. There was an interesting notice on an iron gate of the car park: 'There have been incidents where cattle have damaged parked cars here. Whilst they mean no malice, it appears that electric wing mirrors in particular provide a great place to scratch against'. Fair warning; but whilst acknowledging cattle like a good scratch – who doesn't? – how does anyone know they mean no malice? Maybe wrecking motorists' mirrors is their way of getting back at the human race. After all, we slaughter plenty (without malice, of course).

We reached Longhoughton, passing along the way a place marked on the map as 'Helicopter Station'. Would this be the place the Sea Kings fly from to the Lake District to assist in mountain rescue? I've often thought it weird that rescue comes from the opposite side of the country, but I suppose people need rescuing in Northumberland too.

I must confess that Longhoughton was not a place we particularly aimed to visit. Rather it just happened to be on the way to Alnwick. But, again, it's not till you venture forth into the countryside that you discover things. At Longhoughton we discovered the church. I hadn't even noticed it on the map, but it was there so we followed the path along the line of yews to the porch. The church was open, and inside it is seen that, like the church at Embleton, the nave is built at a slight angle to the chancel. This cannot be a coincidence, the explanation apparently being that this was 'a medieval device recalling the droop of Jesus's head on the cross'.

According to Pevsner the walls of the nave and west part of the chancel are 'probably mid-11th century', whilst the west tower is early 12th. Mid 11th century is pre-Conquest, thus we have Saxon fragments in the building, including the chancel arch. The west tower is Norman, built as a pele tower for defence.

In 1576 it was stated that 'the church is the great strength that the poor tenants have to draw in time of war', meaning they sought refuge in the tower. There's a tale that smugglers brought contraband ashore which was stored in the tower by the vicar. One vicar, the Rev George Duncan, didn't pull any punches when it came to describing some of his parishioners. Writing mainly in

Latin, he remarked that Robert Pringle, a day labourer, was 'the bad son of a bad father', William Gray was 'a very ignorant and obstinate sinner', Henry Elder was 'unhappily married', Anne Wilson, a beggarwoman and a widow, was 'a vile, drunken sinner'. Are they in heaven now, I wonder? Is the Rev Duncan in heaven?

There are many interesting headstones in the churchyard, including one dedicated to Peter Ford Miller, who died in 1882. 'Take ye heed, watch and pray, for ye know not when the time is'. The time you will die, presumably. Another was 'erected in the memory of David Williams, aged 32 years, Master of the Brig, Epsilon of Blyth, who was drowned off Dunstanborough Castle with the whole of his crew. January 4, 1857'. An effigy of a woman is carved on the gravestone, along with an inscription commemorating the loss of the said David Williams:

> Toss'd in the troubled voyage of life
> By many a raging wave
> My weary frame at length hath found
> A harbour in the grave.

Pride of place on our visit to Longhoughton churchyard, however, was something that was alive: scores, nay hundreds, of cowslips, claiming their own special place among the headstones. Never have I seen so many; never have I seen them so lovely.

We took a public footpath that threaded its way across open country to Alnwick, finally arriving at the Percy Tenantry Column, 80 feet high with the Percy lion on top, tail held in the horizontal. My old cat's tail did that when I stroked him. In fact, it went into the vertical. The column commemorates the tenantry volunteers during the Napoleonic Wars, founded by the Duke of Northumberland to deal with any invasion on the coast, a sort of 19th century Home Guard. It was erected by the Duke's tenants in gratitude for a 25% reduction in rents. Legend has it that the next Duke, thinking if his tenants could afford to build the column, put the rents back up again, hence the column became known as the 'Farmers' folly'. The inscription, with date in Roman numerals reads, 'Anno Domini MDCCCXVI' (I make that 1816, shoot me down if I am mistaken), and *'Esperance en Dieu* ('Hope in God'). It is appropriate that a symbol of the Percies greets the visitor. Alnwick was, and is, the Percies' home.

Alnwick is a town of stone. Stone buildings, stone monuments, a stone castle. Kate and I turned for the town centre, where we encountered another legacy of the Percies, the Hotspur Tower, named after Harry Hotspur who, as we saw earlier, was a fighting man, scourge of the Scots who died fighting against Henry IV at the Battle of Shrewsbury.

The Hotspur Tower, or Gate, divides Bondgate, with a narrow arch ill-suited to the passage of present-day traffic. It was built in the 15th century as part of the town wall, the only one left of several. Considering how so much of our history has given way to 'progress' – cars, motorways, etc – it's nothing short of a miracle it hasn't been demolished. It surely won't be now, unless, of course, some bureaucrat in Lithuania or somewhere decides he or she doesn't like it and orders its removal. Let's hope none of our masters on the continent finds out about it.

As usual, we were after tea/coffee. And a fruit scone, of course. Got to have fruit scones. I am partial to the odd slice of carrot cake, but they dish out such risible portions these days I tend to give them a miss. Considering we'd hiked from Embleton without any refreshment it was the least we deserved. A wee café served our needs. Then it was time for perambulation. Kate had never been to Alnwick before, and it had been many a moon since my size 9s graced the streets. I first came here in 1960 by bus from Powburn, one of our summer scout camps. We walked around in our uniforms, as you did then, which, as I mentioned earlier I never seem to see now. Later I came in 1962 with a girlfriend, the one who lived on the Fossway if you remember reading that far back, again by bus. We strolled into the parkland north of the river where I beheld for the first time the castle.

I think, to coin a phrase, Kate was gobsmacked. Here was a wonderful town, with wonderful old buildings, untainted by 'development'. We strolled hither and thither, taking in the market place, with its cobbled slope and trees, the Northumberland Hall with its open-arcaded ground floor, and more, not to mention two lovely churches, all too much to recount here. Finally we turned down Bailiffgate to the castle.

In a county with more castles than any other, Alnwick Castle is possibly the grandest. The Percies, or de Percies as they would have been, followed the Conqueror to England. Before they came to Alnwick, however, another Norman family named de Vesci set up the first stronghold here, a wooden fort. In 1309 the property came into the ownership of Henry Percy, the first Lord of Alnwick, who strengthened it, constructing the keep and towers, after which Alnwick Castle became the strongest fortification on the English side of the border. Thereafter, through many generations, and up until today, the Percy family have been associated with Alnwick. Over the years the castle has been altered, developed and changed to what we see today.

***

A sunny morning. We headed out of Alnwick, past the Tenantry Column, lion's tail still erect. A Northumberland flag fluttered in someone's garden. Are you reading this, Mr Prescott? Probably not. We crossed the bypass to a right of way. Just here, a monstrous black dog, fortunately chained up, barked crazily. A gaggle of geese, cackling away, passed by, hissing, their heads swaying threateningly. Then, mercifully, the path led off across the fields to the Aln. Peace at last.

We walked the riverbank for a mile until we reached the viaduct carrying the mainline railway. It was designed by Robert Stephenson and built in 1849, a grand sight, spanning the gorge, the Aln running serenely by below. Ducklings followed mum in the water. A swan floated, seemingly aimlessly; a heron swooped past and butterflies fluttered in the sunshine. Springtime in England. Wonderful.

Further on we reached the A1068 and walked into Lesbury. Here were stone cottages, an inn, fine trees and a small park. We sat by an ancient pant, the sun shining blissfully on this lovely Northumbrian village. Lesbury was in top form this morning.

St Mary's church is Norman, the chancel and tower accredited to the 13th century. Pevsner describes the interior as 'extremely puzzling', as much of the detail has been 'recut'. Suffice to say the church was restored in Victorian times. The vicars date back to John de Barneburgh, 1306. Later came the Rev Patrick Mackilwyan. He started off by rowing with his parishioners over them having 'tithes in kind', but then won them over during the plague of 1665 when victims were taken out onto the moor and left to die under makeshift tents. He visited them, and prayed for them. He was 97 at the time, and lived to 101. Near death, he reputably declared, 'Of friends and books, good and few are best.' That was his advice to humanity and I wouldn't argue.

On the occasion of our visit there were lots of 'Please pray for…' notelets attached to a small screen. Some of these can be very moving, as was one in particular, dedicated to someone who had lost a daughter in the Bali bombing debacle. Peace by the Aln; terrorism in Indonesia. It is hard to believe the two places occupy the same planet.

Another mile led to Alnmouth. The town started life as a major seaport, set up by William de Vesci around 1150. Its status as such continued, especially for the export of grain, and a turnpike road to the town from Hexham was constructed in the 18th century. But the harbour disappeared in 1806 when a violent storm changed the course of the river, leaving what we see today, a peaceful estuary that serves the needs of small craft and leisure. Across the estuary is Church Hill, now cut off from the village thanks to the storm, where the ruinous 12th century cruciform church, dedicated to St Waleric stood. Nothing remains now.

John Wesley, the evangelist, came here in 1748, describing Alnmouth as 'a small seaport town famous for all kinds of wickedness'. He doesn't seem to have described what the wickedness was, although one might hazard a calculated guess, using just three nouns: 'seaport', 'women' and 'sailors', and possibly a fourth, 'smugglers'.

Another kind of wickedness was perpetrated at Alnmouth in September, 1778, when John Paul Jones, who captained a US ship, *Ranger*, in attacking British merchant shipping, fired a cannonball, apparently at the church. Fortunately it missed. Jones led the last 'invasion' of England when, in April that year, he and others landed at Whitehaven, Cumberland, with intent to burn ships in the harbour. Jones's party captured one of two forts guarding the harbour, and spiked the guns there, but when he went to the other he found the raiding party had gone to a pub. So he spiked the guns there too and set fire to some colliers, after which the entire party escaped back to their ship. (How did he get them out of the pub?). Today he is something of a hero in the United States. In fact his real name was John Paul; he added Jones to it. What's more he was a Scot. I might have known.

The day was sunny and spring-like, but typically cold. We were, naturally, eager for morning coffee. At Alnmouth: Café, yes. Open, no. How is it when you go to France there's coffee and croissants on every street corner in every village, *mais, en Angleterre, il y en a jamais!* Happily we found an hotel for our coffee and braved the cold by sitting in the garden overlooking the estuary. Our view included that of a prominent cross standing atop Church Hill, which we resolved to investigate.

Talking of cafes in England and France, it amazes me that when you enter a café in England (if it's open), you usually have to stand at the counter to order your food and drink, taking a tray (sometimes swilling in tea), then queue to pay, during which time your soup and hot drink are getting cold. I recall visiting a Tesco's, where, having picked up a tray, then a cup, I had to put the teabag into it myself, place the cup under a spout thing and press for hot water; after which when queueing to pay, when the tea was getting cold, I read a notice imploring me, on completion of my cuppa, to kindly take the empty crockery away afterwards.

Why do they stop there? When you've finished the cuppa you've financed and poured for yourself, why don't they tell you to take your now-empty cup to the kitchen and wash up, put it back where it was before you so inconveniently went and moved it and apologise for passing through the portals of the establishment in the first place? I don't like paying for this sort of 'service'; instead I choose civilised places to take refreshment if possible.

We crossed the Aln and headed south. A convenient cycle track led to a sandy peninsula, described as a saltmarsh meadow. At the foot of Church Hill there was a ruined chapel, its four walls still standing, its roof missing. A pile of rubbish lay in the centre of the floor, along with an old fishing net and some logs. The chapel is neglected; it deserves better. At the top of Church Hill there's a fine view across the estuary to Alnmouth, showing off its neat houses and the spire of St John's Church. The cross on top of Church Hill is made of wood with a stone tablet at its base; the weatherworn inscription seems to say, 'Cuthbert, 684 AD'. This may allude to the Great Synod of Twyford, where St Cuthbert was selected as Bishop of Lindisfarne at a place called Adtwifyrdi, although no-one knows where this is. Was it here, perhaps? And could anyone actually say it?

We lingered, then made our way down to a path that threaded its way through the grassy dunes and emerged on to a, deserted beach. Ahead, five miles away, were the buildings of Amble, and offshore Coquet Island; on our left an empty sea, on our right dunes of soft sand; before us lay an empty beach. It was all too wonderful for words.

We walked close to the sea. There was no-one else, not a soul. A mile on was Birling Carrs, a rocky outcrop that had to be crossed to reach the beach on the other side. The rocks were black and slippery, made from a mixture of what appeared to be dolerite and sandstone, fashioned in the way nature intended. We took our time, watched where we put our feet. That was Alfred Wainwright's advice to walkers: watch where you are putting your feet. He was right. And it doesn't only apply to the Cumbrian fells.

We continued on the beach, noting the presence of wartime relics, those square-shaped concrete blocks, part-hidden and somehow not intrusive among the dunes. This would have been the perfect site for an invasion. Flat beach, on through the dunes to open country. Further on the beach widened and there were people, some of whom were suspended in the air on those kite things. There were strollers and dog walkers. It was cold but everyone was happy. A sandy path led inland to Warkworth and a grand sight, Warkworth Castle on its hill. We had time to spare so decided to explore the town, or village as it is, before seeking out our accommodation.

Everything was right at Warkworth. A sunny, spring afternoon, our approach to the town from the north, where we crossed a 14th century stone bridge to the main street rising to the splendid castle, 'one of the most exciting sequences of views one can have in England,' says Pevsner. The narrow bridge across the Coquet is one of the few in the country with a fortified gatehouse. The gatehouse, or tower, has a narrow arch through which, until 1965, all vehicles leaving Warkworth northward had to pass. Happily, the old bridge was spared when they built its modern replacement.

But *one of the most exciting sequences of views one can have in England?* That's one helluva claim, Mr Pevsner, sir. Other places meriting praise for architecture and 'sequences' come readily to my mind: several villages in the Cotswolds, the architecture and layout of Much Hadham in Hertfordshire, Hawkshead and the Vale of Grasmere in the Lake District, Cornish villages, piled up on hillsides above secret coves, tiny hamlets nestling in the Yorkshire Dales and the Chilterns; and many more in the wonderful country that is England, including Blanchland, here in Northumberland. You will no doubt identify many of your own. But, yes, I can see where Pevsner is coming from in Warkworth: the 'main street rising to the splendid castle' that stands atop its grassy mound, in spring awash with daffodils. The street is good; the castle makes the scene glorious.

St Laurence's Church, which is not even part of the scene described above, is Norman, with, internally, 'a display of richness directly derived from Durham Cathedral'. It has one of the few 12th century vaulted chancels in the country. The list of vicars dates back to 1110. A notice inside commemorated the twinning charter with 'Warkworth, Great Britain and Warkworth, New Zealand...Reciprocal links of friendship between the [two] peoples, with the goal that men and women may live together in peace and freedom...ratified 6 February, 1992'.

The church was the scene of a dreadful massacre in 1174, when the Scots, led by Earl Duncan, murdered men, women and children, possibly over 100, who had sought refuge inside. If, perchance, you favour spending time in quiet meditation in a church you may visit, do think of that and try, if you can, to understand the wickedness of such people. I've tried; it is beyond me utterly.

We wandered to the Market Cross, where James the Pretender was proclaimed as King of England at the start of the Jacobite rebellion of 1715. 'The army paused here on its way round Northumberland, recruiting for the Catholic cause and joined here a party from Scotland'. They included James and Charles Radcliffe, of Dilston. The Jacobites went to the church, where the vicar refused to conduct a service for them, riding off to inform the authorities at Newcastle instead.

The castle loomed, but that was for tomorrow.

***

Our guesthouse was typically cosy and welcoming, with our lady host, at breakfast, imparting to us an account of a recent exchange she had had with some 'tourist types' who had stayed there. It had been a rainy morning, with a bleak weather forecast. 'Where can we go today?' she was asked. 'You could go to Bamburgh and visit the Grace Darling museum,' she replied. A museum on a rainy day; a good idea. When, that evening, they returned, she naturally enquired if they went to the museum as she had suggested. 'On no,' she was told. 'We went to Bamburgh, but we couldn't see a grey starling museum anywhere.'

If any location was ideally suited for the site of a castle it was at Warkworth: atop a hill, surrounded on three sides by the natural loop of a river. It seems the first castle here was founded in 1139 by Henry, who was made an earl by his father, David I of Scotland. Little or nothing of it survives. Another was built in the time of Henry II. It was strengthened and became the Percies' home, and the castle at Alnwick became their fortress.

Warkworth Castle was the birthplace in 1364 of Sir Henry (Harry Hotspur) Percy, Northumberland's own Braveheart. It was here that Hotspur, with his father, plotted to set Henry Bolingbroke on the throne, events that feature in three scenes in Shakespeare's *Henry the Fourth*, which are set at Warkworth Castle. In the 1750s the Percies made Alnwick their family home and Warkworth fell into ruin.

Ruinous the castle is today, but this detracts not in the slightest from its appearance. It was another sunny, spring morn, ideal for exploration, as Kate and I climbed the hill and entered the castle by the Great Gate Tower. The central area is grassed, with fragments of buildings and surrounded by the curtain wall; but it's the keep that attracts, 'a work of architecture in the sense that both its mass and inner spaces are beautiful as well as useful…proving the genius of its designer in that it is at the same time a residence of considerable comfort'. (Pevsner). Outside the keep were several groups of young children, 5-year olds, chaperoned by kindly ladies to ensure they would enjoy their visit. How lucky they were, when one considers the 'inner city' kids less fortunate to come to places such as this.

This part of our journey was almost over, but not quite. For I had heard of the Hermitage, a 14th century religious place by the river. Descending from the castle we walked the riverbank for half a mile to find a boat waiting. The boatman rowed us across the river to a spot on the opposite bank, where a series of stone steps led to a ruined chapel, hewn from the solid sandstone rock of the cliff, a scene embowered in trees and hidden from the world. Here lived a hermit, whose prime duty was to pray for the well-being of his patrons. Several features have been carved from the rock: an altar, an ornate window, a south-facing window, the remains of stone figures, a doorway, some 19th century graffiti in Latin. The Hermitage was founded and paid for by the lords of the castle. It is a place unique in England.

The stone figures are that of a recumbent effigy of a woman, with her feet resting on an object bearing the coat of arms of the

House of Widdrington, and at her feet the figure of a man who kneels in sorrow or penitence. Legend has it that they are Isabel, daughter of the Lord of Widdrington, and Sir Bertram, the Lord of Bothal. She, knowing of Bertram's love, sent him a helmet, intimating that he should wear it and 'make as many fresh widows as possible' before she would consent to being his wife. Bertram, under the pretext that a Scots' raid was occurring over the border, went off only to return with a head-wound, probably inflicted by an axe.

Isabel, full of remorse, vowed to nurse her suitor back to health and set off with her brother for Bothal castle. She, alas, was captured by a Scottish suitor and carried off to an unknown location. Bertram and her brother resolved to find her, setting off in different directions. Bertram found the place where Isabel was detained, and saw her descending a ladder held by a young man. Thinking she had been unfaithful, Bertram drew his sword and attacked the man, not realising it was none other than her brother. Isabel, realising Bertram's folly, stepped between them, and was mortally wounded in the chest. Bertram was heartbroken at having killed the woman he loved, and retreated to the hermitage at Warkworth which he fashioned from the rocks in the manner we see today. And there he is, with Isabel, their misery captured in stone.

A sad tale; but sadness was far from our minds as the boatman ferried us across the river once again, after which we took the lovely riverside path back to the village, a scene enhanced by the magnificent sight of the castle, high above the trees.

Part VIII

Coquet to Tyne

When *Mauretania*, pride of the Tyne, passed by on its way to being scrapped in 1935, the folk of Amble waved and her crew declared the town to be the 'friendliest port' in England. Amble wasn't only a friendly port; it was a busy port, too, thanks to coal, mined locally and loaded onto ships at the wooden coal staiths for export, as well as fishing and ship-building and other industries.

I was alone for the final leg of my journey. Kate, alas, was working and in any case had not found the prospect of walking through much of what had been a major coalfield appealing, despite my assurances that it would all be worthwhile nevertheless. It was on a cold October evening when I checked in to my bed and breakfast and went walkabout.

I stood at the harbour and took stock. Here was the Coquet, first seen in Cheviot country and again at Warkworth. At the former the river had cut a dash through lovely Coquetdale; at the latter she was blissfully serene, a romantic place with the castle, in distant view to me now. On this cold autumnal evening the river looked sad, as though sorry after such a lovely journey to have regrettably reached the sea. One or two craft were moored midstream, as though reluctant to sail anywhere. A few people were abroad, braving the cold. It's hardly a tourist's mecca, but then Amble never pretended otherwise. It was a place of work, of purpose. Now there's no coal, no fishing, no 'other industries'.

I went to the town square, where nine flags fluttered from nine flagpoles: the inevitable EU ensign, two Union Jacks, the flags of England, Scotland, Italy, Sweden perhaps and others I failed to identify. Over 100 names are commemorated on the war memorials and there's a bench donated by the people of Amble 'to commemorate the 60th anniversary of VE and VJ Days'.

Two wartime incidents in Amble are worth noting. One occurred in 1940 when a German plane flew over the town and machine-gunned the streets. I wonder if the pilot, if he is alive today, thinks back to that incident and asks himself why he did that and what, precisely, he hoped to achieve. Would he care to come to Amble and explain himself? I doubt it.

Another concerns the Robson family. In December, 1943, Mr Robson, a farmer, was at home with his wife and children when a Stirling bomber crashed onto their farmhouse one foggy night on its approach to RAF Acklington. All five of the children, aged from 19 months to 9 years, died, along with six crew of the aircraft.

Imagine it if you will: the Robsons have got the kids to bed, and they have friends round for the evening, here, in Amble, a million miles from guns and bombs and things. Then bang! A British bomber crashes onto their house, killing their children, all of them. Mr and Mrs Robson, and two friends, who were all downstairs, and the tail gunner of the aircraft, survived. What a tragedy. And if, perchance, you would care to know the names of the children who died in their beds that night, take a walk to a modern housing estate just outside town, where the streets are named after them. I was going there tomorrow, straight after my morning fryup.

***

Breakfast. I'm wearing shorts, just I have done every step of the way from Tynemouth. It's disconcerting, therefore, to see a chap scraping the ice from his car windscreen. Still, there's nothing like getting moving to warm oneself up.

It was sunny morning, with clear skies; hence the frost. The road I took led to a roundabout on the A1068 where I chanced on a pile of twisted metal plates, one of which vaguely resembled a fish. Art, y'see. Foisted on to and paid for by the taxpayer. This one was in the proverbial middle of nowhere, meriting not so much as a glance by the odd motorist who sped past, even though, unusually, a chap wearing shorts and a silly hat graced the scene. Which reminded me: a statue awaited my discerning eye later today, offshore at Newbiggin, a man and a woman, standing on a plinth 300 yards off the coast. I could hardly wait.

The streets I searched for are opposite a school situated on the B6345. The main road through the estate is Robson's Way; the others, named after the children who died that night, are: Sheila's Close, Marjory's Close, Sylvia's Close, Ethel's Close and Williams Close. That should be William's Close, except they omitted the apostrophe, on at least one of the street signs anyway. This suggests a family called Williams rather than a boy's Christian name. And it should be Marjery's Close, if the headstone in the cemetery is accurate. Pedantic? I don't think so. Rather it highlights again the need for correct spelling and punctuation.

To prove my point, is Robson's Way dedicated to one member of the family, or, more likely, all of them, meaning all the children, and maybe Mr and Mrs Robson too, in which case shouldn't it be Robsons' Way? Personally I think Robson Way more appropriate, but that's just my opinion. It's good the names are commemorated here, but a lacking in correct spelling and punctuation is both sad and disrespectful.

The road through the estate – Robson's Way, as it is – led to a right of way leading back to Amble. It passed an avenue of sycamores and a low wall with the iron railings removed. The town cemetery was on the left. I walked broadside on to rows of tall, regimented headstones, all at attention, like soldiers. Every one marks a life or lives. Some looked old, yet were tended with fresh flowers. Cemetery and road were covered with recently fallen sycamore leaves.

There were allotments and pigeon lofts, a reminder, if one were needed, that I was in the North East. I ended up back in town, Warkworth Castle in view, ensign flying proudly. At Queen Street there were shops and banks and business premises. Two old ladies chatted. 'They've ruined this place,' one was saying. I didn't wait to find out what, precisely, was ruined, but all in all, I would like to say, Amble, if that's what she meant, looked OK to me. Back at the harbour seagulls perched on lamp-posts, with 'Look at me' gestures. I wonder why we don't eat them; there are plenty.

Leaving town the path led across undulating grassy links. At Hauxley were wooden dwellings, one I would estimate as no more than 18 ft by 12 ft. Some folk have bigger kitchens but nowhere near as good a view. At Low Hauxley a quiet byroad ran south, ending at a little church and a row of old terraced houses, the sort of place you'd never find unless you were on foot. A footpath continues to Druridge Bay, over six miles of sand backed by dunes. This stretch of the coast is superb. It lies in its natural state, despite the intrusion of man over the years. I remember my only previous visit here, in 1962. The lasting impression in my mind was the sheer length of the beach.

I had a choice: to walk on the footpath on the landward side of the dunes, or the beach. I decided six miles of sand was too far and time was pressing; I had to make Newbiggin today. And anyway I wanted to see the land that was reclaimed from the former opencast coal mining area, and the birdlife. I had the place to myself, save for meeting two young women, then three men and a dog. The latter saw me talking into my dictaphone as I approached, and collectively gave me an odd look. 'Ye divven't work for the DHSS, d'yer?' one asked. Maybe he thought I was recording my thoughts about three skivers. 'Yes,' I replied, just to keep them on their toes. Hopefully they called at the Job Centre, just in case.

It was a grey day now, although streaks of sunshine pierced the clouds over the sea, casting long streaks of silver on the flat surface. At one point three people sat together at the water's edge, perched on small stools, with fishing rods optimistically angled at 45 degrees. Not a bad way to spend the day. Dunno about catching any fish though.

I came to Ladyburn Lake, part of a country park. There was one of those national cycling network columns, 'one of a thousand funded by the Royal Bank of Scotland'. The column had holes where once there would have been coloured discs. Haven't they worked out yet that kids nick them within three weeks of the poles being erected? Behind a fence were four highland cattle, long-horned and shaggy-headed. One of them peered at me through a long straggly fringe. He looked docile. I wouldn't want to encounter one that wasn't.

This wonderful landscape was reclaimed from the scars of coal mining: today there are long grasses, small lakes, all teeming with life, and birds and insects, unseen to the passer-by. There were a few strange-looking huts with slits in the walls, observation hides presumably, and one or two *homo sapiens* carrying cameras. At a point roughly halfway along the Bay I cut through the dunes to the beach. The sand was almost white, and so fine.

A few of those old wartime concrete blocks lay scattered on the beach, almost covered with sand and long, straggly grass. The only sound was the gentle lapping of the small breakers. I lingered, reluctant to leave. When I did I came to a T-junction, where, just over a stone wall near the corner, was a small, tumbledown cairn. A plate with inscription read: 'In 1986 after 17 years of opposition, plans to build a nuclear power station south of here were abandoned'.

The plan to build the power station was abandoned due to changes in government policy on nuclear power, or just as likely no policy, and possibly pressure by those who campaigned against it, either because they didn't want a massive nuclear plant occupying the landscape, or their objection to nuclear power at all. I admire those who campaign against 'big brother' projects, such as the erection of ghastly wind turbines that blight England's otherwise beautiful landscape to no particular gain. We had unsightly pit heaps once, but coal mines were functional and the pit heaps have been removed or landscaped.

I wonder about the wisdom of campaigning against nuclear power, though. There are nuclear power stations all over Europe; what difference would a few more in England make? The only sense in banning nuclear power would be if they were all banned, including abroad. And to those who object to them I say: if you switch on your lights and television and boil your kettle and use a computer, if you want businesses and jobs to thrive, we have to have electricity. If we phase out coal-fired power stations, as we are in the name of global warming, and we don't build nuclear, the only option will be to buy our electricity from abroad at whatever price they charge. So I lament the failure to build a nuclear power plant here; it would have provided work with plenty room left for the flora and fauna – although, let it be said, there may be scope to build one elsewhere, on the former Cambois power station site, say. If we have them they have to be somewhere.

Further on, on a quiet road running adjacent to the beach, I came upon what appeared to be a derelict house at the roadside (map ref 283947). But this was no ordinary dwelling; where there should have been windows there were slits in the walls. It may have been 'ordinary' once, but it had been cleverly converted to a strategically-sited pill box. I stepped inside and found myself looking through one of the slits. Imagine it: Gerry has landed on the beach and now here he is motoring along the road; there's a house ahead but no sign of Tommy when *kapow!!* Tommy's in the house and he isn't firing welcome messages.

At Cresswell there was a shop, where I sat outside in the cold and had an ice cream. Oh, I know how to live well. From where I sat I could see the 14th century pele tower, formerly the home of one of Northumberland's oldest families, the Cresswells. A house was built onto the tower, but was demolished in the 19th century. Here lived the White Lady (another one). It's said she saw her Danish lover murdered on the beach by her brothers, so she starved herself to death.

Another lady, a real one, was Bella Brown, who lived at Cresswell. One wild winter's night in 1876 Bella was at home when she chanced to look out of the window to see a Swedish steamer, *Gustav*, foundering on the rocks. The nearest lifeboat was at Newbiggin. Bella went there directly, but her journey, on foot, was far from straightforward as she struggled for miles along the shore, wading through swollen rivers and clambering over slippery rocks before reaching the lifeboat station. Thanks to her, most of the crew was saved. Her heroics were every bit as dashing and commendable as Grace Darling's nearly forty years before. I know of no monument to Bella. Shouldn't there be?

Beyond Cresswell were some old cottages, protected on their lofty position by the Scars, a long, rocky reef that protrudes out to sea. I could hear the breakers pounding away below. Ahead were the chimneys of the Alcan plant and the wide sweep of Lynemouth Bay and, in the distance, I fancied, the spire of Newbiggin church. By the roadside were more of the concrete blocks left over from the war. I suppose the good folk of Northumberland are stuck with them for good. Twenty or so horses grazed contentedly in a field. I was feeling footsore; a horse would have been handy.

A huge sign by the roadside proclaimed the derelict land hereabouts to be 'reclaimed', thanks to a 'project' by too many organisations to list. Suffice to say the EU flag was depicted and the organisations were taxpayer funded. The date of completion was years before I happened along, yet the land was still derelict. What happened to the project? If the derelict land is an eyesore, it's made worse by the ruddy sign.

Two men with fishing gear stood at the roadside, waiting for a lift. They told me the Alcan plant was still operational, but Lynemouth pit was closed. And here lies a story.

The Alcan aluminium smelter was built in 1972. To meet the electricity demand to power the site a new coal fired power station was built less than half a mile from the smelter, 'the most thermally efficient coal fired power station in the UK'. Coal was supplied locally, from Lynemouth and Ellington collieries. The collieries were a major factor in choosing the site for the smelter. Sensible so far. Unfortunately Ellington colliery had to close when it flooded. That left Lynemouth, plus coal brought in by lorry from drifts around the county. But Lynemouth colliery closed too, along with all other deep-shaft pits in Northumberland – and everywhere else in the UK; so now they have to *import* coal into Blyth from Russia to fuel the smelter. That's Russia supplying coal to Northumberland, where they've closed the pits. Still sensible? I haven't finished…

In 2004 permission was granted to use biomass fuels at the plant: sawdust and wood pellets, mixed in with coal. The station's staff won an award in health and safety, presented by the Royal Society for the Prevention of Accidents (RoSPA) at the Hilton Hotel, Birmingham. However, the future of the smelter and power station are under threat thanks to the EU, who claim Alcan is in breach of its operating licence as it has 'failed to significantly reduce emissions'. They've lost the coalmines, now they may lose the power station and smelter. France, a country I visit, has coal-fired power stations burning merrily away. Are France's coal-fired power stations under threat too? Perhaps by the time you are reading this, the situation may have changed – except that of France's power stations, of course.

The road crossed the Lyne, then turned north-west, in effect around the Alcan smelter and power station. In Lynemouth I passed the Miners Welfare Institute. I remember the Miners Welfare Institutes; every mining community had one. But then we had miners and their families to use them. Later a sign told me I was entering Wansbeck District, 'Twinned with Schalksmuhle and Remscheid'. I wonder how many council taxpayers in Wansbeck District know or care where these places are (Germany), and what, if any, benefit they gain by paying for or towards 'Cross-cultural exchange, celebration of diversity, international friend-ship and civic participation'. Is it value for money? Wouldn't their money be better spent on good causes? I can think of plenty: Hospice at Home, injured soldiers returning home from Afghanistan, the NSPCC, to name a few only. Or filling in potholes in our neglected roads.

A right of way traversed the 'grounds' of the power station. I kept going, curious to see the power station at close quarters. The path led to higher ground, where I looked down at a handful of men working beside rectangular-shaped tanks containing what appeared to water, or in one case, sand. A young fellow stood beside one of the tanks, holding a shovel. Another pushed a wheelbarrow containing a sludge-like substance. He tipped it into another wheelbarrow, which another man pushed to one of the tanks with water in it. What were they doing? I don't know. But from my position of advantage I felt like a spy in a James Bond movie. I moved on.

I tried to reach the sea, but was obliged to negotiate my way through a wasteland marked 'dunes' on the map. Man has made a mess of this place; he should put it right. This is, or was, an industrial site; it's good that men were employed here, but it ought not to be abandoned. My footsteps led to a golf course with a sign: Tee No 7. Par 4. 364 yards. There were some concrete bunker-like structures among the dunes. Leftovers from the war perhaps? Graffiti laced their cold walls: 'Hot Dogs'; 'Fuck the Law'. I glanced back to see a thin, wispy trail of smoke emanating from the tip of the power station chimney, a sort of defiant gesture that seemed to say, 'I'm still working'. Aye, but for how much longer?

My folks had friends who always holidayed at Newbiggin. Every year there'd be a postcard from 'Newbiggin-by-the-Sea', with a picture of the church and its distinctive spire. I was here now, at the church, where I cast a curious eye out to sea to catch sight of the statue of the couple on their plinth, but it was too far away to pass judgement.

Standing on this headland, away from the town, St Bartholomew's dates back to the 13th century. I was curious to see inside, which Pevsner describes as 'archaeologically fascinating'. Alas, life's full of disappointments. Locked, it was. Barred to the visitor. Out of bounds. *Tant pis!* There was always the churchyard to explore. It's huge. Well kept. No laid-down headstones here. Near the main door a solid headstone marked the graves of three children who died between 1865 and 1880, a reminder of the high mortality rate then; but their names are immortal, inscribed in stone. Another marked the resting place of 'Robert, beloved husband of Ann Brown of Newbiggin, who died March 29, 1908, aged 57'. His epitaph:

> Affliction sore, long time I bore,
> Physicians were in vain;
> Till God thought fit to take me home
> And ease me of my pain.

Ann Brown died in 1925, seventeen years after her husband.

Near the churchyard was a granite stone, with the inscription: 'Beneath this stone lies a time capsule containing mementoes of 20th century life in poems, pictures and writing created by children from Newbiggin-by-the-Sea The capsule is to be opened in 100 years' time'. The date was 9th September 2000. I'd love to be there when it's opened, but I don't think it's likely.

I headed for the promenade. The farther I walked, the better the view of the statue, or 'artwork'. Anyway, at a point exactly behind it, by the promenade wall, I looked directly at the man and woman occupying the plinth, looking out to sea. Well, it's different. I had read that the sculptor was 'inspired by the view', but I wonder if anyone in authority considers others might be inspired by the view *without* the statue.

My B&B was directly behind me, and as I climbed the stairs I had an even better view through the window. The perfect view, in fact, for now the plinth aligned with the horizon; the couple were standing on the horizon, that's how it appeared. If they had built the plinth that little bit lower this would have been the view from the promenade. My verdict would have been: good statue but too high (slightly). But then I understand the height of the plinth is set so that the couple are seen apparently standing on the sea at high tide, so maybe they got it right after all.

I hit the town that night; had a few beers and an Indian. Does you good to have a pint or three from time to time (if you can afford it these days). There were signs once, saying, 'Guinness is good for you.' Who could argue? But my favourite sign extolling the virtues of alcohol hangs on the wall, not prominently for some reason, in a pub in Cumbria: 'Beer. Helping ugly people to have sex since 1862'.

***

To maximise guests' views of 'Couple', my host had provided binoculars, a thoughtful gesture as the view from my window looked directly at the statue. He stands with his arms by his sides and wears a shirt, jeans and a flat cap; she has long, black hair and wears a white cardy and tight, blue jeans; her hands are thrust into her pockets. 'Lovely arse' I told my dictaphone. Since my visit I've seen close-up photographs of the statue. The facial features of the two figures are superbly crafted, but as they look seaward no-one can see them. That's a pity, but as the statue's creator said he 'wanted to create an air of mystery' we can consider he succeeded.

The rocks on which the statue stands form a breakwater, constructed to protect Newbiggin's beach. Full marks for the work that's gone on here. Time and tide had eroded the beach so much that a renovation scheme was necessary to recreate a new one. To do this, 500,000 tons of sand was 'imported' from the Lincolnshire coast and pumped ashore to create the new beach at Newbiggin. The breakwater should protect it from further erosion. I just hope the beaches in Lincolnshire are OK.

The vantage point at my window afforded excellent views. On a fresh autumnal morn the beach was deserted. At breakfast I was introduced by my host to two men whom, she said, were Estonian teachers doing a 'cultural thing' in England, whilst their English counterparts went to Estonia. Their English and manners were exemplary. I stepped outside to see dog walkers now occupying the beach along with their charges, including a small white mongrel that pissed here, there and anywhere on the lovely new sand. Give me strength!

I wandered through the town to the Memorial Park, a war memorial opened by the Duke of Kent in 2005. The park is tastefully enclosed within iron railings and a wall. There are trees and flowerbeds and lawns. An inscription in stone reads: 'To the glorious memory of the men of Newbiggin-by-the-Sea who made the supreme sacrifice in the Great War'. In fact, the dead of both wars are commemorated. From the park I took the Woodhorn Trail, into open country. As I progressed I could see the winding wheels of a colliery. It had been a long time since I had seen such a sight; but I knew I was looking at Woodhorn Mining museum. That's where I was going.

Woodhorn Colliery was a working mine from 1894 until 1981. It was one of five pits of the Ashington Coal Company, which at its peak employed over 10,000 men. Entering the museum site one is greeted by the sight of a new building with a roof 'inspired by the monster coal cutting machines' once used underground, and a statue of a pitman holding a miner's lamp, erected in memory of fellow workmen who lost their lives in the Woodhorn Colliery explosion of 13 August, 1916, a reminder of the dangers routinely faced by coal miners everywhere.

'Routine' was what thirteen miners were doing when they died in an explosion deep underground that killed some outright, whilst others died soon afterwards due to gas. It reminds me that when Dad went to work Mam's last words were always, 'Take care of yourself.' I thought it was no more than a phrase, but over 60 miners were killed at North Walbottle Colliery, where he worked, through stone falls, being hit by wagons or explosions.

Today, at Woodhorn, I stood on a concrete plug at the top of one of the mineshafts. A notice said it was 888 feet to the bottom of the shaft, 'the height of the Eiffel Tower', it added, to ensure you get the picture. Another said that coal 'drove the railways, powered our navy, fed our factories, warmed our hearths'. It could still, except they've closed the pits and those who would claim to know say coal-burning power stations harm the atmosphere, causing global warming. I'm not convinced, and until the case is proved 'beyond reasonable doubt', as they say, I see no reason why coal shouldn't be mined in Northumberland pits to fuel power stations.

We've lost the miners, but not the miners' art, to be found in a special part of the museum at Woodhorn. Here are images of the men, naked in their baths, their houses with smoking chimneys, their families, their dogs; the pit heaps. The artists are the miners themselves, men whose paintings tell the story. Stark, grey, grim: I saw these scenes, or some of them, as a kid myself. The artwork at Woodhorn was brilliant!

There was a bus stop, complete with bus, at the museum. I hopped aboard for Ashington.

Ashington is a town, surely. Nevertheless, when coal mining was at its peak it was known as the 'largest pit village in the world'. Whatever, Ashington remains largely unchanged, or so it appeared to me, with its grid-rows of terraced houses and back yards. To me they are synonymous with 'community'; everyone knew one's neighbours, kids played footy in the street. Do they still? Or have television and playstations taken their place? And has the closure of the mines, all of them, destroyed 'community'? I remember Ashington had more workingmen's clubs than pubs. Many miners, my dad among them, refused to drink in a public house. It was always 'the club' with his marras.

Talking of footy, a statue of a true 'local hero' stands in the now-pedestrianised main street at Ashington: Jackie Milburn. He signed for Newcastle United in 1943, turning up for a trial with borrowed football boots, and played for Newcastle and no other club throughout his career, scoring 200 goals and winning three FA Cup winners medals in the '50's. He played a few times for England too; I'm certain it would have been lots more if he'd played for a London club.

I saw Jackie play, but I was too young to recall much. He was my idol, if only because of a striking picture of him in one of my football books. I had my Newcastle United strip and wasn't content until I'd gone to the local rec and rolled about in the mud in front of old, rusting iron goalposts, a necessary duty before driving the ball into an imaginary net. Kids are influenced by their heroes. I don't think I ever 'dived'. I bet Jackie didn't.

There's a story – I don't know if it's true – about a meeting between Wor Jackie and Cardinal Basil Hume, the head of the Roman Catholic Church in England, a Geordie and (naturally) a Newcastle United fan. When they met, they stood in awe of one another until they agreed on an 'autograph'. Both men then stood in silence for a moment, each expecting the other to sign. Of course, we know it was Basil who wanted Jackie's autograph. Wasn't it?

I hung around awhile. Went for a cuppa. I wondered what the men do for work in Ashington, now that the mines have closed. Quite a few occupied the town centre. Once they would have worked down the pit. One fellow was working: a busker strummed a guitar by Jackie's statue. He wore a bushy beard and rabbit's ears and tried unsuccessfully to sing. He was dreadful but he was there so I watched him awhile before heading for a place on the map named Riverside Park. As I left the town centre I noticed a lamp standard with a long, narrow poster hanging from it. It carried a message from Northumbria Police: 'We've got our eyes on criminals'. A pair of enormous eyes stared out from the poster. I'm sure its presence will scare any would-be wrongdoers to death.

A 20-minute walk led to the Wansbeck where a right of way led along the riverbank. The river was wider than I had imagined, with plenty of swans and mallards enjoying a peaceful lifestyle. I encountered a few people, everyone saying 'hello'. I glanced back to see if they were looking back at the unusual sight of a man wearing shorts on a cold day and carrying a rucksack in Ashington. They were. There were old people, youngsters on bikes, women pushing kids in pushchairs. Finally I left the river and climbed through some woods, the ground here covered with autumn's recently fallen leaves. I crossed the A1068, then open country, after which I found myself on the quiet road that leads down to Bothal.

Bothal lies in a wooded hollow, out of sight, out of mind, a proverbial million miles from the rest of the world. The village is barely more than a single street, whose former estate cottages I passed on the way to the church. Tucked out of sight among trees by the roadside is the war memorial. There wasn't enough room to fit all the names on the front, so they went round to the sides: 35 for the Great War, 22 for World War II.

You will have noticed my inclusion in this book of many war memorials. I always acknowledge the debt we owe to men who died for our freedom. Thanks to them I believe I have lived my life at a good time, the best time, maybe. Educated in the 50s, obtained work when there was plenty in the 60s, never had to fight in a war myself and enjoyed a steady increase in the standard of living in this country when ordinary people could buy and furnish their own homes, buy a car, travel. Our forebears were not so fortunate. But in recent times we have experienced erosion of freedom through draconian laws, the threat of terrorism and corruption unparalleled in public life, including in Parliament itself, and the ceding of democracy to the rule of an undemocratic and corrupt superstate.

The worst single event was the ratification of the European Treaty by a British prime minister without asking the British people, despite an election pledge to do otherwise. Members of Parliament do not own us; nor do they own our liberty. If they wanted to hand our liberty, our democracy, to unelected people they should have asked our permission in a referendum. Our soldiers, airmen and seamen fought for the Britain I had as a child and throughout my working life, not the Britain of today, which is no longer a sovereign state; nor, I suggest, would they have wanted the Britain of today. But I live in hope that things will improve. We can begin by becoming a democracy again, governing ourselves and thus becoming masters of our own destiny. I will let the matter rest with Tennyson's words which, I suggest, appertain directly to the England our forces fought and died for: 'A land of settled government, a land of old and just renown…'.

Where was I? In Bothal, where St Andrew's Church has a handsome belfry with three bells, and yew trees guard the entrance to the churchyard. Sadly, the locked door to the church guards against visitors, so I was obliged to explore the churchyard only. One headstone bore the name of Agnes Rogers, village postmistress here for 46 years; another the name of Vera, 'a gay, tender, courageous woman'. As I sat by the war memorial a young lass on horseback approached, riding slowly, as though part of another time. I wandered along the private drive to the castle gatehouse, just to take a peek. In fact, the castle, which is built on a spur above the river, is best seen from the road on leaving the village.

A quarter of a mile along the road led to the woods by the Wansbeck. I went down to the river: three miles to Morpeth. On a grand afternoon I walked on carpets of leaves, heard the music of the river, at times flowing quickly, at times still, with leaves floating on the surface, little flotillas going nowhere in particular. It was cold. There was no birdsong. But, rest assured, all was well with my world.

The path passed beneath a spectacular railway viaduct, high above the gorge. It led to the main road, the A197, which I crossed and entered more woods. Here the leaves were ankle-deep. I kicked them as I walked, and sang Mark Wynter's song: 'I'm kicking up the leaves...' Remember that one? 1960. Not that long ago, eh.

I checked into my accommodation, being interrogated in full hearing of other guests. It felt like checking into prison. Name? Address? What time would you like breakfast and stand to attention when I'm talking to you. Later I wandered into town and leant on the railing by a mini-roundabout near the clock tower. Traffic raced to the roundabout and whizzed round it apace, vehicles just missing each other, their approach timed to perfection. Everyone was in a hurry; no quarter was given, save to give way (just) to the car on the right. I was watching a speeded-up movie, Morpeth's version of the Keystone Cops.

Then I saw them: two polises. No, not on their feet. C'mon. In vans. As I moved my position around the town centre they kept appearing, going to 'jobs' I suppose. Here, there, everywhere. Fire Brigade policing at its worst. They were working hard, probably the only two officers on duty in town and beyond.

There's nowt wrong with the officers. It's the system. What happened to the man on patrol? Rendezvous with the sergeant, and have you checked your property, constable? What happened to the policeman we could talk to and ask what the time was?

***

Morning at the mini-roundabout. Traffic whizzed, late night revellers giving way to early morning commuters. The same people the morning after the night before, probably. According to John Leland, Morpeth was 'a far fayrar towne than Alnwicke'. If it was then, perhaps it is now, so arguably it should be the county town as it claims. I find Morpeth a pleasing place, mini-roundabouts notwithstanding. The name, it seems, is in dispute, possibly deriving from 'moor path' or maybe 'murder path', however unlikely the latter. Still, what's in a name? There's a place in Morayshire, Scotland, called Maggieknocklater. Where did they get that one from, then? Who was Maggie, why had she to knock later and who was asking her to?

The clock tower at Morpeth probably dates back to the 17th century, one of only two of the type in England I believe (the other being at St Albans, in Hertfordshire). It served as a gaol until after 1800. Maybe drunks were locked up here to sober up before being kicked out next morning. Good idea. Saves all that paperwork. Oldgate runs from behind the clock tower. It's a quiet street and here, on the right, is Collingwood House, the home of Cuthbert, he of the statue at Tynemouth. He moved here when he married the daughter of the mayor of Newcastle, spending just one year's leave at home in the seventeen years between 1793 and 1810. Collingwood once wrote: 'How I long to have a peep into my own home and walk in my own garden'. He never saw it after Trafalgar (1805).

The main bridge in Morpeth, built 1829-31, is accredited to Telford; but Hodgson, Northumberland's historian, says that although Telford chose the site and supervised the work, John Dobson designed it. It carried the A1 before the town was bypassed. Not far away an iron footbridge stands on the foundations of a previous, medieval bridge, which was so dangerous the mailcoach knocked away the parapet and fell into the river. The riverside path below could be better; nettles and weeds growing wild when I visited.

From the bridge it's a short walk to the strangely-named Ha' Hill, the mound upon which Morpeth's first castle was built, probably a wooden stockade. It's within Carlisle Park, where you can walk in solitude among pleasant gardens and climb steeply to the second castle, probably built in the 13th century. The gatehouse and some sections of curtain wall remain. This castle was held by the Scots during the Civil War, but was captured for the king after a 20-day siege, after which it was described as a 'ruinous hole'.

South of the castle is the 14th century St Mary's Church. Described by Pevsner as 'a picturesque sight', this is an understatement. St Mary's stands splendidly behind trees on rising ground known as Kirkhill. The church is big, and quite magnificent inside. It was the parish church until the 1840s, when attendances fell, probably due to its location: a mile out of town, on high ground, difficult for parishioners to get to in winter. Another church, St James's, was built to replace it.

There are too many medieval artefacts to describe here; suffice to say it is worth anyone's visit, as is the enormous churchyard: there's the 'watch house', built to house those guarding the graves against body snatchers, and the memorial to Emily Wilding Davison, the suffragette, who went to prison for the cause she believed in, and apparently died for it when she fell under the hoofs of a horse at the Epsom Derby on 4th June 1913.

Emily Davison was born in London, but her parents were both Northumbrians. Her cause was a commendable one: better opportunities for women and the right for women to vote, in keeping with the suffragettes' belief that being denied the vote made women second-class citizens Of privileged stock, Davison joined the Women's Social and Political Unit (WSPU), founded by Emmeline Pankhurst. But where extreme measures were necessary to get the political establishment to take notice, Davison's conduct resulted in imprisonment for criminal activity.

Her first sentence, one month for attempting to hand a petition to Herbert Asquith, the Prime Minister, was hardly likely to hurt anyone; and when she hid in a cupboard in the Palace of Westminster overnight to claim that she could give her place of residence as the House of Commons, no-one was liable to get hurt. But thereafter her conduct was violent: throwing stones at a car taking David Lloyd George to a meeting, setting fire to letterboxes and, worst of all, a violent attack on a vicar in the mistaken belief he was Lloyd George. In prison she went on hunger strike and threw herself down an iron staircase.

Davison's conduct proved to be self-defeating, so much so that many of the suffragettes themselves thought she was making their cause worse, not better, and members of the public regarded her as a sort of fanatic. She was obviously a determined woman, but what she had in mind when she stepped onto Epsom racecourse on Derby day is not known. In any event, as most of the field galloped by, Davison appeared from behind the guardrail and deliberately stepped in front of the King's horse, Anmer, The horse struck her with full force and fell to the ground, throwing off its jockey and seriously injuring Davison who died four days later. She was forty years old. It seems she may have been trying to plant a flag on the horse so that when it crossed the finishing line it would be flying the flag of the suffragette cause, but no-one can be certain.

Whatever she was about, Emily Davison paid for her actions with her life. Thousands of suffragettes, dressed in white, paid their respects as her coffin was taken to King's Cross station in London, from where it was taken to Morpeth. The inscription on her memorial, 'Deeds not Words', is a fitting epitaph for someone who had courage and determination. Whether these commendable qualities were always best applied is open to question. She was a foolish woman; there were better ways to further her cause.

Lingering in Morpeth had taken up much time. So I caught the bus to Bedlington. I've got a bus pass and, make no mistake, I use it, even though the photograph makes me look like someone who's just escaped from Durham prison.

Until 1844 Bedlington was the capital of Bedlingtonshire, in the County Palatine of Durham. Bedlington was an agricultural village until they built an ironworks, then, from 1870, the coal industry became the main employer.

I headed directly for the town cemetery. I considered, as a retired policeman, I could not perambulate Northumberland without visiting the granite memorial 'erected by the officers and men of the Northumberland County Constabulary' to the two policemen murdered on Tuesday, 15 April, 1913, shot dead by John Vickers Amos: Constable George Bertram Mussell and Sergeant Andrew Barton.

Jocker Amos, as he was known, was licensee of the Sun Inn, Bedlington, and when told he was being evicted he sent his son to the shop to buy some cartridges for his shotgun and refused to quit the premises, even as his replacement and his wife, Mr and Mrs Grice, were waiting to take up occupation. PC Mussell attended where he confronted Amos and tried to reason with him. Amos's response was to discharge both barrels of the gun into the constable's chest, killing him instantly. Amos then shot Mrs Grice, despite her pleading for her life.

Outside, Sergeant Barton heard the shots. Despite the danger he went inside where he urged Amos to give himself up. Amos shot him dead on the spot. Amos fled, but was found hiding in a culvert. At his trial the jury took just eight minutes to find him guilty of murder. When asked by the judge if he had anything to say, he replied, 'I don't remember anything. They [the policemen] were good friends to me.' That he was not in control of his senses when he murdered three people seems certain, and over 60,000 people signed a petition asking the home secretary to commute the sentence, but Amos was hanged in Newcastle that July. I pass no judgement, save to say how easy it is for those who have access to firearms to kill, as we have seen in recent years, notably at Hungerford, Dunblane and West Cumberland, and more recently still in those infamous events in the Northumbria Police area that culminated at Rothbury. Without a firearm none of these men could have murdered so many people.

I went down Front Street, to the Trotter memorial, a fountain 'erected by public subscription to the memory of Dr James Trotter who died in Bedlington, July 8, 1899'. Dr Trotter was a county councillor who worked hard to improve living conditions, including the improvement of water supplies and sanitation: 'Loved by the poor and respected by his political opponents'. The latter headed a public subscription list to erect the fountain in his memory. Typically, the fountain was dry, despite Dr Trotter's 'improvement of water supplies'. How ironic.

Further down the street is an obelisk, the Market Cross, 'thought to have been erected here in 1782 and used as a public gathering place for political speakers in Victorian times'. Nearby Piggly Wiggly's was well-popular, with the locals queueing for their coffee and sarnies. Popular with me too, before setting off for Blyth. On the way I passed the aforementioned Sun Inn. My greatest memory of Front Street is its width and its trees. Bedlington's a canny place.

Bedlington once hosted the Miners Gala, an annual festivity of brass bands, and banners representing the various lodges. There were speeches by miners' leaders. People wore their Sunday best clothes. The men had a wee drop of beer. Everyone had a good time. That's what mining communities did; let their hair down once a year, and who could blame 'em? Now the coalmines have gone. Other work, maybe, has replaced it; but not all of it. Time moves on. Things change. But I still can't get my head round Mr Hesletine saying we didn't need coal when now it's being imported.

The road led down to the river, which is crossed here by a bridge of 1996. It's built in stone, 'old style'. They made a good job of it. Inevitably, graffiti adorned its parapet. Such a shame to see something so aesthetically designed defaced by small minds. A good path led through the woods, the river looking small considering it's only about a mile or so to the estuary, then the sea. The sun came out. There wasn't a soul about as the path climbed steeply above a gorge, the river snaking lazily below. And then I saw, ahead, what appeared to be two people. But no, it was Janus.

Janus turned out to be two 'half people', made of steel, whose heads face opposite ways. The work of the sculptor, Peter Burke, Janus is named after the Roman god of gates and beginnings and endings. 'The sculpture is located on the site of the Bedlington Ironworks (1736-1867) and symbolises the change throughout Wansbeck, looking back to traditional industry, such as coal mining, and looking forward to a greener environment, with new parks and open spaces...It conjures up the way in which the character and values of the communities and individuals have been moulded by the industries of the area'.

The sculpture makes one stop and hopefully reflect that here, for over a hundred and thirty years, men worked in the ironworks in the conditions of that time. Today all was peaceful. It was as though there had never been anything here but trees and birdsong. Janus reminds us otherwise.

The path led down to the river, which I crossed to be greeted by a sign: 'Welcome to the Borough of Blyth Valley, twinned with Solingen (Germany), Ratingen and Gelendzhik (Russia)'. More cultural exchange visits! The river had turned into an estuary now. The tide was out, leaving a huge expanse of black slurry as a riverbank. Further on were old, rotting jetties sticking out of the mud. Mud isn't pleasant to look at but that doesn't mean it's no use. As the information board said, it's mud that makes the Blyth estuary so important. There were images of oystercatcher, redshank, cormorant, curlew, and ragworms and lugworms. 'Mudflats may seem bleak, inhospitable environments. Only the wormcasts provide clues to the creatures that lurk beneath the surface...'.

Further on, where the estuary widens, a number of small craft was moored midstream, including cobles and pleasure boats. I was reminded of the two occasions I was taken out to sea from Blyth to go fishing. There were four of us. This chap had a 22-foot boat complete with engine, which drove us offshore for a couple of miles. I was OK until he switched the motor off. From that point we would simply drift, rising and falling on the swell, our fishing lines dangling in the water, angling for fish we could not fail to catch. A hook without bait was enough for cod or mackerel to swallow, and there were plenty of them. Why I wanted to catch fish in the first place escapes me, except to take one or two home and give the rest to the neighbours (we didn't have the luxury of a freezer). This was all very well, but as the boat rolled with the swell my stomach, my entire insides in fact, couldn't cope. I spent the first half hour or so vomiting over the side, the remainder of the day retching, with nothing left to bring up. 'Look at the Alcan chimneys,' I was told, the idea being to take my mind off the sea. It did no good. How I ever went for a second dose I don't know. I didn't venture a third.

Today two tall derricks came into view. There was a boatyard. Across the harbour was a tanker, being loaded by a crane that turned slowly, like a strange, prehistoric beast, before opening its jaws to deposit a sand-like substance into the hold. Blyth Harbour still functions.

Blyth grew through coal. There were coalmines in the area, and coal was exported from Blyth. In the late 19th century Blyth developed as a shipbuilding port, and in 1914 the Royal Navy's first *Ark Royal* was launched here. The harbour also served as a submarine base in both world wars. Blyth power station was also part of the industrial scene. But then came change: the power station was demolished, the mines closed, shipbuilding disappeared. It still has its 'industrial estates', and the onshore and offshore wind turbines. Industrially, Blyth is a shadow of its former self. But then, industrially, so is England.

I walked as far as I could by the estuary before turning inland for the town centre. It was market day and the square was a-busy. Lots of young men stood on the pavement. Time was they would have been working down the pits, or at the harbour, or maybe in the shipyards. I lingered, reflecting on the three former industrial towns I had visited in the past two days: Ashington, Bedlington and Blyth. From being the 'workshop of the world', England has become, or is becoming, an industrial desert, with modern goods being manufactured elsewhere: China, the Far East.

I had reserved a room at the Steamboat, a brick edifice that has seen better days. I was received courteously by a young man who told me my room was on the top floor and he would take me to it, at the same time beckoning a young lass from behind the bar: 'Have you ever seen upstairs?' The question was asked in such a way that upstairs was special, or maybe different. So it was, on both counts. An old, springy bed (with clean linen), a TV without remote; the shower was decrepit but water flowed; the wallpaper had had it and the carpet I won't comment on. As far as I was aware no-one else occupied this enormous 'hotel'. Still, I had a grand view out to sea, where a solitary boat occupied the azure main and the sails of a nearby wind turbine peeped above the rooftops.

Refreshed and showered I set forth for the fleshpots of town. Just up the road was the police station, a huge Victorian building that must have served Blyth throughout her busy, industrial days. Size doesn't matter, though, for it was closed. A notice gave the opening times, 9 to 5 basically, and a telephone was available for anyone who wanted to call for help: 'When closed please contact the Helpline for routine enquiries or 999 for emergencies and we'll send a polis from Morpeth'. (I made the last bit up). But there was more: 'The enquiry office at Bedlington police station is open 24 hours daily'. Blyth is the biggest town in the administrative county of Northumberland and the nick was closed. As I turned to leave the Marie Celeste a couple of cars sped by at around 50 m.p.h. What the hell.

As a retired rozzer, I'm bound to take more than a passing interest in the police. So I might as well get this off my chest.

The police force has changed. But the change we have seen in the police force is not good. The fact is, the police have given up the streets. No matter we hear chief constables say officers are 'on the beat': they are not. They're not on the beat because the culture of being on the beat no longer holds. Police officers don't patrol on foot because they don't want to and they aren't trained to. They spend their time driving around aimlessly in cars. It's not the officers' fault. It's the fault of a system going back to the introduction of 'panda' cars. I thought pandas were a good idea, brought in to complement the beat officer; instead they replaced him. Supervisory officers don't patrol either, and they should. Supervision isn't confined to within the police station.

Don't tell me police officers are inundated with paperwork. I know they are. But not for entire shifts, every day, to the exclusion of patrolling the streets. They should be on the beat, on foot. I don't mean dropped off in some town centre for a couple of hours to show the flag. I mean working a regular patch, where they get to know the local toe-rags and the public see a reassuring presence. I live near a small Cumbrian town and I see local officers every week. Not on the street, but in a freebie booklet that's delivered through my letterbox, unknown faces along with messages about locking your car and cracking down on drinking in the park. Where I don't see them is where I want to see them: on patrol, on foot (including in the park).

Look at crime today. We hear of people being driven to distraction and even suicide through yobs taunting them and attacking them if they are challenged when damaging property. Police on the beat with the power to act with discretion and backed by the courts would go a long way to curing this and many other ills. I didn't see a copper on foot patrol in Blyth, or anywhere at all on my perambulation throughout Northumberland, including Newcastle city centre. How shameful.

Also shameful is racism in the police force (as well as in any organisation). A few years ago the McPherson enquiry into the murder of black teenager Stephen Lawrence, in London, concluded that the police force was institutionally racist. 'Institutional' meant all police officers, which was nonsense in my opinion. In my experience your everyday copper deals with everyone equally, regardless of race.

But now racism has filtered into the police, as it must be regarded when an organisation such as the Black Police Association is sanctioned; and racism it will remain until there's a White Police Association. That, surely, is a day that will never dawn, as it shouldn't. Similarly, one reads of local city and county councils advertising for 'black and ethnic minorities only'. No offer of work, or anything else for that matter, should depend on the colour of one's skin or ethnic background. I'm digressing again. I said I would.

There's one final point. When it comes to dealing with major incidents and major crimes, I believe our police forces are the best: organised, focused, fair and determined. And in other, specific departments too: the motorway patrols who deal in danger and gruesome deaths, child protection units who deal with victims of some of the most serious crimes, and more. These continue to serve us well. It's the basics where the police have lost it: smartly dressed in uniform (including their hats; excluding ghastly reflective jackets), on the beat, in contact with the public. For any copper reading this, let me tell you that as someone who reads and watches the news like anyone else, you are now held in very low esteem by Joe Public. For any chief constable reading this, stop saying your officers are on foot patrol when they aren't and get them out on to the streets. That includes sergeants and inspectors along with their superintendents. Read my lips: 'On the streets.'

No polis in Blyth, but what I did see was a restaurant, 'The China Cook'. It was empty when I plonked myself at a table, my needs attended to by two smart waitresses. They stood close to my table, smiling but holding off tactfully until it was time to quietly step forward and clear the table before bringing me another plateful of nosh, then standing by, still smiling, ready for action again.

Here I must digress (again) to mention something that has amazed me for years. Why is it, I have always wondered, that a people who date from one of the world's oldest civilizations, who built one of the great wonders of the world, the Great Wall of China, who now populate the fastest growing economy and industrial power on earth, why is it that they persist in eating rice with two sticks? And, just as mystifying, why do they think an English person would do the same when a spoon is a far more efficient tool for shovelling it in, along with copious quantities of sweet and sour chicken and whatever other Chinese goodies are ordered. The courteous young women who waited on me now, of course, were not concerned in the slightest about my food-eating technique, only that my requirements were attended to without fuss. Chopsticks, had I chosen to use them, were available on the table, as were spoons. I have seen English people choose the former. Why they do so is beyond me.

Throughout all the time I ate the other tables remained empty. It was as though I had commandeered the place for myself on this particular evening. I mention this because in a lifetime of consuming Chinese food, including when I was a beat polis in Newcastle, when we would slip into a Chinese for a natter with the management and gratefully accept a portion of chicken fried rice when we were at it – it's a great way to get to know your patch and the villains on it, and beats driving around aimlessly in cars, believe me – that meal, in Blyth was the best Chinese ever.

***

'Staiths' is not a noun readily found in dictionaries. It might have been if coal had been mined in Surrey, say, and loaded onto ships on the Thames, but on the Tyne at (Lemington) and Coquet (Amble), places far removed from the attention of the compilers of dictionaries, it seems to have escaped notice. But staiths are perhaps most associated with what once was the biggest coal exporting port in Europe: Blyth.

Staiths were huge, wooden structures, along which wagons ran, carrying coal that was deposited into ships' holds. Since coal is no longer mined in Northumberland, at least not in the quantities it was, and is not exported, the staiths have either fallen into disuse or have been demolished. At Blyth, however, some of the existing timbers have been utilised to fashion a new promenade, despite having been in the river for over 100 years, with new timbers being incorporated where necessary. They've made a great job of it. In addition, to commemorate Blyth's historic past, as well as its 'renaissance', an artwork, 50 feet high, was constructed.

I sighted 'The Spirit of the Staiths' as I strolled along the new promenade. At first glance I would describe it as a meaningless tangle of metal. Having looked at it closely, and read the notice that explains its purpose, I would describe it as a meaningless tangle of metal. The artist, we are told, was 'trying to capture local history by representing the original timbers of the staiths as thirteen steel legs...supporting the panels of a train cut from polished panels of stainless steel'.

It seems to me that if he was trying to 'capture' these qualities, he might have done better, if he could have, to have fashioned something in the shape of these things. Evidently if viewed from a nearby park, you see a life size image of train towing coal trucks, set at the height of the original timber ramp. Unfortunately people promenading on the staiths aren't standing in the park.

To me an artwork should show what it is supposed to represent. If it's an abstract work and isn't meant to represent anything, then fair enough; it may still be attractive or different. This artwork cost around £300,000, funded by the Northumberland Strategic Partnership, Blyth Valley and Northumberland County Council with arts and business. That's taxpayers, mainly. I hope the taxpayers of Blyth Valley are happy with what their money was spent on. 'The Spirit of the Staiths' may be loved or hated or regarded with indifference. But if, as we are told, this 'artwork' is meant to capture 'this slice of local history', then it fails in the humble view of the author. In times when we hear of old people's homes closing and the like, imagine what £300,000 could have been used for.

If I found tangled metal unattractive, at least I had the sight, now close at hand, of some wind turbines, standing in regimented line on the opposite side of the river. When I'd had a good view of the sails of a wind turbine from my window in the Steamboat, to measure its efficiency I carried out an experiment by timing the revolutions over a period of one minute. Yesterday evening it took one of the sails 12 seconds to make one revolution. This morning it took 19 seconds. Will someone on planet earth please tell me how these machines create electricity? I understand the basics: cutting through the magnetic field, etc, but how are they supposed to power homes, offices and factories (those that are left)?

In a survey conducted by Ofgem in 2010 the windfarm at Blyth Harbour was the least efficient in Britain, producing just

7.9 per cent of capacity. The survey said they are too low, that wind farms need to be on high ground, where the wind, if it's blowing, can turn the blades. We knew that without a survey, surely. But placing them on high ground blights the beautiful English landscape. Alfred Wainwright complained of unsightly radio masts on distant hills; what he would have thought of these monstrous machines one can barely imagine. Anyway, I had lingered long enough among tangled metal and wind turbines. I took the bus to Seaton Sluice.

This was the final leg of my journey: six miles along the coast to Tynemouth. It was a cold, dank sort of day. I resolved not to eat a thing until I arrived at Tynemouth, when I would gorge myself on fish and chips, which I would consume outdoors, no matter what the weather. But it would be remiss of me, in an area that was once a great coalfield, and as the son and grandson of coal miners, not to mention the New Hartley pit disaster.

New Hartley is situated just a couple of miles from where I now walked. It was here that Northumberland suffered its worst mining disaster when 204 miners died, 199 of them asphyxiated, deep down the mine where they had put in a full shift before making ready to come to the surface. Coalmines were privately owned then, and only one vertical shaft led down to the mine. At the top of the shaft was the engine room housing the engine for pumping water out of the pit. The engine was supported by a 42-ton, cast-iron beam: solid, strong, built to take the weight. But on Thursday, 16 January, 1862, the beam snapped, and huge sections of it hurtled down the shaft where they collided with the upcoming cage carrying eight men who had just finished the nightshift. Five of those men were killed.

The shaft was then completely blocked, and on top of that the falling beam destroyed the wooden partition in the shaft, which divided the shaft to maintain airflow. One hundred and ninety-nine men and boys were now entombed, their supply of air cut off, and to make matters worse fumes from the ventillating furnace was consuming whatever oxygen remained.

The miners, although hoping for rescue, would have known their fate. One of them, James Armour, aged 43, trapped with his son Richard, 14, wrote a brief message: 'Friday afternoon at half past one. Edward Armstrong, Thomas Gledson, John Harding, Thomas Bell and others took extremely ill. We held a prayer meeting at a quarter to two, when Tibbs, Henry Sharp, J. Campbell, Henry Gibson, William Palmer. Tim Tibbs exhorted us to God. Sharp also. James Armour'. Armstrong was 12, Bell was 13. Two of the boys who died were ten years of age; many others were teenagers.

Those on the surface worked tirelessly to clear the shaft, but it was the following Wednesday before they succeeded. When they did they found the bodies of men and boys lying in rows, as though they were asleep. Fathers and sons and brothers lay with their arms around one another. Joseph Skipsey, the 'Pitman's Poet', wrote:

> 'Oh father, till the shaft is rid,
> Close, close beside me keep;
> My eyelids are together glued,
> And I – and I – must sleep.'

60,000 people attended the funeral, on 26 January. The procession of coffins was four miles long. Nearly all the bodies were buried in Earsdon churchyard, with a neighbouring field used to accommodate so many. As a result of the disaster, from 1865 coalmines, by law, had to have two shafts to increase the chance of escape. In that sense, at least, the men and boys at Hartley did not die in vain.

The tide was out today, and twenty or so boats languished in Seaton Sluice's black, muddy harbour. I headed south, passing the huge Waterford Arms and arrived at the war memorial, a tall, granite cross, dedicated 'To the memory of the men of Seaton Sluice and Old Hartley who fell in the wars'. In the Great War, 23 men died; in the Second, 27. It's unusual to find the total greater in World War II.

Seaton Sluice was deserted. There was only me. Things weren't always so. This was a place of industry, with a port so important it had its own gun battery. Coal was mined locally from the 13th century, and was used to fire huge saltpans, where sea water was evaporated to produce salt for export. Coal was shipped from the harbour, which, unfortunately, kept silting up. A pier was constructed, with sluice gates that trapped seawater at each high tide. At low tide the gates were opened, flushing the sand from the harbour, a practice that gave Seaton Sluice its name.

In the mid 18th century a channel, 300 yards long, was constructed by blasting through solid rock. It was known as 'The Cut', and could be sealed off at both ends to facilitate loading of ships no matter what the state of the tide. Other industries flourished: glassworks and bottle factory, brickmaking. Sadly, it couldn't last. The silting in the harbour was always a problem; glass and bottle production fell victim to other, rival areas; coal was exported from nearby Blyth and Tyne; salt was killed off by the salt tax of the 1790s.

The cold spurred me on, and I set off for my next objective, St Mary's Island. There was but one person in view: someone fishing at the sea's edge. A brave soul on such a day, I thought. The tide was out, the sea flat-looking, undisturbed by the elements. The only movement in view was a solitary jet on its descent to Newcastle Airport. I've flown in this way myself, with grand views of the coast. To be on the coast was better. The path led along a broad headland, passing a caravan park with well-cropped grass, altogether very trim. In sight was Whitley Bay and, beyond, Tynemouth pier, where I had started my journey. The bracing air, the sea, the view; what more could anyone ask? A cup of tea, that's what. There would be none for a while, and no food until journey's end.

The dominating feature ahead was the tall lighthouse on St Mary's Island. The island, like Lindisfarne, is cut off at high tide, and since I intended to walk over to it I would have to keep an eye on things to ensure I wasn't marooned. The sea was a long way off; but time and tide wait for no-one, not even me. I reached Curry's Point, named (presumably) after Michael Curry, a glass worker from Seaton Sluice who was hanged on 4 September, 1739, for murdering Robert Shevil, licensee of the Three

Horseshoes, Hartley. In keeping with the practice of the time his body was brought here and suspended from a gibbet, within sight of his crime and as a reminder of the fate of murderers. Today the site is occupied by a scattering of benches, all bearing plates with commemorative names, many of whom 'so loved this view'.

In medieval times there was a chapel here, dedicated to St Helen. Inside was St. Katherine's Light, later wrongly ascribed as St. Mary; so we have St Mary's Island. In 1898 the lighthouse was built on the site of the chapel and was first lit on 31 August that year by the builder's two daughters. It's 120 feet high and cost £8,000. The light was decommissioned in 1984. How many lives it saved over its 86-year history we can never know.

I crossed the short causeway to the island, and climbed the steps up to the lighthouse, to an old anchor and more benches with commemoration plates. A helpful information board explained much of the history of this coast, mentioning the offshore wind turbines at Blyth, 'Britain's first offshore wind farm', as though it's something to be proud of. Lots of little buildings are clustered on the island, including a shop and, inside, a super museum, with lots of model ships: 'Between 1968 and 1977 the Swan Hunter yard built eight giant oil tankers. One was Tyne Pride, able to carry 262,000 tons of oil, the biggest ship ever constructed on the river'. The loss of industry, lamented again.

I'd forgotten all about the tide, of course, but happily I was able to stroll back to the mainland and continue south. I took the path along the clifftops for Whitley Bay, crossing a little stone bridge over the Brierdene Burn, and continued, with a choice of route: a lower or elevated section of promenade, or the links. I chose the lower promenade. A few brave souls strolled the beach with the inevitable dogs, along with courting couples, hugging one another for warmth. And then I was in the part of Whitley Bay we all know and love: the Promenade.

For me, Whitley Bay is synonymous with the Spanish City, the collective name to the former amusement park dominated by a white-domed, concrete edifice, erstwhile place of loud music, the big dipper, the waltzer and the ghost train – but not, as I recall, a tunnel of love, and never mind Mark Knopfler's words.

Believe me, as a 17-year old with ultra-active hormones, if there'd been a tunnel of love I'd have found it.

And to here we'd come, Sunday evenings, on the bus, to meet our girlfriends for a stroll on the links and a ride on the waltzer, etc. Put a year on this lot, then: *Runaway*, *Runnin' Scared*, *Halfway to Paradise*, *She-she-she little Sheila*... This was the music blaring out in the Spanish City, always more than one song at a time from different speakers as the waltzer waltzed and the dodgems dodged. Noise? Today's kids don't know the meaning of the word. We were swingin': Keith, Robert and me; Lilian, Jackie and Sandra. Innocents all in the progressive world of the early sixties.

My memories of these madcap rides are quite specific. On the dodgems, if we were with our girlfriends it was fun to drive at speed whilst avoiding other dodgem cars, so proving our driving skills; if we were free 'n' easy we did the opposite, driving deliberately into dodgems driven by girls – I did, anyway – in the hopeful attempt to chat them up, a manoeuvre that never actually worked, but never mind.

I was always a bit scared of the waltzer, sitting on a spinning whirligig hurtling around at 100 m.p.h., at the same time going round and round and up and down on wooden boards, an altogether violent, crazy experience as we hung on grimly to an iron bar, liable at any moment to be cast forth into the midst of those who stood at the side waiting their turn. It was done to a cacophony of throbbing noise: the waltzer's engine, the mechanism of the thing, the clattering boards, voices of Elvis, Cliff, Gene Vincent and Del Shannon, mixed in a blaring cocktail of pop music.

But what sticks most in my mind about the waltzer is that in these five minutes of spinning and noise, with serious injury just a millisecond away at any given point, when you couldn't do anything save hang on to that iron bar for dear life, the young bloke who collected the money you had to pay before savouring this wonderful experience, strode effortlessly across the boards, navigating between whirligigs and going out of his way to look so bloody clever. Then, at some point, he would stand side-on, feet astride, in a gesture of utter nonchalance, as though he were located in some rural landscape looking at rolling fields of yellow corn, perhaps casting his eye into the far distance, studying the woodlands on the distant horizon.

The big dipper, or roller coaster if you like, I recall venturing on to but once. I sat next to my girlfriend, Sandra (naturally) as we were dragged slowly up the steep incline at the start, before careering down and then up again, and round about and hither and thither. This was a good reason to place a supporting arm around Sandra's shoulders, an 'it's all right, girl, you're safe with me' gesture. Sadly, I have to admit, on one sharp turn, when it seemed we could be cast henceforth from a great height, I released my hold of her shoulder and grasped the rail of the car (if that's what it's called), a manoeuvre amounting to self preservation. Nearly half a century later, if you're reading this Sandra, I'm sorry. It won't happen again. Honest.

Today I stood on the sea front at Whitley Bay and looked over at the forlorn sight of that white dome. I think it's being redeveloped. I hope so. How many folk must have memories of their visits there: when in their youth, with their kids, when they met so-and-so. As for the rest of this part of Whitley Bay, what I saw of it, the beach looked clean, and the links looked as spacious and neat as ever. I gather the town has a vibrant nightlife. Whether they dance romantically to *As Time Goes By* or if it's young men and women on the 'Strip', so-called, I believe, because in some way it resembles the Strip at Las Vegas (however doubtful) I wouldn't know. I couldn't care less. Whitley Bay, to me, is 1961, Del Shannon *et al*. Great place. Great memories.

Near the beach was a small café. I went in and bought a coffee. A woman with what appeared to be her daughter were the only other customers. We sat in silence, the three of us, gazing out to sea, sipping our drinks. It's not the quite the Costa Brava, Whitley Bay in October, and I wouldn't want it to be. I resisted the temptation to eat; those fish and chips at Tynemouth were tasting better with every step. Emerging from the café it occurred to me that on a cold, late October afternoon Tynemouth's amenities might be closed. It was a Saturday, so I lived in hope that it wouldn't be. Ever the optimist.

I took to the prom. A solitary fisherman sat by his rods, staring out to sea, waiting... There was lots of dog poo on the pavement. You need to be careful taking in the view when you walk along the prom in Whitley Bay. When Alfred Wainwright advised us to watch where we put our feet he meant when fell-walking; but his advice holds good here, albeit for different reasons. On the pavement were yellow, stencilled dogs and even stencilled poo, along with stencilled lettering: 'Clean it up'. If only they would.

The North East's favourite comedian, Bobby Thompson lived at Whitley Bay for a time. As he said in his best 'posh' accent, 'We live in a detached house. It's falling away from the one next door.' Bobby was born at Penshaw, and not surprisingly spoke with a north-east Durham accent. A dimin-utive chap, he was unique, standing at the microphone, wearing his flat cap, Woodbine poised for a drag between jokes. He never really made it big beyond his native North East, probably because no-one could understand what he was saying, especially in London and the south. I used to listen to him on the wireless when I was a kid. We understood you, Bobby. You never relied on foul language to make people laugh; you were the little waster who relied on natural talent to be funny.

I liked Bobby's 'war' jokes. 'I'll never forget the war. How I fought and fought and fought. An' I still had t'gan.' And his telephone call to the Queen. 'Is that thou, Bob? Just a minute, I've got a pan of chips on.' Here's a good 'un to sign you off. 'Me an' wor lass was at Buckingham Palace. The Queen comes ower an' says t'me, "Bob, would you like a scone or a meringue?" Ah says, "No, it's ah reet. I'll hev the scone.".' Get it? Maybe not, if you're from south of the Wash, or even west of the Pennines. Bobby died in 1988.

As I rounded the point Cullercoats came into view. An old rowing boat lay in a flower bed, white paint peeling from its sides. A few straggly primroses struggled for life in soil amidships. Here was the harbour and beach and a stone building, the

Cullercoats Fisherman's Lookout, built 1879. It has a clock turret and belfry. Cullercoats, like Seaton Sluice, was a place of coal mining and salt panning, but afterwards became an important fishing port, with its 'cobles' and two piers constructed to protect them in the harbour. The men went to sea, the women baited hooks, mended nets and sold fish on the streets of Tyneside. Today an information panel said 'the fishing industry is not what it was'. A gross understatement.

There are many stories about Cullercoats. Two incidents I highlight here. The first, in 1848, was the loss of a coble that capsized with loss of all hands. The grave of three men of the same family is in the cemetery in the grounds of Tynemouth Priory: George Lisle and his sons, George and Robert, 'Fishermen and pilots of Cullercoats who formed part of a boat's crew of seven men, lost on the Bar of Cullercoats Haven when going off to pilot a vessel on the morning of 2nd February, 1848'.

Most people, I imagine, when thinking of lifeboats, think only of the men who crew them. But women played their part too, in 1860, when the *Lovely Nelly*, a collier that regularly took coal from Seaham to London, foundered off the coast. She had set sail, fully laden, from Seaham on 28 December, but at Flamborough Head was forced to turn back due to a 'heavy leak'.

The captain tried to 'run' for Sunderland but the ship was forced north, past the Tyne and past Cullercoats. Observers watching from the shore saw her flying a distress flag and called for the 'coastguardmen' to 'do something'. The ship's crew, realising they were losing the battle against elements, struck out for Whitley Sands; they must have hoped to beach her, but the ship struck a reef.

When the call for the lifeboat went up – it was New Year's Day, 1861 – the lifeboatmen and fishermen of Cullercoats ran through the snow, harnessed six horses to the carriage and brought the lifeboat to the sands. The women of Cullercoats helped drag the lifeboat through the blizzard, a scene enacted on the BBC's *Coast*, in an apparent attempt to see if this was possible. A painting, *The Women*, by John Charlton, depicts the scene.

The Cullercoats men rowed the stormy sea to the *Lovely Nelly* and fastened the lifeboat to her with a rope. The crew was rescued, save one, the cabin boy, Thomas Thompson, aged 12, whose cries for help would have been heartbreaking to the men who wanted to rescue him. They tried, but as the boy held on to the rigging they were forced to abandon rescue for fear of the main mast falling on to the lifeboat, in which event no-one, including the lifeboatmen, would have survived. Even as they left the stricken ship, the mast fell, and the lifeboat turned again to the ship but young Thomas was swept away. One imagines the scene: the roaring wind, the sea, rising and falling, the spray, the cries of men...

And so to Tynemouth.

Tynemouth has been in my bones for almost as long as I can remember. Or, more accurately, Long Sands and its environs: the boating lake, the amusements and the Plaza, now gone. It was to Tynemouth every summer we came on the Club Trip, ten double deckers (the first 'trip') and ten more (the second 'trip') from Westerhope. Kids were given four bob, courtesy of the club funds – eight bob in 1953, Coronation year. We sang all the way, there and back. We played on the beach from the moment we arrived until we left, not leaving it except to go boating on the lake and visit the Plaza.

I was at Long Sands now, the north end that is, which was unfamiliar to me, never having ventured this far on the Club Trip. Over the road was St George's Church, whose tall steeple I recalled as part of the scene from the beach. Long Sands looked in good nick, I thought, before continuing to the amusement and shops opposite the lake, and the spot where once stood the Plaza. Built in 1878 as The Palace of the North, the Plaza burned down in 1996. I remember its size, the noise and the roller-skate rink.

I couldn't find a loo, so crossed the road into the park and went directly into a café. 'Have you a toilet?' I enquired. The woman looked at me suspiciously. 'Will you be having something?' she asked, meaning if I wasn't clear off. 'Of course,' I told her in my best of course voice. 'It's through there,' she said, indicating. When I returned she'd disappeared, and so did I. Sorry missus. I wandered around the lake, the scene largely unchanged since my rowing-boat days except today's paddle boats were tied up, which was hardly a surprise. They looked as though they'd been there for 40 years. If so, they would still have post-dated my ventures onto the lake. A dilapidated canoe filled with soil but no plants lay in a flower bed. The scene was drab, I thought, but no doubt will liven up with sunshine and children's voices in the school holidays. Do they still come here on double-decker buses?

I returned to the prom and surveyed the beach where we pitched those box-shaped tents – they were freezing inside – and ate our egg, tomato and sand sandwiches. The word 'sandwich' derives from sandwiches eaten on Tynemouth beach. Long Sands would be packed with people just like us, folks who'd come to the seaside for the day. Old photographs depict the scene perfectly. How grand it was to arrive at Tynemouth on the Club Trip, that thrilling moment when everyone on the bus cried, 'There's the sea!' Just as they did every year, from the same place! The buses pulled up somewhere near the Plaza and we all spilled out, running down the steps to the same spot we had the year before, and the year before that. There were few people on the beach today; a few of the inevitable dog walkers, a couple of kids kicking a football about with their dad, a man here, a woman there. A kayak graced a calm sea. There was no sign of candyfloss. The shuggyboats have gone. Without fail I threw up on them. I located the old stone steps leading down to the beach, the same ones I trod barefoot over half a century before.

My final thoughts as I stood at the top of the steps were of my parents. This place was their escape, their big day out. Dad worked down a black hole in the ground for nearly half a century; he must have loved it here. Mam too, an away day from routine.

Beyond King Edward Bay were the Priory ruins, the end of my journey. On the right, set back, the crescent-shaped Percy Gardens, mid-Victorian houses with superb views. They don't build 'em like that any more. More's the pity. I'd walk past them with my parents on those Club Trips, to the end of Front Street, where, I recall, there was a huge mine that was used as a moneybox, just like the one on Holy Island. From there we'd walk on to the pier, but where we never went was to the ruins of the priory, close by but shunned by Mam and Dad. I guess they just wanted fresh air and a stroll, and who could blame them? The ruins stand on a rocky promontory known as Pen Bal Crag, and I had always intended this to be the grand finale of my journey.

But first a stroll along Front Street, beginning at the sandstone clock tower that stands in the road. Built in 1861, it was restored in 1999. It would have been so easy to remove it for the benefit of traffic flow; how good they kept it for the benefit of the public. Just across the road, behind the railings of 'The Old House', lies a doorhead in the form of the Borough Arms. It came from Tynemouth's old police station in Oxford Street. Its Latin inscription reads *Messis Ab Altis*, meaning 'Harvest of the Deep', a motto relating to pitmen and seamen: the former worked deep underground, winning coal, the latter, as fishermen, fished in the depths of the sea. I'm using past tense, perhaps inappropriately.

A plaque on the wall at 57 Front Street bears an interesting inscription: 'Harriet Martineau, novelist and England's first woman journalist, regained her health here, 1840-1845'. Martineau was a writer who suffered 'chronic ill health' and came to live at Tynemouth, of which she wrote: 'When I look forth in the morning the whole land may be sheeted with glistening snow, while the myrtle-green sea tumbles. There is none of the deadliness of winter in the landscape; no leafless trees, no locking up with ice, and the air comes in through my open upper sash, but sun-warmed. The robins twitter and hop in my flower boxes. What an expanse of stars above, appearing more steadfast the more the Northern Lights dart and quiver!' Harriet Martineau left Tynemouth for Ambleside in 1845. She regained her health, and lived until the age of 74. If she could return to Tynemouth, she would see that the myrtle-green sea still graces Tynemouth's beaches, and doubtless robins still hop into flower boxes too.

It was time, at last, to complete my journey. I crossed the road for the Priory.

There were monastic buildings on the site in the 7th century, after which the monastery was repeatedly attacked by the Danes; in AD 865, when the church and monastery were destroyed, the nuns of St Hilda, who had come here for safety, were massacred. God knows what other horrors they suffered. In 1090 the priory fell under the jurisdiction of St Albans, Robert de Mowbray, Earl of Northumberland, having fallen out with the Bishop of Durham. It seems the monks sent from St Albans were 'difficult to manage'. What, I wonder, did they think of their posting to this rocky headland?

Three kings were reputedly buried on the site: in 651 Oswin of Deira was murdered by soldiers of neighbouring Bernicia and was brought here for burial, although his remains were probably removed later; in 792 Osred of Northumbria was murdered, and buried here; and Malcolm III of Scotland, who invaded England in 1093, was killed at Alnwick and buried here, although it seems likely his remains were moved to Dunfermline. The three kings were commemorated on the Tynemouth Borough coat of arms, represented by three crowns, which appear today as part of North Tyneside's coat of arms.

The ruined monastery fell victim, along with all monasteries, to the dissolution. Thereafter the nave was used as the parish church until the 17th century, hence the extensive cemetery. The site, a natural defensive strongpoint, was occupied for at least 400 years as a coastal fort.

The impressive Castle gatehouse still stands, and today you pass through it to explore at your leisure – having first paid for a ticket (concessions apply, as they say) at the little shop run by English Heritage. This I did, and exploring went. First, directly to the ruined priory, whose towering walls suggest an impressive building. An information panel depicts the scene as it might have been, the sun's rays streaming through the windows onto the monks within. The *piece de resistance* surely is the Percy Chantry, a tiny vaulted 15th century chapel, restored by – who else – John Dobson, in 1852. Outside is the solid, perpendicular Monk's Stone, dating back to the 9th century, and beyond are gun emplacements, where today a gun, now (presumably) decommissioned, points out to sea in the direction of would-be invaders.

Having sated my exploratory appetite, I took a stroll to the south corner of the site for a view over the mouth of the Tyne and the piers, and upriver. Out at sea, and on the river: no ships, nothing at all. My journey over, I took a last, lingering look at Lord Collingwood, high and proud on his plinth. And, on the horizon, shiver me timbers, there was Penshaw Monument in the distance.

So...

I'd walked Northumberland. Could I be proud of my native county? Has it changed since my schoolteacher held up a book entitled, 'England's Farthest North'?

Well, for a start, I didn't actually 'walk' Northumberland. I walked a corridor through it. A corridor that passed through selected places but didn't take in everywhere, as it couldn't. In particular I regret not visiting Staward Gorge and Rothbury; and there were, inevitably, other notable omissions: huge swaths of central Northumberland; the country around Capheaton and Kirkharle, the Ingram Valley, Stamfordham, Belsay, Etal, to name but a few randomly.

There have been changes. Since I was a kid New Towns, Cramlington and Killingworth, have developed; Newcastle and other places have expanded. Kielder Reservoir has been created. There has been the sad loss of industry, particularly the Northumberland coalfield, fishing and the shipyards. All are gone and not likely to be replaced. But Northumberland is still a county of space, of many visible signs of history, especially those castles and pele towers, and wonderful churches. Hadrian's Wall, where it still stands, is as isolated as in the time of the Romans. The beaches are empty and magnificent. So are the Cheviots, at the time of writing still free of ghastly windmills blighting their rolling skylines. As for the future: who can say?